Mennonite Entrepreneurs

Mennonite Entrepreneurs

CALVIN REDEKOP

STEPHEN C. AINLAY

ROBERT SIEMENS

THE JOHNS HOPKINS UNIVERSITY PRESS
Baltimore and London

Published in cooperation with the Center for American Places,
Harrisonburg, Virginia

© 1995 The Johns Hopkins University Press
All rights reserved. Published 1995
Printed in the United States of America on acid-free paper

04 03 02 01 00 99 98 97 96 95   5 4 3 2 1

The Johns Hopkins University Press
2715 North Charles Street
Baltimore, Maryland 21218–4319
The Johns Hopkins Press Ltd., London

Library of Congress cataloging-in-publication data will be
found at the end of this book.
A catalog record for this book is available from the
British Library.

ISBN 0-8018-5003-7

Contents

III ❖   Theoretical Reflections

Preface and Acknowledgments

This is a book about Mennonite entrepreneurs—a curious hybrid we would admit at the outset. It is a study of people who adhere to a religious-ethnic tradition that is on the periphery of the world economy and, for that matter, North American religious life. Furthermore, it is a study of people who have been, until recent times, somewhat on the margins of the Mennonite world itself. Having said this, one (especially if he or she is not a Mennonite businessperson) is certainly justified in asking, "So what's in this for me?"

We will not, of course, be able to answer this question fully in our prefatory remarks and must, therefore, beg for patience. However, we believe that the Anabaptist-Mennonite experience with the emerging entrepreneurial role is instructive for both Mennonite and non-Mennonite alike. It is our conviction, in other words, that the Anabaptist-Mennonite tradition has something extremely valuable to contribute to all of us. Part of our job in the pages that follow will be to convince the reader of this.

This book traces the ways in which Anabaptist-Mennonites have interpreted the role of economics in their society. As we will detail, this interpretation of economics and economic activity has not been as uniform as either popular stereotype or even Mennonite self-understanding would have it. Thus, one of our goals is to set the record straight on this point. Beyond this, however, we are interested in capturing something of the stories of Mennonite entrepreneurs—economic pioneers of sorts—who have lived lives of struggle and achievement. As will be seen, these are also stories of people who have had to balance self-advancement with community membership, finding a path between individualism and commitment. It is here where the non-Mennonite and Mennonite reader alike will find something of themselves in this book. Similarly, one need not be in business to appreciate how difficult it is to find this balance or path amid the confusion of modern life. By understanding members of this religious-ethnic group—a group that arguably carries a pronounced utopian impulse deep within its historical group consciousness—we will come to understand something of the tension and the balance with which we all must come to terms.

The book is divided into three parts. Part I frames the project by introducing the reader to Anabaptist-Mennonite culture, theology, and history. It also introduces the entrepreneur as a sort of modern type, unpackaging important aspects of the entrepreneurial role. The two chapters in Part I provide a sense of the tensions that are played out in greater detail in the remainder of the book: the tension between religion and economic activity, between the Anabaptist-Mennonite world and North American society at large, and within the Anabaptist-Mennonite community as to acceptable forms of economic activity.

Part II is the empirical heart of the project. These six chapters take the reader into the world and mind-set of the Mennonite entrepreneur. Using a combination of quantitative and qualitative interview data, we explore the ethos and rationale of Mennonite businesspersons. We learn of their struggles to fit in with the church and local community, their anxieties about upward mobility, their attempts to articulate an Anabaptist vision in the face of worldly material success, and their heroic conformity to community values and priorities.

Part III examines the theoretical significance of the project. In the first of two chapters we look at extant theoretical treatments of Mennonite economics, beginning with Max Weber's classic treatment of them in *Protestant Ethic and the Spirit of Capitalism*, revealing the power of their insights as well as their respective misunderstandings of Mennonite life and culture. The final chapter of the book articulates the theoretical synthesis of religious and economic activity which is lived out in the day-to-day activities of the Mennonite entrepreneur. It considers the implications for Mennonite ethics and theology as well as for the non-Mennonite world.

We would like to acknowledge a number of people and organizations which made this project possible. Calvin Redekop thanks Conrad Grebel College of the University of Waterloo, which generously provided him with a sabbatical leave during the 1985–86 academic year. He also thanks the Social Sciences and Humanities Council for funding support (grant 410-84-1217). Stephen Ainlay thanks the Professional Standards Committee, College of the Holy Cross, for awarding him a summer fellowship. He also acknowledges the Lilly Endowment for financial support (grant 900760), which enabled him to participate in this project. All three authors express their appreciation to Johns Hopkins University Press and, in particular, the helpful comments of their anonymous reviewers and the support and encouragement of George F. Thompson, president of the Center for American Places and our editor. Finally, we also thank the one hundred entrepreneurs who participated in the Redekop Entrepreneurial Research. We hope that they recognize themselves and their experiences in the pages to follow. Their help was truly indispensable to the project.

PART I

Mennonites and
Entrepreneurial Activity

CHAPTER ONE

Historical and Theological Perspectives

If the juxtaposition of *Mennonite* and *entrepreneur* means little to you, take heart, for you are certainly not alone. Mennonites, with the exception of the Amish, simply have not captured the popular imagination—or that of sociologists, for that matter—so books about anything Mennonite seem somewhat esoteric.

The term *Mennonite* defies easy definition.[1] It is applied to a host of specific religious groups that trace their origin to the radical wing of the Protestant Reformation; however, not all of these groups accept the designation. The founding figures have been dubbed *Anabaptists* (a derogatory term in its original application, meaning *re-baptizers*) who preferred to use the term *Brethren*. Various subgroups—often located in different geographical areas of Europe—chose the name (or had the name thrust upon them) of their leaders (e.g., the followers of Jacob Hutter were called Hutterites, the followers of Melchior Hoffman were called Melchiorites, the followers of Obbe Philips were called Obbenites). The term *Mennonite* eventually came to be applied to the whole movement and was an elaboration of *Menist*, referring originally to the followers of Menno Simons. *Menist* was in turn elaborated into *Mennonist* and finally *Mennonite*.[2] Redekop suggested that this last term came to refer to the entire group probably because of Menno Simons' extensive writings on the faith and doctrine of the movement.[3] Such a generalization, however, conceals important theological, historical, and social differences among various Anabaptist subgroups. Furthermore, some who take the name *Mennonite* have debated as to which group is the rightful heir to the title.[4] All of this conceptual confusion makes it necessary to begin with a general discussion of the Anabaptist-Mennonite movement and then work toward greater definitional precision.

One image almost certain *not* to come to most people's minds is that of the Mennonite businessperson. Nevertheless, it is likely that they have consumed goods manufactured by Mennonite businesses or enterprises founded by people who were Mennonite. Sauder computer desks and other furniture products, Smucker jellies and jams, and Musselman applesauce are just a few examples of these goods. And if you add the names of companies founded by descendents of Mennonite immigrants to the United States, such as the Hershey chocolate company founded by Milton Hershey, the list is even longer. Stories of business ventures—both those that end up with national markets as well as those that don't and are therefore less recognizable—are intrinsically interesting. Risk taking, successes, and failures are the stuff of good storytelling and make good reading. Yet Mennonite entrepreneurs prove instructive for other reasons.

Behind the stories of Mennonite businesses and businesspeople lie tales of individual and collective struggles: the struggle to reconcile the accumulation of personal wealth with responsibilities to the collective good; the struggle to reconcile the autonomy and self-interests of the individual with a traditional submission to group authority; the struggle with individualism and commitment.

These are not uniquely Mennonite struggles. We were reminded of this by Robert Bellah, Richard Madsen, William Sullivan, Ann Swidler, and Steven Tipton in their best-selling book, *Habits of the Heart*. They insisted that the entrepreneur—whom they described as self-sufficient, competitive, tough, and freed by wealth from external constraints—is an important modern North American character.[5] They also argued that the entrepreneur must struggle, like most contemporary people, to reconcile the various aspects of life, especially work and family, and to find moral meaning and direction without clear linkages to religious and civic institutions. The entrepreneur, in other words, brings into relief the characteristic dilemmas of our time.

Mennonites who pursue business are instructive because they bring the struggles of the entrepreneurial character into relief. Their theological and cultural traditions, emerging from more than four hundred years of collective experience, exaggerate the dilemmas posed by entrepreneurialism. In this sense, the emergence and history of the Mennonite entrepreneur are far from esoteric but rather strike at the heart of our common experience. Thus, the lessons to be learned from the Mennonites concerning individual interests and collective good are important.

We are motivated to tell the story by a second consideration as well. Mennonites themselves have been silent about the place of economic activities in both their history and their contemporary circumstance. The economic dimensions of the early Anabaptist experience, especially communal tendencies, have been all but ignored, and there is a reaction bordering on embarrassment to economic success among contemporary Mennonites.[6] Mennonites seem to be ambivalent and ambiguous about the relationship between their system of belief and economic activity. The discussion that follows attempts to clarify this relationship as well as the reasons that Mennonites have difficulty addressing it, bringing economic issues within their community into full light.

Finally, the story of Mennonite entrepreneurial activity necessitates a reexamination of the relationship between religion and entrepreneurial activity more generally. This places the project squarely within the tradition of classical sociology. That capitalism and the role of religion were central concerns of the major classical writers is well established.[7] Among the founding figures, Max Weber was especially concerned with uncovering the relationship among religion, rationalization, and the development of modern capitalism. His classic work, *The Protestant Ethic and the Spirit of Capitalism*, established a link (or elective affinity) between the teachings of ascetic Protestantism and the conduct of individuals pursuing their economic activities. The story of Mennonite entrepreneurial activity reaffirms the importance of the classical project but also calls for a critical reexamination of the Weberian thesis.

THEOLOGICAL AND CULTURAL PERSPECTIVES

The story of Mennonite entrepreneurial activity is far more involved than one might imagine, covering the whole of Anabaptist-Mennonite history. For more than four hundred years, the so-called radical left wing of the Reformation has struggled to reconcile economic life with living in the kingdom of God. This struggle involves a sort of collision of theological premises, cultural arrangements, and socioeconomic necessities.

Origins in the Reformation

Mennonites trace their origins to the intellectual ferment and social unrest set in motion by the great events that transformed the European world during the Protestant Reformation. Specifically, they find their beginnings in the Anabaptist movement, which took the form of a protest movement against Roman Catholic and Reformation groups alike over a range of interrelated religious and theological, political, social, and economic issues.[8]

The Anabaptist movement originated between 1520 and 1530 in the regions now known as Switzerland, Austria (especially the Tyrol), Germany (especially south Germany), France (Alsace), and the Netherlands. It was spearheaded by young intellectuals (mostly students in their twenties) who idealistically carried the Reformation to its logical conclusion by demanding that the committed individual become the basis of the religious community.[9] Among the early leaders of the movement were Conrad Grebel, Felix Manz, Georg Blaurock, and Simon Stumpf. Influenced by Erasmus, they were early supporters of Ulrich Zwingli's reforms, believing that these demands could and would be adopted by the Reform leaders in Zurich. But when Zwingli and the other Reformers began—in their eyes—to equivocate and temporize, the young radicals became impatient and on January 21, 1525, broke away, committing the heretical act of self-baptism without sacerdotal continuity.

Because the Anabaptist movement was so diverse in its regional peculiarities, it is difficult to provide a concise definition of its central genius. It was considered a utopian movement, motivated by an impulse to give the ideals of the Christian faith expression in everyday life. The Anabaptists were distinguished from other movements by their radicalism and by their literalism in the biblical interpretation of basic issues.[10]

The symbolic significance of re-baptism (which gave the Anabaptists their name *Wiedertäufer*, or *one who re-baptizes*) was that it represented the constitution of the religious congregation on the basis of adult conversion and baptism.[11] Acts that in today's world seem relatively insignificant, such as pouring water over each other's heads, were viewed as despicable and dangerous because adult conversion and baptism involved theological issues that threatened the stability of European society and concerned the nature of the church/community (*Gemeinde*). Anabaptists maintained that the Christian Church could only be a voluntary association of persons who, as adults, repented of their carnal life and were regenerated through the power of Christ's saving grace. As Menno Simons put it, "They are the true congregation of Christ who are truly converted, who are born from above of God, who are of a regenerate mind by the operation of the Holy Spirit through the hearing of the divine Word, and have become the children of God, have entered into obedience to Him and live inblamably in His holy commandments." [12]

The critical divergence from the accepted ecclesiology was that the Anabaptists made adult baptism an external sign by which one could distinguish believers from unbelievers. This distinction was critical for determining membership in and exclusion from the religious community. In medieval European Christendom, everyone was assured of temporal as well as eternal salvation by belonging to the religious community and by receiving the necessary sacraments, which were considered effective for salvation regardless of the personal attitude of administering priest or receiving penitent. The Anabaptist view diverged significantly from this position.

The Anabaptists' claim to establishing a new church on the basis of personal regeneration, independent of the established states and their affiliated churches, was not something the authorities of the time were ready to tolerate. Not only were the material interests of the clergy and nobility threatened but so too was the very conception of society (family, polity, church). Contrary to the established view in which one belonged by birth, Anabaptists saw community membership as a matter of personal commitment.

The political consequences of this heresy for both the secular and ecclesiastical authorities were that it threatened the very foundations and authority of the Christian religion (and Roman Catholic Church). Young radicals demanded a number of seemingly unrealistic reforms, including the eradication of the tithe in its manifest exploitative forms; the reformation/abolition of the oppressive priesthood and the institution of a lay ministry; the separation of the religious life from the control of the state; absolute nonresistance (pacifism), which meant that the state could not coerce Christians to use force; total lay control of congregational life including excommunication of the recalcitrant; freedom from any constraint in matters of belief and faith; communal ownership of property; and mutual assistance and support for members in need.

What was the catalyst that precipitated the Anabaptists' rejection of the established order? The social and economic forces at work in the Anabaptist movement were many and complex. Increasingly, it is recognized that social and economic conditions figured prominently in the protest: the wealth, pomp, and power of the Roman Catholic Church and the corrupt lives of its clergy contributed to a very widespread anticlericalism; social and economic oppression of the peasantry by the nobility and by the Roman Church, which owned much of the land on which peasants toiled, figured prominently in creating general unrest.

The German Peasant Revolt, the Muenster Rebellion, and other lesser social revolts were signs of this unrest and the level of people's disaffection. The German Peasant Revolt, which ended in May 1525 with the killing of thousands of peasants by the military forces of well-armed nobles, was orchestrated by Thomas Muntzer, whom some have called the forerunner of modern socialism, which may be something of a misnomer.[13] What is certain, however, is that Muntzer's radical program of social and religious reforms alienated nobility and Martin Luther alike. Yet he was successful in appealing to the general disaffection of the time and organized an armed force that participated in numerous uprisings.

The Muenster Rebellion, partly the result of a millenarian impulse within early Anabaptism, became one more tragic episode of the sixteenth century. Jan Matthijsz, an Anabaptist leader who had been converted by Melchior Hoffman, tried to establish a new societal order, the New Jerusalem, in Muenster, a north German city undergoing profound economic and religious conflict and change. The city became a center for radical Anabaptism and proved responsive to Matthijsz's vision.[14] Stirred by the Peasant Revolt, the residents of Muenster had called for improvements in social, religious, and economic conditions. Matthijsz and his representatives assured them that the Lord had selected Muenster to establish His kingdom on earth. In February 1534, the city hall was seized, and all those who refused to be baptized were expelled from the city. In response to these developments, Bishop Franz of Waldeck, ruler of the territory, embarked on a siege of the city. When Matthijsz attempted to disperse Waldeck's army, he was killed and was succeeded by Jan van Leyden, who carried on the notion of armed resistance (a position in sharp contrast to the nonresistance of other Anabaptist groups) and instituted two other programs, the community of goods and polygamy. Ultimately, Waldeck's army gained entrance to the city, and most of the remaining male population was put to death. The leaders were cruelly tortured, executed, and displayed in cages hanging from the tower of St. Lambert's Church.

However tragic, it is not surprising that communalistic tendencies developed in Muenster and elsewhere during this period. Benjamin

Zablocki pointed out that all communal movements draw their members from a larger pool of dissatisfied people, not all of whom become communalists.[15] The greatest sociological significance of communal movements, Zablocki argued, is that they take shape during periods of intense social upheaval, and individual communalists are drawn to them as vehicles to stabilize their lives. The Anabaptists themselves emerged in the context of the disintegration of medieval Europe.

The German Peasant Revolt linked the economic fortunes of the peasantry with the religious reforms of the day. Although the association of the Anabaptist movement with events in Muenster would become a millstone around the necks of the more pacifist among them, it served to link their religious ideas with the issues of social and economic change and provided an ideological vehicle by which the oppressed peasants could articulate their socioeconomic grievances.

A History of Persecution and Migration

So threatening were the ideas and practices of the Anabaptists that members were thought to deserve banishment, imprisonment, prolonged torture, and even violent death. Many of the leaders were put to death. The first to be martyred by Catholic authorities was Hippolytus Eberle, executed in the spring of 1525. The first killed by the Protestants was Felix Manz, drowned in Zurich in January 1527. A number of Anabaptist leaders met in Augsburg in August 1527 for what has become known as the Martyrs' Synod, so named because many of those attending were put to death soon after the meeting.[16] So effective were the pursuit and persecution of early Anabaptist leaders that they led to what has been termed *rustication*, the loss of leadership talent through persecution.

Striking are the lengths to which those who persecuted the Anabaptist leaders would go to ensure that punishment was served. The case of Hans Hut is an example.[17] An effective preacher, Hut apparently won numerous converts to the Anabaptist movement. He was captured in Augsburg in 1527, tried, tortured, and died in a fire in his cell.[18] His body was carried to the judgment hall, tied to the executioner's cart, and his corpse sentenced to death by burning.

Persecution continued for leaders and followers alike. In the Netherlands alone, more than two thousand martyrs gave up their lives for the faith between 1530 and 1578.[19] Their stories fill the pages of *The Martyrs' Mirror*—a 1,290-page volume first published in 1660.[20] The harsh reaction to Mennonites derived both from theological (ideological) issues and as the social consequences of Mennonite actions, the latter of which appear to be the real reason for their brutal suppression by the state and church-states.

Persecution scattered the Anabaptists into other parts of Switzerland, south and north Germany, Alsace, Austria, and the Netherlands.[21] Many became evasive and retreated into the most inaccessible hinterlands where the Anabaptist hunters would have difficulty finding them.[22] The migrations, given the widespread grassroot unrest and support for the Anabaptist cause (at least in its economic and political implications), resulted in the spread of the movement all over Europe and produced conventicles and other forms of religious expression which have influenced the Mennonite movement to the present. In south Germany, Anabaptists were recruited from among those involved in the Peasant Revolt; in north Germany, they were chosen from the Muenster Rebellion.[23] Related uprisings in Amsterdam and Utrecht and the Hutterite communistic movement in Austria and Bohemia were all offshoots of the original revolt.[24]

The dispersing of Anabaptist-Mennonites all over Europe resulted in their becoming a religious minority group very quickly, developing a defensive and separatistic stance against the world at large. Enclavic communities grew in the backwoods and corners of the European continent, from the Bernese Juras to the Prussian swamps. The subcultural tendencies of ethnicity very soon emerged as these hunted groups lapsed into linguistic and social isolation.

Mennonites in North America

Even remote areas of western Europe did not provide safe havens for Anabaptist-Mennonites, and over the years they continued to migrate to Russia, North America, South America, and elsewhere.[25] North America, in particular, proved attractive.[26] In 1677, William Penn accompanied Quaker founder George Fox on a preaching tour of the Netherlands and Germany.[27] Penn and Fox shared the idea that North America might prove a haven for the persecuted religious minorities of Europe. Although some Mennonites were nervous about associating too closely with Quakers, they founded the first permanent German settlement in America at Germantown, Pennsylvania, in 1683.

Over the next two hundred years, eight thousand Mennonites migrated to North America alone.[28] This migration has been separated into six distinct phases, during which many Swiss and southern German Mennonites crossed the Atlantic. Between 1873 and 1884, some 18,000 Mennonites left Russia to settle in the United States and Canada; another major migration of Russian Mennonites occurred after World War I. Less than fifty years after the Amish-Mennonite split in 1693,[29] the first major contingent of Amish settlers arrived in Philadelphia. Amish immigration peaked between 1727 and 1770, and today no Amish remain in Europe. Between 1856 and 1859, all Hutterites left the European continent, founding three colonies in South Dakota (see Figures 1-1 and 1-2).

After first arriving in North America in the late 1600s, Anabaptist-Mennonites continued to move both internally and internationally, westward and north to Canada. They were often drawn more by the prospect of good land at low prices than by a specific aim of establishing model religious communities.[30] Large tracts of land, out of the question in southeastern Pennsylvania, were still available in places like Virginia, where Mennonites settled in the early to mid-1700s. Good land at low prices also drew Mennonites to Ohio, Indiana, Illinois, Iowa, Kansas, and Nebraska.[31]

Mennonite Diversity in the New World

Varied settlements in search of tolerance and peace created the climate of subcultural differences which in time developed into subgroups, eventually resulting in misunderstandings, conflicts, and schisms. The many conferences during the first several decades of the Anabaptist movement were able to hammer out relatively similar statements of faith, but they were not sufficient to prevent schisms. Many but not all of these occurred while the Anabaptists were still in Europe. Some formed gradually and persist to the present day.

Figure 1-2 illustrates the proliferation of the Anabaptist-Mennonite family, which today consists of some twenty-five groups in North America alone (see Table 1-1). They range from very traditional Old Order groups such as the Amish to highly assimilated groups such as the Mennonite Brethren. Important attitudinal and behavioral differences separate the major subgroups,[32] notably, between those Mennonites of Swiss versus Dutch origin.

Today, the North American Mennonite community totals more than 600,000 persons, including 405,713 baptized members (see Table 1-2). De-

Figure 1-1. Anabaptist–Mennonite family tree

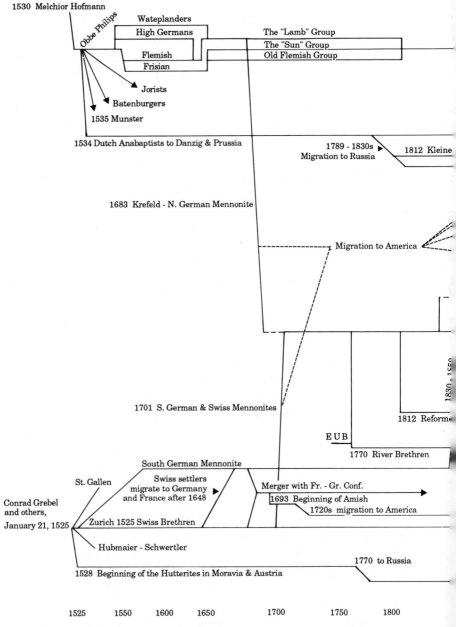

Vertical lines denote schisms or reunification; diagonal lines denote migration.

1874 - 80   1945 End of Danzig - Prussian Settlements

1881 Evangelical Mennonite Conference
Mennonites in Russia
1867 Krimmer Mennonite Brethren
1874 Bergthaler (Chortitzer) Mennonite Church
1889 Evangelical Mennonite Brethren

1890 Old Colony Mennonite   1958 Reinland
1892 Sommerfelder Mennonite   1936 Evangelical Mennonite Mission
Converence of Mennonite in Canada
60
Mennonite Bretheren Church
hurch of God in Christ Mennonite
Founding of General Conference Mennonite

1968 Eastern Pennsylvania Mennonite
1978 Fellowship Church
Mennonite Church

1957 Orthodox Mennonite
1917 David Martin
1940 Waterloo Markham
1871 Old Order Mennonite
865 Evangelical   1898 Missionary Church Association
ennonite Conference

1947 United Missionary Church
1883 Mennonite Brethren in Christ

1872 Stucky Amish   1946 Join CG
1910 Conservative Amish Mennonite
1925 Beachy Amish

1870s to S. Dakota, Manitoba, Alberta

1875   1900   1925   1950   1980

CE: Redekop (1989), 32–33. Expanded and revised from Dyck (1981).

Figure 1-2. Mennonite migrations to and within North America

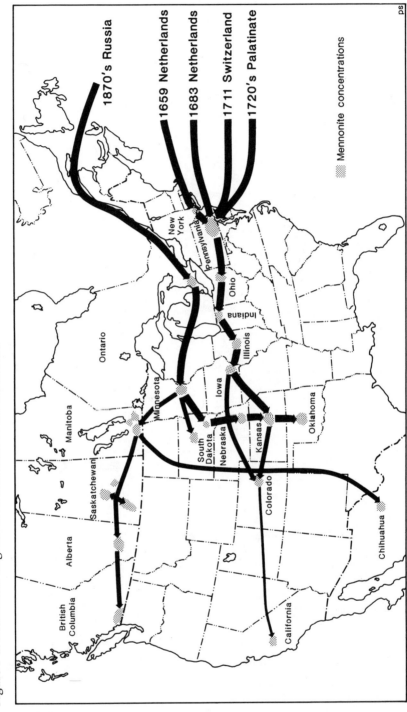

1870's Russia
1659 Netherlands
1683 Netherlands
1711 Switzerland
1720's Palatinate

Mennonite concentrations

New York
Pennsylvania
Ohio
Indiana
Illinois
Iowa
Minnesota
Ontario
Manitoba
Saskatchewan
Alberta
British Columbia
South Dakota
Nebraska
Kansas
Oklahoma
Colorado
California
Chihuahua

ps

SOURCE: Map drawn by Pamela Schaus. From Redekop (1989), 18.

TABLE I-I
Congregations and Membership of Mennonite and Brethren in Christ
Church Bodies in North America, 1990

Name of Church Body	Congregations			Membership		
	Canada	United States	Total	Canada	United States	Total
Beachy Amish Mennonite Fellowship	—[a]	—	105	—	—	7,238
Bergthaler Churches in Alberta, Saskatchewan	11	0	11	900	0	900
Brethren in Christ General Conference North America	—	—	225	—	—	19,853
Chortitzer Mennonite Conference	11	0	11	2,400	0	2,400
Church of God in Christ, Mennonite (Holdeman)	34	77	111	3,424	9,999	13,423
Conference of Mennonites in Canada[b]	156	0	156	28,994	0	28,994
Eastern Pennsylvania Mennonite Church and related areas	—	—	55	—	—	3,255
Evangelical Mennonite Church	0	26	26	0	3,888	3,888
Evangelical Mennonite Conference, Canada	48	0	48	5,813	0	5,813
Evangelical Mennonite Mission Conference	—	—	24	—	—	3,470
General Conference Mennonite Church[c]	0	258	258	33,812	—	33,812
Markham-Waterloo Conference	10	0	10	1,035	0	1,035
General Conference of the Mennonite Brethren Churches	—	—	317	—	—	43,452
Hutterian Brethren	—	—	353	—	—	14,000
Hutterian Brethren (Society of Brothers)	0	6	6	0	800	800
Mennonite Church General Assembly	—	—	1,055	—	—	102,276
Mennonite Church (independent and unaffiliated groups)	—	—	288	—	—	13,878
New Reinland Mennonite Church of Ontario	3	0	3	464	0	464
Old Colony Mennonite Church	21	0	21	6,150	0	6,150
Old Order Amish	—	—	784	—	—	56,200
Old Order Mennonites (Canada)	17	0	17	2,470	0	2,470
Old Order Mennonites (U.S.)	0	49	49	0	10,000	10,000
Old Order River Brethren	0	7	7	0	326	326
Reinland Mennonite Church	8	0	8	1,590	0	1,590
Sommerfeld Mennonite Church	26	0	26	5,500	0	5,500
Totals			3,974			381,385

SOURCE: James E. Horsch (1992), 215.

[a] —, Information not available.

[b] Affiliated with the General Conference Mennonite Church.

[c] Affiliated with the Conference of Mennonites in Canada.

TABLE I-2
Mennonite and Brethren in Christ

Continent	Country	Membership	Organized Bodies or Groups
Africa	Angola	2,600	1
	Burkina Faso	63	1
	Ethiopia	50,018	1
	Ghana	1,500	1
	Kenya	11,682	7
	Malawi	240	1
	Mozambique	22,900	1
	Nigeria	7,251	2
	South Africa	199	2
	Tanzania	19,486	1
	Zaire	136,200	3
	Zambia	8,362	1
	Zimbabwe	16,152	1
	Total	276,653	23
Asia and Australia	Australia	40	1
	Hong Kong	94	1
	India	84,195	8
	Indonesia	60,709	3
	Japan	3,460	5
	Philippines	1,059	2
	Singapore		1
	Taiwan	1,400	1
	Vietnam	100	1
	Total	151,057	23
Caribbean, Central and South America	Antigua and Barbados	795	1
	Argentina	2,885	3
	Belize	2,429	7
	Bolivia	6,664	6
	Brazil	5,974	5
	Colombia	2,134	3
	Costa Rica	1,725	2
	Cuba	45	2
	Dominican Republic	2,163	4
	Ecuador	213	1
	El Salvador	262	2
	Guatemala	3,971	5
	Haiti	901	3
	Honduras	9,841	5
	Jamaica	505	2
	Mexico	20,478	9
	Nicaragua	5,093	3
	Panama	710	2
	Paraguay	22,512	19
	Peru	323	2
	Puerto Rico	596	1

TABLE I-2
Continued

Continent	Country	Membership	Organized Bodies or Groups
	Trinidad and Tobago	86	1
	Uruguay	887	3
	Venezuela	244	3
	Total	91,436	94
Europe	Austria	350	1
	Belgium	85	1
	CIS	3,350	
	France	2,000	1
	Germany	24,414	7
	Great Britain	88	2
	Ireland	6	2
	Italy	160	1
	Luxembourg	100	1
	Netherlands	15,500	1
	Portugal	14	2
	Spain	265	3
	Switzerland	2,800	1
	Total	49,132	23
North America	Canada	117,932	15
	U.S.	287,781	6
	Canada/U.S.		10
	Total	405,713	31
Summary			
Africa	276,653	13	23
Asia and Australia	151,057	9	23
Caribbean, Central and South America	91,436	24	94
Europe	49,132	13	23
North America	405,713	2	31
Total	973,921	61	194

SOURCE: Roth (1994), 15.

spite traditionally large families, the Anabaptist-Mennonite movement has not grown as rapidly as other religious traditions that emerged from the Protestant Reformation, primarily because of the opprobrium attached to membership in a rather despised minority. Although the vicious attacks of the Reformation gave way to other forms of persecution from other sources, many "birthright" Mennonites continued (and continue today) to forgo their heritage to be accepted by the larger society.

HISTORY OF MENNONITE
ECONOMIC ACTIVITY

The proliferation of Anabaptist-Mennonite communities was accompanied by a multiplication of economic arrangements within them. Real life brought dramatic variation to the way in which a theology of economics expressed itself. Old Order groups, for example, maintained a relatively rural existence with a traditional economic system, which, if not totally communal as among the Hutterites, was at least nearly so, as illustrated by the close economic sharing in the Amish or Old Colony society.[33] By contrast, the more assimilated groups moved into the dominant societal institutions and operate in an economic milieu not much different from that in the non–Mennonite world at large. These communities have been exposed to an erosion of the religious/utopian values and commitments that were part of the early Anabaptist movement. They are composed of Mennonites engaged in activities outside the traditional economic order and for whom Mennonite economic theology has failed to keep them faithful.

The Utopian/Communal Impulse in Early Anabaptism

The Anabaptist-Mennonite movement had a utopian and, at times, chiliastic emphasis. Achieving their utopian ends often meant separation from the world and creating a society in which there would be absolute brotherhood, an objective expressed by a majority of early Anabaptist leaders. Wolfgang Brandhuber, martyred in 1529, expressed his communal sentiments in the following manner: "If God permits and enables, all things should be held in common love, should compel him [the believer] to contribute faithfully to the common treasury."[34] Brandhuber's teachings are regarded as foundational to the practice of a community of goods, instituted among the Hutterian Brethren in 1528.[35]

The social and economic aspects of this utopian movement formed a curious profile, no doubt partly the result of the severe persecution. The radically communistic form that developed at Muenster finally disintegrated through brutal internal events and external opposition. The Hutterite branch took a middle of the road approach and practiced New Testament communalism in very isolated retreatist societies. Most adherents to the Mennonite movement, however, developed a form more benign, familistic, and withdrawn though still strongly communal, so that for several hundred years the Mennonites were called *die Stille in Lande,* the silent in the land.

In all branches, economic factors were under the strict surveillance of the congregation. One of the earliest references to economic practices is found in a report of the Strasbourg Conference of 1557. Representatives from fifty or more congregations in Switzerland, Moravia, Alsace, and south Germany attended this meeting and concluded that "all types of work and business enterprises were permissible for the Christians if they were not offensive and were not contrary to the Scriptures."[36] This item was couched in a discussion of how strict the process of excommunication should be for backsliders.

Beyond Utopianism

The Anabaptist-Mennonite movement was originally composed of a cross-section of society, including noblemen, teachers, lawyers, and other professionals, a goodly number of artisans, and peasants, who, after all, made up 90 percent of the population. There was some regional variation in the occupational profile of early Anabaptists. W. L. C. Coenen's study of 161 Anabaptist martyrs in the Netherlands, for example, revealed no farmers. Those who were martyred were businessmen, craftspeople, and industrial workers, including weavers, tailors, shoemakers, sailors, carpenters, goldsmiths, hatmakers, bricklayers, bakers, leather dealers, teachers, saddlers, and potters.[37] The occupations of Dutch Anabaptists can be contrasted with those in Switzerland, where the overwhelming majority were peasants.[38] Over time, however, the movement was universally driven out of the cities and towns by the persecution, and it became a peasant movement, with the few artisans that remained providing the leadership.

After the Mennonite movement settled into the epoch of community and institution building (circa 1580–1880), its energies were turned toward building community institutions (including facilities and personnel for schools) nurturing the family, and securing the material welfare of the community. The Hutterites especially are known for their educational achievements,[39] but the Russians also developed some impressive educational institutions, reviewed briefly below.[40]

The nurture of the family—in many ways the most impressive institution of the entire Mennonite community—has an equally strong history. The bulwark of the Mennonite society and almost synonymous with the religious community, the family also contributed to the order, solidarity, communalism, and religious base of the community at large.[41]

Mennonites moved into the economic sphere with vigor and ingenuity as soon as they were allowed to do so. Political and religious oppression restricted the Hutterite, Swiss, south German, and Alsatian Mennonites mainly to agricultural activities because there they were the least visible and contentious. In any case, in spite of severe early persecution, they developed an impressive and varied economic industry, beginning around 1540.[42] This included the introduction of crop rotation, the use of fertilizers and manure to produce remarkable crops, the introduction of legumes (especially alfalfa), and haying rather than grazing for cattle. Mennonites in France and south Germany thus became known far and wide as the best of agriculturalists. These Mennonite innovations became so famous that at the beginning of the nineteenth century an agricultural professor at the University of Heidelberg told his students to go to Mennonite farms, "where they could learn more than their professor could teach them."[43] Individual Mennonite agricultural innovators such as Klopfenstein and Moellinger became almost household words in Alsace and south Germany.[44]

The Dutch and Prussian Mennonites in the first decades were also hounded and persecuted and thus settled in rural areas where they innovated in remarkable ways, especially in land drainage in the lowlands areas of the Netherlands, north Germany, and Prussia. But the Mennonites in the Netherlands and north Germany, especially in the seacoast regions, became actively involved in nonagricultural economic activities as soon as persecution began to abate. By the middle of the seventeenth century, Mennonites were among the leading groups in the lumber trade and in shipbuilding, herring fisheries, and whaling. Mennonite merchant fleets monopolized the Baltic shipping for generations, including Iceland and Greenland; they also reached Riga and the Levant. Families associated with this industry include the de Rijpps, van Warendorps, van Eeghens, and the van Lenneps.[45]

Mennonites also became leaders in the banking and insurance business, flour milling, distilleries, weaving, and textile and dye factories. For example, in 1768 the Leyen family silk industry in Crefeld utilized 724 machines and employed three thousand workers.[46] Textile and flower export and grocery chains were also created. Many of these houses still exist, such as P. Sehoen, W. Middelhoven, and ten Cate, although few are under direct Mennonite ownership.[47] The Dutch and north German Mennonites thus were predominantly commercial and have remained so until the present day, though a strong rural contingent has persisted especially in Friesland.

The migration of Prussian Mennonites to Russia, on the invitation of Czarina Katerina, resulted in an unusual socioreligious phenomenon. The Mennonites were invited to settle in an isolated block of land, ostensibly totally free of other people, thus creating a veritable church-state within a church since the Mennonites considered themselves a religious people.[48] Although agriculture was their economic mainstay (as was the case throughout the world until the Industrial Revolution) the emergence of a Mennonite enclave soon developed a great need for nonagricultural institutions.

A unique dual authority system developed. On the one hand was the religious authority that included a *Kirchenkonvent*, a council of the ministers and elders of all the congregations, which was responsible for the spiritual life of the Mennonite society. On the other was the secular arm, consisting of a colony authority system (*Gebietsamt*), constituted by all the landowners who elected a mayor (*Oberschulze*) and several assistants (*Beisitzer*).[49]

The secular order pertained to the entire realm of social activities, including economic, social, educational, and political, and provided the setting for a complex socioeconomic structure. This secular political organization, emerging as a response to very practical and pragmatic necessity, developed into a complex structure with considerable scope and concentration of power. Hence the *Oberschulze* slowly began to accumulate power, which included taxation, public works, and law enforcement. This contributed to the development of a considerable Mennonite society, which at the end of the nineteenth century totaled about 120,000.[50]

An educational system grew in response to the need to supply the entire cultural education for the Mennonite society. Eventually it included a universal elementary system for all children, consisting of 450 elementary schools, a teacher training institution, and a number of secondary as well as several business/commerce schools (*Kommerzschule*) and an agricultural school.[51]

Business and industrial activities and organizations flourished. Of course, agriculture was the original predominant activity, but with the growth in population—due largely to very large families but also to the continuing immigration from Prussia— alternative economic pursuits were the only viable solution to the problem of an expanding population. Hence, a variety of businesses and commercial ventures emerged. One was the flour milling industry, which found a niche in the great demand for the Red Turkey wheat, developed by the Mennonites.[52] By 1908, the major Mennonite settlements had seventy-three motorized and steam-driven mills.[53]

Cornelius Krahn reviewed the extent of industry among Mennonites in 1957[54] and noted that other industries emerged, including silkworm raising and silk processing. Mennonite foundries and agricultural machinery factories produced more than 10 percent of the total output of south Russia in the nineteenth century. A tally at the end of that century is impressive: twenty-six factories of agricultural machinery, thirty-eight brick factories, and twenty other industries. There were a number of large corporations; the largest, Lepp and Wallman, employed 270 persons in 1911.

The entrepreneurial thrust obviously thrived in the Russian context, as it did in the Netherlands. Many could be listed as leading entrepreneurs, but foremost is Johann Cornies, who assumed almost mythic proportions in Russian Mennonite memory. "Cornies achieved more than anybody else in the realm of cultural and economic advancement in Russia. But in dealing with the opposition of religious leaders, ignorant conservative farmers, or personal opponents he could be ruthless."[55] There were many other entrepreneurs, including P. H. Lepp, J. G. Niebuhr, J. Siemens, and many lesser ones as well.[56]

Mennonite migration to North America, which began with Palatinate and lower Rhine region emigrants, brings us to the setting in which the rest of this book will unfold. The Germantown settlers overwhelmingly belonged to the artisan and yeoman classes.[57] Most of them were linen weavers, but they also included cloth and fustian weavers, tailors, shoemakers, locksmiths, and carpenters. With the opening of the frontier, many Mennonite immigrants settled on rural lands, bringing with them the advanced farming practices already in use in Alsace and ultimately contributing extensively to the present-day Pennsylvania German culture, especially that of Lancaster County. From there, Mennonites and Amish continued to filter to western Pennsylvania, Ohio, and states beyond. They migrated north to Ontario, partly in protest to the Revolutionary War, and south to Virginia in search of land. A massive immigration of Mennonites from southern Russia, beginning in 1874, to the midwestern United States and Canada developed a Mennonite presence that soon expanded to British Columbia in Canada and the coastal states of Washington, Oregon, and California.

The major economic activity these Mennonites undertook was agriculture, and the conservative and especially Old Order Mennonite groups remain rural and agriculturally based to this day. But soon nonagricultural activities attracted Mennonites, especially in eastern Pennsylvania, which had become urbanized by the beginning of the twentieth century. Fretz stated that by the end of the Civil War, Mennonites in Franconia conference were merchants, supplying Philadelphia and neighboring cities with produce and related services.[58]

By 1900, sizable industries emerged, such as the Miller-Hess Shoe company in Akron, Pennsylvania. Several apple butter and canning businesses were on the scene as well, including C. H. Musselman and J. M. Smucker in eastern Ohio. Other Mennonite communities housed many smaller industries—milling, retailing, banking, and service stations and garages.[59]

By the 1940s, Russian Mennonites had established themselves securely on the prairies and in the West, and business and industry flourished in almost every Mennonite community. Their variety is illustrated by a random selection of substantial organizations: Jacob A. Shenk Hatchery, Harrisonburg, Virginia; Saunder Woodworking Co., Archbold, Ohio; Ulrich Products Corporation, Roanoke, Illinois; Hesston Corporation, Hesston, Kansas; Snyder Potato Chips, Cambridge, Ontario; Friesen Printing Co., Altona, Manitoba; and Enns Farms, Reedley, California. Not included in this list are other areas of Mennonite activity, such as wholesaling, retailing, financing, land development, and building and contracting.

THE MENNONITE DENIAL OF THE UTOPIAN-COMMUNALISTIC ETHOS

Today the Mennonites are extremely ambivalent about their original utopian and egalitarian emphasis. Ever in the disputations and inquisitions at the hands of the Catholic and Protestant authorities, some Anabaptists had denied that they were communistic, but according to contemporary observers their life betrayed it. It is generally agreed that much of the Anabaptist denial of communism derived from fear of imminent persecution if they confessed. Hence, Ambrosius Spittelmayr "maintained that it might be correct to speak of a community of goods, but this had no overtones of an organized communism, for it was only the economic expression of a love ethic that could not disregard the needs of others."[60] The resulting and curious historiographical and methodological quirk is that non-Mennonite scholars are more insistent on the communal aspect of the movement than are the insiders.[61]

Present-day Mennonites continue to resist considering themselves radically communal; their scholarly community largely ignores or even denies the communal aspects of their heritage,[62] resulting in a contradiction in modern Mennonite belief and practice. Guy F. Hershberger, a leading interpreter of Mennonite political and social thought, stated that "one cannot accept the identification of communal ownership with the way of the cross in economic relationships," but continued, "[there] is no doubt that modern Mennonitism has far too much fallen under the spell of materialism."[63]

The contradiction is that even while they deny the communal nature of original and present-day Anabaptism, conservative scholars lament the materialistic nature of contemporary Mennonitism and call for a return to the more mutually sharing aspects of the Gospel. The world has grown more seductive, and in the arena of mutuality and economic sharing, the discipline is lax. Hershberger believed, in fact, that economic prosperity might destroy the movement and often quoted a Dutch Mennonite leader: "After the devil failed in his attempt to destroy Dutch Anabaptism by means of persecution, he almost succeeded when he changed his tactic and made them rich."[64]

Thus, although the world had been resisted fairly easily in the areas of pacifism, political separation, mutual assistance, lay congregational life, and nonconformity, the area of economics has been a different matter. Mennonites have participated according to the rules of the market economy, have become assimilated, and are losing their identity. Today there is a growing awareness among educated lay people as well as professional scholars that material culture—which makes a capitalist society possible—holds a place of central significance in human history. Mennonites themselves have largely ignored the significance of their material conditions in shaping their ideology even though they have become deeply involved in material life.

The continuing derision the movement suffered for its communal thrust—especially the Hutterites who continued the tradition and who suffered continuously for it—must have contributed to the general evasion of looking critically at the centrality of economic factors in social life. The material culture, or economy, of modern North America is based on principles directly antithetical to those of Mennonitism. Insofar as Mennonite history and practice are "spiritualized," the worlds of economic practice and religious belief run on separate tracks.[65]

Regardless of how thoroughgoing the separation has been, the selective presence of the world or the larger environment has been just as real. Mennonites have known instinctively and intuitively that the world is necessary both as reality from which they need to separate and one on which they depend, thereby putting into question their very reason for being. This dualism—or dialectic, depending upon one's point of view—stems from the early Mennonites' realization through their agonizing persecution that their utopian/apocalyptic cultural blueprint could not be completed.

In a larger sense, however, the meaning of *separation* is that of becoming a people, an *ethnos* in which family, church, and economic community form an indissoluble unity. The Mennonites became such a people in the crucible of persecution. Peoplehood brings self-consciousness; and self-consciousness, if we can trust what our dialecticians (Paul, Augustine, Cusa, Hegel) tell us, is originally consciousness of alienation (that Adam and Eve knew that they were naked meant that they were conscious of their alienation, according to Sartre). The Anabaptists established a new people spiritually—ideologically, by imposing their religious beliefs onto the material of their everyday existence—and then failed miserably to cope with the natural peoplehood that grew up as the material result of their ideal community.

Therefore, although the world was resisted with relative ease in the areas of warfare (pacifism) and selfishness (internal discipline and mutuality), in the arena of the material culture/economic sphere, the world's claim had been much more aggressive and incessant. Mennonites participated in the expanding trade, commerce, and industry as soon as they were sufficiently tolerated to establish themselves. In North America, this process took another step. The secular environment of North American materialistic culture, and especially its high valuation of the acquisitive impulse and its gratification, has been very powerful in shaping Mennonite identity, albeit very unevenly among the various groups.

It is reasonable to propose that the Mennonite ambivalence regarding the communistic protest in economic life must be seen as the gradual rejection of the utopian/eschatalogical nature of its original vision. Mennonites were unable to master all the conflicts and outside pressures arising from their rejection of a wide range of societal values and institutions, not

to mention the internal hemorrhagings from members becoming fright-
ened by the severity of the persecution and seduced by the attractions of
materialism. Mennonite communities, in the ensuing years, yielded to the
temptation to reject communalism as having ever been a part of original authentic Anabaptism. More serious than the historically established
loss of the utopian stance is the theoretical conclusion that rationalizes the
loss as gain on the assumption that communism is fundamentally incompatible with Anabaptism because withdrawal from the world ostensibly
impairs the church's "prophetic witness."[66] Here Hershberger, of course,
begs the question of whether communalism implies physical and social
withdrawal.

The dogged retention of communalism by the Hutterites thus gives
considerable weight to its place in the early Anabaptist movement. What
is needed is an explanation of how they were able to adhere to the communalism while most other Anabaptist groups relinquished it in practice
while adhering to it theologically. The answer must lie within the larger
cultural/historical forces. The individualistic cultural milieu of the dominant society is an important factor that immigrants from all religious-
ethnic groups must address. Many studies have been written on the His-
panic, Italian, Jewish, and Armenian responses to their new American
environment. The Mennonite response, because of the group's emphasis
on congregational autonomy, has been one of great tolerance, with Mennonites defending practically the entire economic spectrum in the name
of orthodoxy.

The great hiatus between early Anabaptist-Mennonite beliefs in and
practice of a radical communal economics and modern practice has created
a great conflict in the basic identity of Mennonite society. Hans Jürgen
Goertz speaks of a "crisis of the Mennonites' cognitive center [which] has
dissolved and created a vacuum into which outer, nontraditional viewpoints have flooded."[67] Goertz maintained that only by returning to the
traditional understanding of its faith and purpose will modern Anabaptism recover its identity and purpose. There is no question, according to
Goertz, that the economic issue is at the center, for he says, "It was not the
primitive Christian principle of sharing everything with one another that
triumphed, but the domination of man by man, persecution and destruction, the striving for wealth and the misery of war." He concluded, "The
Mennonites have made their accommodation with bourgeois capitalist
society."[68]

MENNONITE UNEASINESS WITH ECONOMIC SUCCESS

Over the past four hundred years, Mennonites have developed a disquiet about business activities generally and economic success more specifically. Guy Hershberger noted that some early Anabaptist leaders considered it quite impossible for a Christian to engage in trade (e.g., Peter Riedemann, a successor to Jacob Hutter). Although Menno Simons left this door slightly ajar, "granting that some merchants and retailers were God fearing and righteous,"[69] many Mennonite writers, including Hershberger, wanted to slam it shut.

The Anabaptist-Mennonite antipathy toward business flies in the face of what Max Weber would have predicted for them. In his 1958 *Protestant Ethic and the Spirit of Capitalism*, Weber argued that capitalism would flourish among the Mennonites (whom he called Baptists) because their theology justified prosperity as a sign of grace (theodicy) and because their lifestyle and scrupulous integrity enhanced their business opportunities. Weber's sociological hypothesis of Mennonite propensity toward capitalism is in direct contradiction to the anticapitalistic theological and community tradition.

Where does this uneasiness about business and success originate? Some of it undoubtedly results from the contradictory views of Anabaptist-Mennonite communalism discussed above. Other, historical/ideological factors are also important. Because of the persecution and the resulting justification of the movement, a peasant tradition developed in which the most orthodox Mennonites became those who conformed to the *Gelassenheit-Gemeinschaft* type of social organization based on the experience of rural life, whether actual or idealized. Entrepreneurship was present in communities organized according to the principles of this ideal, but it was very circumscribed and standardized. *Gemeinde, Gemeinschaft,* and *Gelassenheit* all referred to the basic elements of the "covenanted Community or the "colony of Heaven" based on submission to the Lordship of Christ.[70] *Gelassenheit* was the term the early Anabaptists used for submission to the will of God and the community, downplaying the individual striving and acquisitiveness of materialism.[71] The central role of private property and self-advancement in the breakdown of community was keenly recognized by Anabaptists and was resisted strongly.

Anabaptist ideology was forged as a response to the emergence of modernity as the dominant worldview. Modernity is characterized by the market economy, individualism, private property, and materialism. Anabaptism, properly understood, is not *reactive*—maintaining antiquated social forms in the face of shifting realities—but *proactive*—based on an understanding of community as *Utopos*, or nonplace, the community yet to be realized and which any existing historical community is by definition inadequate to express.

Sebastian Franck, a contemporary of the Anabaptists, though no friend, described their life as follows: "Not only must a Christian not seek worldly pleasure but he must flee it, and take joy in the cross, misery and poverty, seeking only what is above and nothing on earth. He counts taking as giving, dying as living, privation as possession, poverty as riches, and possessions as though he had none."[72] An analysis of the *Gelassenheit* theme, especially in relation to the acquisitive impulse and private property, reflects the traditional communal ethic in which family, church, and polity form an indissoluble union. The local normative Mennonite entrepreneur's activity is restricted to meeting the satisfaction of his traditional needs; the interests he recognizes as his own are those of his religious community. Robert Friedmann, in an analysis of *Gelassenheit* and communalism, quoted Hans Denk: "When we truly realize the love of God, we will be ready to give up for love's sake even what God has given us. It is by this *Gelassenheit* that a true disciple is first recognized. Only by overcoming all selfishness will communion of love become possible."[73]

This communion/community of love is precisely how Hegel characterized the family in his *System Der Sittlichkeit* and *Rechtsphilosophie*, which forms the "natural" base of all forms of higher culture.[74] Civil society, the arena of individual liberty and the site of the market economy's activity, is, in this scheme of things, not the result of a natural state of affairs, but the culmination of a *Bildung* (education, *paideia* in Greek) which begins in the context of the family. The next stage of development is that of traditional peasant society in which the familial affinity is extended to a larger, fictive, kinship network in a village context, and which forms a number of such fictive kinship groups, from the totems of primitive clans to the patronage networks of surviving peasant cultures in modern societies.

Social relationships in all premodern societies were patterned after the model of the family and were either patriarchal or patrimonial. In time, these families adopted outsiders with the effect of the family remaining a model long after those who considered themselves members of such a family could demonstrate affinal relationships. The traditional example is the Sons of Israel and Jesus' and Paul's elevation of the fictive kinship (children according to the Spirit) to higher status than biological (children according to the flesh) kinship. We arrive at the problem of whether society created the natural spirituality of the family (Durkheim, Levi-Strauss, Gottwald) or whether the natural spirituality of the family gave rise to society, as a one-sided reading of Hegel and the modern, individualistic, myth of human origins has it.

The rustication of the Anabaptist movement idealized the natural spirituality of family feeling and extended it to the peasant culture that was being threatened by the rise of modernism. Peculiar, acultural individualism was perceived as the destroyer of the natural spirituality of religion or the family, wherever its effect became manifest.[75]

Tension in the lives of North American Mennonite communities and individuals comes from the diametric opposition of the *Gemeinde, Gemeinschaft, Gelassenheit* ethic that was reinforced by persecution when the European Anabaptists rejected the ecclesiastical authority of the state religion and the emerging economic individualism under its cloak. In North America, no state religion exists. Also missing is the traditional structure of authority on which the peasant society survives as an independent culture. The external compulsion of the state as enemy, which traditionally reinforced the communal ethic and simultaneously discouraged Mennonite cosmopolitanism, is therefore lacking. In North America there is no material basis for peasant culture—the inalienable right to the land as an incentive to remain in the traditional community. In the end, the structural inversion of the Mennonites' social position from communal peasant to individual capitalist took place upon immigration to America. American society encouraged entrepreneurial activity by eroding the agricultural base, which was protected in Europe by traditional considerations, and by creating an open, entrepreneurial political system, as opposed to the closed, persecuting society of European experience.

Mennonites in North America have tolerated certain forms of business activities. Most have assented to an informal distinction between legitimate (or normative) and suspect (or nonnormative) business activities (e.g., Mennonite grocers selling cigarettes, selling on Sunday). The dark side of the overt acceptance of the normative Mennonite entrepreneurs by the rural congregation was the tacit agreement among themselves that the Mennonite businessmen, especially those in town, were "different" and could not be quite as loyal to Mennonite principles as the rural folk in the traditional role of farming. Lifestyle and the types of contacts and relationships businesspeople developed with "outsiders" became evidence of disloyalty to the traditional community. Aggressive involvement in business conflicted with loyalty to the church in the minds of the traditional interpreters of Jesus' words that one "cannot serve God and Mammon," with all the disastrous consequences (alcoholism, tobacco use, divorce and unemployment) of assimilation to follow.

This situation created a series of what might be termed *push* and *pull* factors. A sociologist at one of the Mennonite colleges stated the case as follows:

As a small boy some thirty-five years ago, I asked my parents why a number of families who had become successful in business and professions left the Lititz [Pennsylvania] Mennonite Church to join a neighboring denomination. . . . With a bit of thought, I can compile a long list of persons who, along with their success financially and professionally, chose to leave the Mennonite Church. . . . There are characteristics within the Mennonite Church that *push* successful persons to leave and there are characteristics that *pull* them. (italics added for emphasis) [76]

The *push* factors deal with the inhospitable attitudes of many Mennonites to the successful business person and the expectations of conformity to seemingly rigid community norms. The *pull* factors refer to the perceived greater hospitality among non-Mennonite or progressive Mennonite communities.

Mennonites have recognized the tension, and several church-business organizations have emerged as part of an attempt to bridge the gap between the increased number of people in business-oriented occupations and the church, reducing their feelings of alienation. The first president of Church-Industry and Business Association (CIBA) stated the problem in the inaugural editorial of the organization's *Newsletter*:

In Chicago, October 25, 1969, CIBA was born. The ninety persons who met together as a brotherhood had a common concern—that a vehicle might be provided to communicate the problems and visions of business and industry people to one another and then to the church. The future holds much opportunity for us to develop love and understanding of one another . . . and to communicate this to people involved in our everyday lives. [77]

But the question of business's compatibility with Mennonite heritage, theology, and values remains. It was posed quite eloquently by a leading Mennonite entrepreneur, who queried, "Is it possible for the Christian to consider seriously a life in business? From my vantage point as a business person it appears that our concerned Christian community often·lives in two different camps . . . [illustrated by] the apparent dichotomy between business and Christianity." [78]

CHAPTER TWO

Religion and
Entrepreneurial Activity
Congruous, Contradictory, or Paradoxical?

THE UBIQUITOUS QUALITY OF THE
ECONOMIC ENTERPRISE

The book of Genesis tells us that we will earn our daily bread by the sweat of our foreheads. This bit of ancient wisdom reveals a sociological truism: economic activity is a ubiquitous part of human life. Acquiring sufficient resources to feed, shelter, and otherwise make life worthwhile has occupied the waking hours of most people throughout time and in all civilizations.[1] Anthropological research supports this view and indicates that humans have been resourceful in this "occupation" and have overcome seemingly insurmountable obstacles in it. As Raymond Firth noted, although nature has not been totally stingy, it "obviously sets broad limits to the possibilities of human life. . . . Groups have managed to adapt themselves to very rigorous conditions which at first sight seem impossible for human existence."[2]

People's relationship to nature is, to a large degree, dictated by the social world into which they are born. Firth maintained that the physical environment plays an important part in regulating the food supply of a people, but he inserted an immediate proviso that "to a considerable extent social factors influence the situation."[3] He went on, "It is sometimes imagined that the main drive to the economic activity of a tribal people is their immediate desire to satisfy their material wants. But it would be untrue to interpret their economic organization as a simple response to their requirements for food, clothing, shelter, and the like. In the first place, it is a socialized and not an individual response."[4] Every society and its culture affect the way food, shelter, and life in general are derived from nature.

In describing the Dahomey of Africa, William Goode stated that "every Dahomean man must know three things well: How to cut a field, how to build a wall, and how to roof a house."[5] But Firth pointed out that these sorts of activities are not directed merely "to satisfy hunger, but in the use individuals can make of it to express their obligations to their relatives-in-law, their chiefs, their ancestors; to show hospitality; to display their wealth; to initiate or marry off their sons."[6] In other words, economic activity is not a series of simple actions (such as hunting or fishing) alone, but rather is bounded by social, cultural, and ideological restrictions that ensure that the individual's acquisitive impulses remain subject to the group's interests.[7]

Thus, there is a vital connection between the economic activity in society and its values, beliefs, and institutions. Not surprisingly, the nature and uses of the connection have been studied for millennia. "The fact is," Pitirim Sorokin once maintained, "that since immemorial times, thinkers were aware of the important role played by 'economic' factors in human behavior, social organization, social processes, and in the historical destiny of a society."[8] As a result, a massive legacy of thought and theory has emerged which attempts to rationalize the relationship between economics and society. This legacy includes the theories of Confucius (China), Aristotle and Thucydides (Greek), Polybius and Seneca (Rome), Machiavelli and Harrington (middle to late Middle Ages), Adam Smith and Turgot (eighteenth century), Marx and Engels (nineteenth century), and Max Weber and Joseph Schumpeter (twentieth century), to name only a few.[9]

The technology developed as a result of the Neolithic revolution in agriculture, which has remained basic to human culture as we know it, enabling humans to place the procurement of food, shelter, and all the other elements we understand to be part of human species survival and growth on a new basis.[10] These "biological functions" increasingly became involved in, and controlled by, complex politically, religiously, or ideologically determined economic institutions. Eventually, the invention of coinage and writing provided the institutional basis for ancient empire building.[11] Finally, with the emergence of the modern world economy and the Industrial Revolution (which characterizes the modern world economy for the popular imagination), further specialization of the workforce has removed even more people from primary production than did ancient civilizations' need for scribes and administrators, warriors, and merchants.

In modern societies, because fewer persons are directly involved in food production or the construction of houses, it is often assumed that fewer people are involved in economic activity. Nothing could be farther from the truth. Almost everyone is involved in producing food and shelter or other less directly economic goals. In the increasingly specialized division of labor characteristic of Western civilization, the activities of any one individual may not appear to serve any economic function, but an argument could be made that all human activity has an economic contribution to make, "for all human relationships may be discussed as exchange transactions." [12] As Karl Marx insisted, all human activity is class-oriented activity based upon control, or lack thereof, of the means of production. [13] This is especially true of modern society, where the status groups of traditional societies are replaced by economically based social classes. Max Weber also recognized the range of economic activity and its centrality to human social life, arguing that "all action will be said to be 'economically oriented' so far as, according to its subjective meaning, it is concerned with the satisfaction of a desire for 'utilities' (*Nutzleistungen*)." [14] People's need to satisfy desires (to have children, to eat, or to sleep) demand economic activity as Weber defined it.

RELIGION AND THE REGULATION OF THE ECONOMIC ENTERPRISE

All human societies have been concerned about the economic processes of assuring survival and the "good life," but each social grouping has interpreted its economic activity in the context of the origins, purposes, and destinies of its own history and ethos. Generally, it can be said that through their specific cultures (blueprints for living) all societies have had a great deal to say about how, when, where, and why members engage in acquisitive behavior. The Hammurabi Code and Karl Marx's writings, although widely separated in time and space, present but two interpretations of the need to regulate this human impulse.

In part, the need to regulate economic activity flows from the fact that humans are "biologically incomplete." As Peter Berger and Thomas Luckmann put it,

Man's instinctual organization may be described as underdeveloped, compared to that of the other higher mammals. Man does have drives, of course. But these drives are highly unspecialized and undirected. This means that the human organism is capable of applying its constitutionally given equipment to a very wide and, in addition, constantly variable and varying range of activities.[15]

Berger and Luckmann concluded, therefore, that human survival becomes dependent on social arrangements, through which human activity is regulated and social chaos and conflict minimized. Berger and Luckmann suggested that "human existence, if it were thrown back on its organismic resources by themselves, would be existence in some sort of chaos."[16] Yet empirically we see that human existence manifests order, direction, and stability because of the human environment socially constructed for people and by people.

Among other things, the human environment regulates economic relations and activities. As Kingsley Davis said, "If men obtained goods solely through unrestrained cunning and ruthless struggle, there would ensue a state of social chaos in which actually they could obtain no goods at all."[17] Like many theorists, Davis presumed that human beings are motivated by self-interest and want to maximize their own happiness. According to Sorokin, this produces scarcity, the source of human conflict.

Conflicts take place in three different fields: (1) between man and nature, (2) between man and man, and (3) between the different interests of the same man. If things were not scarce, no one would think of claiming property in anything . . . the economic problem is the fundamental one, out of which all other social and moral problems have grown.[18]

Economist Robert Heilbroner put it this way:

Since he came down from the trees, man has faced the problem of survival, not as an individual but as a member of a social group. . . . It is hard to wring a livelihood from the surface of this planet . . . But the very fact that he has had to depend on his fellow man has made the problem of survival extraordinarily difficult. Man is not an ant conveniently equipped with an inborn pattern of social instincts. On the contrary, he is pre-eminently endowed with a fiercely self-centered nature. If his relatively weak physique forces him to seek cooperation, his untamed unconscious drives constantly threaten to disrupt his social working pattern.[19]

Heilbroner also felt that earlier, the struggle between personal aggression and social cooperation was assisted by the environment; but in a culturally and technically advanced society, the environment is no longer so restrictive. Other forces have emerged to control individual self-interest. According to Heilbroner, these are three in number: (1) *tradition,* which has controlled the economic behavior of people for many millennia; (2) *the rule of centralized bureaucratic administration* of political empire, operative for centuries; and (3) the most recent development, *the market system*, by which society assures its own continuance by allowing individuals to do exactly as they see fit—provided they follow a central guiding rule. "The game was called the 'market system' and the rule was deceptively simple: each should do what was to his best monetary advantage."[20] Over time, the sources of control over economic behavior have shifted from tradition to the more individually tailored rules of the market system. A peculiarly modern view of economic activity grew to predominance in much of Western society: strongly self-centered human individuals, each faced with the need to cooperate in order to survive, tolerate the social bond, however precarious that bond may be, which encourages people to work together rather than against each other. The challenge for capitalism was to harness all the selfish traits of human nature for the realization of social ends with a minimum of interference, with each individual pursuing its own ends.[21]

Enter Religion

The main vehicles by which tradition controlled people's economic impulses for millennia, as Heilbroner put it, were religious ideologies, myths, or dogmas. In fact, economic activity is one of the most important areas of life to be regulated by religion.[22]

Typical of the historical role of religion, it provided answers to questions—ranging from the pragmatic to the abstract—so that humans could get on with the business of living.[23] In addition, religious institutions and traditions long served to interpret the world for them and to ensure that they would carry out their lives in a prescribed manner. Along with this *legitimating* function (Weber), religion often defused, as Marx argued, the revolutionary potential of disenfranchised members of society by justifying the place of the have-nots as well as that of the haves, thereby securing the status quo. The karma-samsara complex of Hinduism, for example, specifies a person's cycle of rebirths and also legitimates and regulates the Indian caste system.[24] Furthermore, not only have the relations among strata been regulated by religion but so too have the production (the procedures and conditions under which goods needed by human societies are made available), distribution (way in which goods, once produced, are exchanged or allocated), and consumption (way in which goods are used up and the roles of property and wealth in lives of consumers) of goods.[25]

The development of capitalism was stifled by traditional communal values that imposed restrictions on acquisitive activity and economic inequality alike. But, as Heilbroner correctly assumed, under the sway of the modern market system, the regulating role of religion diminished. Indeed, this is a critical aspect of what is termed *modernization* and is often discussed by sociologists under the rubric of *secularization*. Industrial capitalism (along with other carriers of modernization—urbanization, mass education, mass media, etc.) fragmented life. Most fundamentally, it fragmented it into private (homelife) and public (worklife) spheres,[26] which have been further subdivided many times over. Bellah et al. concluded that "under such conditions, it is not surprising that the major problems of life appear to be essentially individual matters, a question of negotiating a reliable and harmonious balance among the various sectors of life to which an individual has access."[27]

Alongside this fragmentation, a certain disenchantment of the world has also occurred, removing more and more areas of life from the control of religious institutions and authorities.[28] Christianity, in general, contributed to individualism through its emphasis on personal salvation,[29] but Puritanical Calvinism gave it its modern meaning. This insight is, of course, the brilliance of Weber's analysis in *The Protestant Ethic and the Spirit of Capitalism*. The Protestant Reformation gave moral purpose to the capitalist endeavor. People's professions became God-given tasks, making this arrangement available to all rather than only to priests. Economic success became a sign of God's acceptance. The coming together of industriousness, thrift, and a denial of things luxurious enabled the accumulation of capital. According to Weber, a further by-product of all this was the rise of secular rationality. In sum, capitalism had found its perfect ideological/religious match!

Salvation in a Market Economy

Many religious denominations have transformed the concept of "being saved" into a market economy institution, employing all its elements and activities: advertising to attract customers, serving the needs of the customers with entertainment, providing an attractive interpretation of human experience, etc. This orientation, which has been called *religion as business*,[30] was fostered by the Lutheran theology of *justification by faith*, which made salvation, until then a communal affair (i.e., the individual attained salvation by adhering to his community's norms and could expect supernatural rewards—whether in this life or the next—for carrying them out in an exemplary fashion), into something intensely private. As Peter Berger notes, "In this situation it becomes increasingly difficult to maintain the religious traditions as unchanging verity. Instead, the dynamics of consumer preference is introduced into the religious sphere."[31]

The American evangelical conception of personal salvation has approached that of the market economy by intimating that a Christian can be free to do anything, as long as it is in keeping with the rules of the free market, which are, in this case, those of the prevailing doctrines of the Christian Church. Developments in the contemporary Christian world, especially in North America, have neared the laissez faire philosophy of Adam Smith.[32] Analyses of evangelicals, especially those on television, suggest that a sacralized form of secular capitalism has emerged.[33] Evidence for this abounds. Scandals have recently rocked televangelism to the point of secular state intervention in the public fleecing that was the PTL Club.[34] On other fronts, the New Age movement has met with considerable success in selling its wares, and cults prove far more persistent than most would have expected, disclosing a healthy market for all religious persuasions from Wicca to Zen Buddhism. All that is required is religious virtuosi to sell the goods.

Weber predicted that the logical conclusion to this development would be the "iron cage" of post-Christian secularization of Western civilization.[35] Weber was right in suspecting that this secularization would succeed nowhere as well as in modern North America. However, the process did not move in the direction Weber anticipated, and instead of an iron cage it produced a "cosmic playpen."[36] Rather than culture being secularized, Christianity was capitalized.

REENTER ANABAPTISM–MENNONITISM

At first glance, it would seem that the Anabaptist concept of being saved as an individual choice and act and as a personal responsibility matched up well with the requirements of the modern market economy— the ideological rationalization of which was beginning to occur just about the time when the Anabaptists arrived at the notion that a personal commitment, adult confession, and submission to baptism were *conditio sine qua non* for the establishment of a true church.[37] It is for this reason, in fact, that Weber considered Mennonites (or Baptists, as he often called them) to be extremist individualists.

This may seem straightforward enough, and it certainly was to Weber, but the individualistic emphasis and secular rationality that modern capitalism presumes and fosters are, in many ways, directly antithetical to the religious ethos and teachings of Anabaptism.[38] Anabaptism presumed that human beings are by nature self-centered, aggressive, and antisocial, but it argued that the individual could only be saved from the self-destructive tendencies of selfishness or egotism by becoming a member of the religious community and submitting to the collective will.

Anabaptists have not been alone in this emphasis. The Dahomean community (mentioned briefly at the beginning of this chapter), for example, stands in contrast to the world of secular rationality which Weber described. The myths and collective rites of Dahomey society do not educate the individual to self-consciousness but rather deliberately suppress all self-awareness by maintaining the individual's group awareness at all times. In industrialized North America, the Shakers and Oneida communities attempted to develop this extreme "group think" in an effort to maintain a radically different social order.[39]

The "biblical myth," however, educates the individual to self-consciousness as something that must be consciously overcome. This, for Weber as for other thinkers (McLuhan, Polka, Frye, Hegel, Kierkegaard), is the critical difference between biblical and natural religion. Empirically, this means the difference between other-worldly and inner-worldly asceticism. Economically, this translates into a difference between fleeing from economic involvement as something contaminating or sinful, and religious regulation of acquisitive behavior, which permits and even encourages the expression of self-interest to the extent that such activity falls within the moral guidelines and interests of the religious community.

Mennonites and the Market Situation

Mennonites have not been immune to these economic forces. In fact, the economic question is the anvil upon which the Anabaptist-Mennonite society has been forged and upon which its utopian dream was shattered. The capitalization of biblical religion, which has eroded their collective emphasis, is perhaps the single greatest threat to Mennonite identity in North America today.

We contend that the original charisma of the Anabaptist vision has been routinized into two antithetical economic idealizations: the traditional peasant village reconstituted on biblical grounds, on one hand; and assimilation to the North American evangelical market economy Christianity, on the other. Although both extremes claim to embody the true spirit of Anabaptism, they are in tension with one another if not mutually exclusive.

The Mennonite entrepreneur has become the visible symbol of the latter extreme, but only when the entrepreneur moves his or her sphere of activity from the Mennonite village community to the world at large and to the pursuit of personal interests according to the rules of the market economy.

Three consequences, for the entrepreneur and the Mennonite community, follow. First, because the entrepreneurs exemplify all the dangers the Mennonite society faces from the greater world, the entrepreneurs have become scapegoats for more conservative groups as well as for the conservative elements of liberal congregations.[40] Second, because they have been typecast as potential deviants, entrepreneurs are prone to leave the church and assimilate into the secular culture. Third, the general malaise of the Mennonite society (the permeation of its moral environment with capitalistic individualism) goes unrecognized because attention is focused on the entrepreneur's troubles. Furthermore, the society deals with them in such a way that the purity (traditional authority) of the congregation (as defined by the wielder of traditional forms of social and economic power) is safeguarded.

A CONCEPTUAL MAP OF MENNONITE ENTREPRENEURIAL ACTIVITY

To discuss the place of entrepreneurialism in the Mennonite world, it is first necessary to map out the conceptual terrain of the entrepreneur more generally. Mark Casson, in his review of literature on the entrepreneur, noted that most studies of the phenomenon make no attempt at definition but rely simply on stereotypes,[41] with that of entrepreneur as a "swashbuckling business adventurer." A simple dictionary definition of the *entrepreneur*, which reflects our common usage of that term fairly well, says the entrepreneur is "a person who organizes, operates, and assumes the risk for business ventures, especially an impresario."[42] Although a coherent theory of the entrepreneur has proven elusive, we can add some additional precision to our use of the term by reviewing several major conceptual concerns that have arisen in the literature.

From Classical to Neoclassical Entrepreneur

It has been argued that the entrepreneurial role has existed from the beginning of human history,[43] but it has become an organizing principle for society with the genesis of the modern world system and the transformation of traditional peasant society into a modern market economy. Indeed, the word *entrepreneur* itself is old, although it has only recently come into vogue. Adam Smith, David Ricardo, and Karl Marx gave the term its classical meaning. For each of these writers, *entrepreneur* referred to a small, elite group of capitalists. According to Smith, greater division of labor led to greater worker dexterity, more available time, and the invention of new machines. For Marx, the profit motive drove the bourgeois capitalist. Ricardo saw the decisions of the capitalist as key to the creation and resolution of economic problems.

The changing cultural historical context of *North American* capitalism, and of an economic world system, has demanded that the meaning forged in the context of political world empires be reconsidered. Weber explicitly pointed out that North America represented, for the European peasant/laborer, the dream of social and economic advancement through enterprise. As a result, everyone in America could become a successful entrepreneur, initially through the capitalization of land, which produced a capitalistic urban culture along with its supporting ideology. Thus, a democratization of the entrepreneur occurred, and a *de facto* neoclassical definition of the entrepreneur—as anyone who accepts an exceptional level of risk taking, is creative and innovative, and "goes all out" in the accomplishment of goals—emerged in the popular imagination and the social scientific literature.

Entrepreneurial Activity: Personality or Behavior?

It has long been argued that entrepreneurial activity is ultimately motivated by a personality type or trait. A counterdefinition suggests that entrepreneurship is the result of social conditions and structures that literally create the entrepreneurial organization or person. The former position is obviously psychological, and the latter is championed by sociologists—specifically, structural sociologists such as Friedrich and Aiken, who stated:

The term "entrepreneurship" refers to a kind of behavior which is characteristic of certain organized associations of individuals (usually business firms). It is only in highly exceptional cases that the presence of this characteristic can be imputed to the actions of personalities of single individuals. The general rule is that it is the *association*, not the individual which exhibits entrepreneurship. The search for individual entrepreneurs rests on a fallacious logic, tends to result in biographical antiquarianism, and adds little or nothing to our understanding.[44]

Survey research on this sociological approach to entrepreneurship uncovered several elements that help explain the entrepreneurial event. (1) *Initiative taking*: an individual or group starts the process. (2) *Consolidation of resources*: an organization is formed or restructured to accomplish an objective. (3) *Management*: the organization is run by those who took the initiative. (4) *Relative autonomy*: resources are disposed of and distributed with relative freedom. (5) *Risk taking*: the organization's success or failure is shared by the initiators.[45]

However compelling the sociological argument, it still begs questions about the origin of an association's principle of organization, which brings the entrepreneurship into operation. Certainly the structural organization cannot create business *ex nihilo* without a supporting value system and actors involved in both the creation and maintenance of it.

Peter Drucker dismissed the extreme structural position and suggested that entrepreneurship can be defined by both individual and organizational actions and that the organization is usually the result of an individual's entrepreneurial action. In this scholarly discussion a dialectic seemed to be emerging in which an existing traditional structure created entrepreneurial opportunities that would be utilized by individuals who, in turn, would affect the structure of the community that produced them, most likely in a proentrepreneurial way.

The entrepreneurial event is, therefore, neither entirely individual nor totally determined by social structures. The individual, the social structure, and cultural factors are operative in creating a milieu in which the entrepreneurial event can emerge. Max Weber's study of the world religions supported this view, concluding that material conditions alone are insufficient for capitalism to develop.

Toward a Definition of the Entrepreneur

Bearing these conceptual debates in mind, we can begin to develop a workable understanding of the entrepreneur. Peter Drucker, representative of the neoclassical point of view, suggested that "the entrepreneur always searches for change, responds to it, and exploits it as an opportunity. . . . Entrepreneurship . . . is enormously risky . . . it needs to be based on purposeful innovation."[46] Consistent with Drucker's definition, a survey of the research on the entrepreneurial phenomenon reveals that the entrepreneur exhibits a cluster of traits, including self-confidence, perseverance or determination, energy or diligence, resourcefulness, an ability to take calculated risks, a need to achieve, creativity, initiative, flexibility, a positive response to challenge, independence, foresight, and dynamism or leadership. This list is not exhaustive, but it includes most of the personal characteristics commonly associated with entrepreneurship.[47]

Furthermore, we would advocate a dialectical approach to the entrepreneur which resolves the personality versus structure debate over the origins of entrepreneurialism. Clearly some type of *both/and* notion is possible, plausible, and probably most accurate. It also moves us closer to a workable definition of the entrepreneur. As Fredrik Barth noted in this context, focusing on the entrepreneurial role may be helpful.

It is essential to realize that "the entrepreneur" is not a *person* in any strict sociological sense. . . though inevitably the word will be used. . . . Nor does it seem appropriate to treat entrepreneurship as a status or even a role, implying as it would a discreteness and routinization which may be lacking in the materials we wish to analyze. Rather, its strict use should be for an *aspect of a role*; it relates to actions and activities, and not rights and duties, furthermore it characterizes a certain quality or orientation in this activity which may be present to a greater or less extent in the different institutionalized roles found in the community. To the extent that persons take the initiative, and in pursuit of profit in some discernable form manipulate other persons and resources, they are acting as entrepreneurs.[48]

Barth also exemplified the neoclassical definition of the enterprise as anyone who, in any culture, exploits the values of that culture to enhance first his or her own, then his or her family's and nation's, and ultimately all people's, interests.[49]

The personality trait/social structure conflict can also be avoided by accepting the conception of the entrepreneurial event developed by Albert Shapiro and Lisa Sokol.[50] According to them, the following activities take place in the context of an aggregate of individuals: (1) initiative is undertaken; (2) consolidation of resources (an organization is formed to achieve some objective) occurs; (3) management is implemented; (4) autonomous action is undertaken; (5) risk is taken. Innovation is not included in the definition because all of the five points are innovative; for that matter most people are innovative who deviate from the group norms, including criminal deviation (which is why prisons are such good schools for crime). The critical factor is the positive or negative reward the group (traditional authority structure) gives to the innovators' activities.

Defining the Mennonite Entrepreneur

If one carries the neoclassical definition of the entrepreneur to its logical extreme, there were many individuals in the early Anabaptist-Mennonite movement who were entrepreneurial. Some of them even fit the classical definition of the entrepreneur. Most Anabaptist-Mennonite leaders were, however, actually very poor capitalists by virtue of the fact that they became martyrs for the truth through their entrepreneurial efforts. Yet, Muenster Rebellion leaders such as Jan Matthijsz and Bernard Rothmann were outstanding entrepreneurs if the focus is on risk taking, creativity, innovation, and going all out in pursuit of a goal.[51] The same could be said of Jacob Hutter, who managed to coalesce a disparate group of refugees from the Tyrol of Austria into a relatively unified people now known as Hutterites.[52] We can consider other early Anabaptist leaders— Grebel, Blaurock, Mantz, Sattler, Hubmaier, Marpeck, Hofmann, and Simons—to be entrepreneurial spirits as well. Seen more conventionally, these figures are charismatic leaders rather than entrepreneurs.[53] Only by accepting the neoclassical revision of the entrepreneur can these men be claimed as such. Nevertheless, this revision establishes that although entrepreneurialism is conventionally associated with the world of business, it is more than a mode of economic production. It represents a way of life. For the purposes of our study, however, we will limit the definition of Mennonite entrepreneurialism to the "creation of a business organization and activity that did not exist before."

From the individual's perspective, realization of the enterprise enables transformation of the very nature of labor. In the classical Greek pattern, enterprise was the slave's opportunity to earn the capital to purchase freedom; and in this, it was an educational process. Individuals learned to understand themselves not only in relation to nature (as in an economy oriented to primary production), but also in relation to their colleagues with whom they had to cooperate to achieve their personal ends. The Mennonite situation is somewhat different from this model in that the Mennonite is not forced by a state of bondage to cooperate with his fellow entrepreneurs but finds enticements that awaken dissatisfaction with the traditional way of life, the traditional level of consumption, and the traditional means of production.

Max Weber considered North American capitalism distinct in that it is based on this ever-heightening level of consumption—called the *standard of living*—which fuels the economy and generates the taxes that bloat the state bureaucracy and the consumptive form of life by which it is supported. Mennonite experience will provide another opportunity to test Weber's hypothesis in the laboratory of history.

We can understand more fully the symbolic significance of the entrepreneurial role to the Mennonite community by considering the surreptitious capitalization of it in North America. Modern society and economy are so constituted that communal groups, unless they withdraw and become independent territorial entities, are forced to come to terms with their larger social context. For that matter, the same can be said of any cognitive minority (a group that strays significantly from the prevailing cultural norms and ideology). This coming to terms has been termed *cognitive bargaining*. According to James Davison Hunter, this poses a dilemma for contemporary evangelicals: "Adherents of a religious world view may either attempt to resist the compromising realities of modernity or attempt to make the best of the situation by giving in to modernity's cognitive pressures."[54] Since leaving Europe, Anabaptist-Mennonites have had to negotiate between their idealized communalistic-utopian roots and the realities of living in the middle of North American culture. Some have tried, in fact, to steer a course closer to withdrawal than accommodation (e.g., the Hutterites). Others have attempted to retain the core of their belief system while giving in on what they deem to be less significant issues (e.g., the Amish of Lancaster County).[55] Still others have seemingly gone much further in accommodating to secular culture and the market system.

This conversation or negotiation with non–Mennonite society must also be understood in terms of a sort of internal contradiction with Mennonite life. The traditional Mennonite community with its traditional level of consumption and its traditional means of production provided only a limited range of opportunity for its aggressive, creative, and productive farmers and craftsmen. In the context of the market economy model of society, on the other hand, the traditional authority is that of liberal economic individualism, which has innovation embedded in its very structure. Thus, Mennonites have struggled with this built-in contradiction, which provides the basis for what we have called the *push-pull theory* of Mennonite enterprise in North America.

The Mennonite community in North America lives, therefore, with the tension between the heightened self-assertion and drive for success by taking risks and making innovations that are essential to the entrepreneur's survival in the context of accumulative capitalism *and* the ethic of discipleship that repudiates all property and wealth as summed up in *Gelassenheit*. *Gelassenheit*, a central tenet of Anabaptism-Mennonitism, refers specifically to the submission of the human will to the will of Christ.[56] It has been understood more generally as humility. Thus, *Gelassenheit* stands in contradiction to much of the individualistic impulse in contemporary North American life.

Local and Cosmopolitan Mennonite Entrepreneurship

The original charismatic expression of Anabaptist-Mennonite ideology took a form of enthusiastic communalism which, except for the Hutterites, has been efficiently extinguished by the combined forces of persecution and history. And yet, like the Apostolic community of the New Testament church, this Anabaptist-Mennonite communalism has had a lasting effect on Mennonites' economic ethos. Even today when Mennonites become businesspeople they bring a unique character to this role. In later chapters we will attempt an outline of this character, but first we must discern the central distinguishing features of the *local* and *cosmopolitan* Mennonite entrepreneur.

The distinction between them derives from Robert Merton's reference group theory, which attempted to determine "under what conditions associates within one's own groups [are] taken as a frame of reference for self-evaluation and attitude-formation, and under which conditions do out-groups or non-membership groups provide the significant frame of reference."[57]

In the Mennonite context, the local entrepreneur would be the one who serves the Mennonite community and is dependent on its good will for economic survival. The cosmopolitan entrepreneur is one who has transferred his dependence onto the larger impersonal market economy and whose lifestyle and business practices tend more to conform to the host culture's norms. As Kallen and Kelner state the case,

The local are bound by existing ties and obligations to their community; they continue to respect community values and they see their own activities as increasing community profits. They play an active role in community affairs and gain prestige through their commitment to egalitarian norms and neighborly relations within the community. In contrast, the cosmopolitans have broken the ties and obligations to their communities of birth. They seek the status and financial rewards of the secular state and its market economy. The cost of becoming cosmopolitan is repudiating existing relationships within the community to forge new ones outside it.[58]

Many Mennonites have undertaken entrepreneurial activities within the Mennonite community context, but they did not deviate from group norms in lifestyle or belief. In fact, they often helped determine the direction that local interpretation and practice of the traditional Mennonite beliefs took. This is a distinguishing characteristic of local Mennonite entrepreneurs. They do not extend their activities far beyond the Mennonite community because their local mind-set is threatened by the greater world, and they are unwilling to risk the disapproval of the members of the Mennonite community which would be the inevitable response to any deviance from Mennonite economic norms.

Disapproval by the community proves a strong and resilient force in many of the more traditional communities, especially the conservative and plain Mennonite groups like the Old Order Mennonites and the Amish. Although some amazingly creative and innovative practices and businesses have emerged in these groups, restrictions are clearly imposed. John Hostetler noted, "When Amish enterprises become large—successful by worldly standards—they also constitute a liability to the Amish way of life. The determination to maintain a small-scale operation dictates that if the business becomes 'too large' it must be sold to an outside company."[59] Donald Kraybill, a sociologist who examined the "riddles" of Amish culture, quoted an Amish businessman as follows: "My people look at a large business as a sign of greed. We're not supposed to engage in large businesses and I'm right at the borderline."[60] Calvin Redekop interviewed an Amish entrepreneur in Arthur, Illinois, who had built up a very successful and sophisticated construction firm, employing more than thirty persons.[61] At a certain point he held a family counsel and sold his business to a local Mennonite at a very reasonable price. He subsequently opened up a harness shop that employed his two sons and himself. When asked why he had done this, he replied, "I saw that the business was running away with me. I saw that the business was interfering with my relationships with my family and church, and so I had to make a choice."

When Redekop asked, "What kind of profit were you making when you owned the construction business?" the Amish entrepreneur cagily replied, "plenty."

The difference between the local and cosmopolitan entrepreneurs is that the latter are willing to venture out and yet are unable to resist the many life changes that entrepreneurial success brings. Whether the Amishman was fearful or wise is not up to us to judge; but his actions illustrate perfectly the distinction between cosmopolitan and local entrepreneurs.

Local entrepreneurs, then, tend to be more *normative*; that is, they tend to operate according to community norms. Cosmopolitan entrepreneurs tend to be *non-normative* or deviant, and consequently they often function as scapegoats for community problems. Mennonites with entrepreneurial inclinations and drives therefore face a choice of sorts: they will be directed inward to conform to agrarian community values (local), or they will be directed outward to conform to secular organizations and practices, depending upon the degree to which the individual has accepted external values and norms (cosmopolitan).

In summary, entrepreneurship in Mennonite contexts can be expressed in one of two ways: either in taking the entrepreneurial expression as far as conformity to agrarian community norms and values permits or in disregarding community standards and practices to compete in the larger market economy according to its rules. Both types of entrepreneurship are significant and relevant for our discussion, but the cosmopolitan type may provide more insight into the way a utopian religious system accommodates itself to the economic systems of the larger social environment.

Two Illustrative Cases

Consider the cases of two Mennonite entrepreneurs.[62] The first is an example of a traditional (i.e., noncosmopolitan) congregation producing a cosmopolitan entrepreneur. This individual came from a very conservative community and family, finished only grade school, and slowly made his way toward establishing his own business. He was considered a bit dull by some of his peers. He turned out, however, to be a very creative and inventive entrepreneur. He developed a successful business, went bankrupt, and began over again. The congregation to which he belongs is quite conservative. When asked "What did your church say about your being involved in business?" he responded,

I heard a lot about how bad businesspeople are. That was in the [name of his church] and that is what they told me straight to my face, even the ministers. I was the only businessman in their church who persisted, even though the church did not want it. The ministers came to me and told me that they didn't really want businesspeople in their church and that they hoped I would not be too offended if they dealt with me like that. To them a businessman was a crook right from the start. But I was always a bit skeptical about the way the church operated. I had been in MDS [an inter-Mennonite assistance organization] and I got together with other people and saw that there were other people who wanted to be just good Christians, like me. But our church couldn't see this. The agricultural way of life was the righteous position, and business was always looked down on. Even my uncle said that I was making too much profit until I went down [went bankrupt] then he changed his attitude a bit. I asked him one day if making 100 percent profit was wrong, and he said yes. I asked, "What about if you get sixty bushels an acre of wheat? You only put one in to begin with." He replied that the Lord sent him that. I had nobody behind me in business in the church. In the world things were different. Companies would come here from Toronto or Winnipeg. In my twenty-fifth year as a Massey dealer I told them I was quitting. They came flying out and wanted to give me a bigger area. I had good jobs offered to me as credit union manager. Massey wanted me in Toronto. Minneapolis [another company name] wanted me in their business. Inventing and developing have been my life. I couldn't have done anything else. I never dreamed [as a youth] that I would even own a garage and get into manufacturing. My problem was that I didn't have a high enough opinion of myself. So that is why I said no to a lot of things.

When he was asked whether or not he had mellowed through these experiences, he responded,

What really happens if you are an aggressive man is that you may walk all over people without knowing it, and when the time comes that they can strike back, they will because they haven't forgotten. It has helped me a great deal that I went through this [the bankruptcy]. I grew up a lot.

This example illustrates very well the tension that many Mennonite entrepreneurs experience. On the one hand they must contend with the traditional (local) restrictive norms of the congregation, framing a worldview from the perspective of the rural agricultural way of life. On the other, they often face encouragement from the members of the host society, which pulls them toward cosmopolitan assimilation. It is interesting to note as well that rejection by traditional Mennonite Churches, which this person experienced, appears to be the common denominator around which cosmopolitan Mennonites are beginning to create a new identity. This particular entrepreneur was excommunicated from his church for a few years because he went bankrupt, and it was assumed that he had been engaged in bad or immoral business practices. He claimed that he had not lost his faith in God but indicated how the local congregation misunderstood business.

This case points to the problems of cognitive bargaining faced by Mennonite entrepreneurs and also illustrates the issues congregations face as they try to arrive at appropriate cultural understandings of Mennonite business experience. In the traditional understanding of personal relationships, bankruptcy is considered a moral affront because it is an excuse to shirk paying one's debts. Under the cultural terms of modern society (Mennonite and non-Mennonite alike), business ventures are an indispensable part of producing, distributing, and consuming the commodities of a free market economy, and business failures are part of the process of establishing the fair price of all the various commodities (the economic equivalent to the biological survival of the fittest). We would add that the case begs further and perhaps even more profound questions about the morality of the market economy; and here the traditional Mennonites have the Marxists on their side morally, if not epistemologically (Marxist epistemology is materialistic, Mennonite epistemology utopian). Cognitive bargaining then is not necessarily easy for individual or community.

The second case concerns a younger entrepreneur who distributed commercial products. He became active in business enterprises while he was still in high school, selling candy and organizing a sales force of his school chums. He was very popular among his peers and was encouraged by his parents to attend college and graduate school. His parents came from Russia and wanted to compensate for their own restricted opportunities. His story illustrates just how acclimated some Mennonite businesspeople have become to the entrepreneurial role.

I guess my father had something to do with my getting interested in business, by being self-employed himself as a farmer. Being raised on a farm was a real asset, learning work habits and learning to be a jack of all trades. My father said when something broke down you either had to walk all the way home or you had to figure out some way to fix it, and usually you figured out how to fix it. I've never figured out why I got into business. Opportunity was one factor. The product I started with was already being used in the United States. Luck was also involved. Pieces fall into place sometimes, and you don't know why. I would say the people we picked up [hired] helped very much. I enjoy the distribution business; the challenge is that there is a big market out there. Plus I enjoy being close to agriculture. I enjoy work. I'm not sports minded. I golf, but work is my primary enjoyment. It was just the satisfaction of accomplishment. In sports it is winning, and in business it is winning. As far as providing guidance for my business, there is no one except the local banker in whom I confide. There is no one else on a personal basis. I read a lot of books on various people who have succeeded in business. My objective has been to develop a market. We weren't first. There was another company here, but they were very high priced, and we were very competitive because we kept our overhead as low as possible.

This entrepreneur belonged to a rather progressive local congregation of the Mennonite Brethren. The congregation was reasonably cosmopolitan in its orientation. The entrepreneur, who held a Ph.D. degree from a prestigious university, adhered to some universalistic values but was basically committed to, and accepting of, the values, beliefs, and practices of his church community.

From Local to Cosmopolitan

We are not simply interested in determining which Mennonite entrepreneurs are local and which are cosmopolitan. The local entrepreneur who *becomes* cosmopolitan is of even more central interest to our study because he or she appears to be a critical mechanism of cognitive and cultural bargaining, of the importation of alien cultural traits into the traditional community. If local entrepreneurs can make the transition to cosmopolitan status without offending or being offended by the local community/ congregation, the entire group will become more cosmopolitan. If, on the other hand, these entrepreneurs feel obligated to change their reference groups and are lost to the community/congregation, the group will remain traditional.

"The majority regard Christ very highly . . . they do not believe in him externally from afar, but put him on and believe *in* him, following him in all [*Gelassenheit*], as they speak of it."[63] This majority of Mennonite believers, able to express traditional faith within the constraints of modern society, has been a hindrance to the non-normative cosmopolitan entrepreneurial drive to make deeper inroads into Mennonite life. The cosmopolitan reference group, however, has considerable influence on the emergence of entrepreneurship and thus is a source of tension for the orthodox community. Local entrepreneurship, usually organized according to a matriarchal kinship system (*unter die sanfte Pantoffel der Frau*) only serves the interest of ruling families and their clients, creating another source of push toward the cosmopolitan reference group.

The Mennonite cosmopolitan entrepreneur often moves beyond the Mennonite community and adopts the capitalistic ethic (as seen from the perspective of those who remain insiders). To the extent that more Mennonite entrepreneurs become cosmopolitan, Mennonite community life will be profoundly affected.

Some writers note that American capitalism has had a profound influence on the development of the Mennonite economic ethos and that this influence can be gauged by the rate of emergence of cosmopolitan entrepreneurs out of traditional congregations and by the transformation of entire congregations from traditional to modern styles and values. Frank Epp identified the changeover from "family-style" to "cathedral-style" worship services, from meetinghouses to sanctuaries, from chairs and benches to pews, "from multiple ministry and collective leadership" to the single-ministry antiprofessional administration, and from a participatory style to performance-oriented liturgy as the indicators of this transition.[64]

THE EXTENT OF LOCAL ENTREPRENEURIAL ACTIVITY

The extent of local entrepreneurship in the North American Mennonite community is massive. Practically every Mennonite community can identify numerous businesspersons who have become unusually wealthy and successful while operating within the norms of the Mennonite society, especially in farming and related activities. Hence, innovating and taking risks in expanding milking, feeding, and cash-cropping operations are almost standard. But related activities such as milling and manufacturing, merchandising of almost every agricultural commodity, manufacturing of agricultural implements and materials, constructing buildings, and servicing machinery and horses, are also extensive.

Successful primary industry, the closing of the frontier, and the urbanization of society have accelerated the development of local entrepreneurs, especially among the Old Order groups, so that even the Amish have produced handbooks of Amish business establishments which list a vast variety of goods and services.[65] A recent research report indicates that there are more than 950 microenterprises in Lancaster County, Pennsylvania, operated by Old Order Amish (which translates into about nine microenterprises per district). Of these, 60 percent were begun between 1980 and 1992. Of the total number, 14 percent did business of greater than $500,000 per year, and 7 percent did business of more than $1,000,000 per year.[66] This growth of local entrepreneurships among the Old Orders is clearly the result of the push of land scarcity and the pull of the opportunity for occupational outlets among the surplus population. One of the most extensive studies of this phenomenon was conducted by J. Winfield Fretz in Waterloo County, Ontario, Canada.[67] Fretz noted that early in the history of Berlin (the center of the early settlement), "not one of the 82 businessmen could be identified as Mennonite by [his] name."[68] In 1978, Fretz collected information on the occupational distribution of all Mennonites. Fifty farm-related industries were listed, with harness and shoe shops most predominant (6), followed by farm wagon builders (5), and buggy builders and repairers (4). The list also included blacksmiths and furniture makers.

Local entrepreneurship has developed much more routinely and extensively among the non–Old Order Mennonites. The few community studies that have been done, which include accounts of economic activities, document the extent of this development. Esther Epp-Tiessen's *Altona: The Story of a Prairie Town*, for example, provided an excellent description of a typical Mennonite community and included an account of the development of the business-commercial and industrial sector of Altona, Manitoba.[69] Epp-Tiessen reported that beginning with the early years from 1895 to 1914 and continuing until the present, a count based on Mennonite names reveals that thirty-eight out of a total of sixty-two businesses in Altona were initiated and controlled by Mennonites.[70] The types of business and the proportions are suggestive of the types of business which seem to be more in accord with Mennonite community norms. Those enterprises requiring broader connections such as banks, lumber yards, and elevators were run by non-Mennonites.

Because very few Mennonite communities are strictly segregated (i.e., there are always non-Mennonites living within the confines of the enclave, as only the Hutterites are totally homogeneous), it is difficult to analyze Mennonite communities in a controlled environment. The Old Order groups are more cohesive, but even they have not managed to keep their culture entirely intact and immune from the influence of the greater society. Altona, Manitoba, is probably one of the most homogeneous Mennonite communities, since it emerged out of an area reserved for Mennonite settlers in the 1870s.

Mountain Lake, Minnesota, is another example of a Mennonite community that has been subjected to some scrutiny. Originally settled by Mennonites, it was soon "invaded" by non-Mennonites including

Lutherans and others. The city of Mountain Lake was probably settled by Mennonites, who still comprise about half of the population. Both Altona and Mountain Lake, however, were clearly predominantly Mennonite in influence and ethos, as are many communities that have been known as Mennonite through the years.

A survey of all Mennonites of Mountain Lake, conducted by Calvin Redekop in 1952, revealed that the number of Mennonite farmers totaled 398, whereas only 22 were businessmen in the town.[71] Although some of the businesses, such as barber shops, were rather small and might not be considered entrepreneurial, by and large these persons could be counted as entrepreneurs. Redekop, having grown up in the community, knew many of the persons, and it is clear that many, if not most of these persons were aggressive and creative risk takers. As an example, A. P. Balzer, president of Balzer Manufacturing, was an inventor, developer, organizer, and financier whose products were sold in most parts of the United States and Canada in the 1950s and 1960s.

Altona, Manitoba, Mountain Lake, Minnesota, and Waterloo, Ontario are quite representative of Mennonite communities in Canada and the United States. The data from the studies of each community confirm that there has been local entrepreneurship in all Mennonite communities (echoing Weber's thesis), although it is most extensive among the more progressive groups.

These findings also suggest that all traditional societies are compelled to tolerate a certain level of entrepreneurial activity among their members, if only to mediate the exchanges that the market economy, society, and state demand in the form of taxes and essentials that the community cannot provide for itself (iron from the Philistines). Of course, local entrepreneurship can be distinguished, at this level, between activities that conform to the norms of the religious community and those that do not. Some business activities clearly have not been tolerated. For example, "exotic dancers" in Abbotsford, British Columbia, have raised considerable community debate, and both sides have flooded the Abbotsford city council with petitions. This is an extreme example of entrepreneurial activities that are either questionable or offensive to widely perceived norms of Mennonite faith and commitments.

THE MENNONITE MOVE TOWARD COSMOPOLITANISM

Have Mennonite communities become more cosmopolitan in orientation? Peter Berger once spoke of the cosmopolitan motif as being intimately linked to an urban and urbane worldview.

Going back to very ancient times, it was in cities that there developed an openness to the world, to other ways of thinking and acting. Whether we think of Athens or Alexandria, of medieval Paris or Renaissance Florence, or of the turbulent urban centers of modern history, we can identify a certain cosmopolitan consciousness that was especially characteristic of city culture. The individual, then, who is not only urban but urbane is one who, however passionately he may be attached to his own city, roams through the whole wide world in his intellectual voyages. His mind, if not his body and his emotions, is at home wherever there are other men who think.[72]

Are Mennonites becoming urban? Are they becoming urbane? Are they equally "at home" outside their Mennonite communities? The increasingly urban quality of Mennonite life and the inroads that mass communication and education have made into their community would predict it. So too would the integration of individual Mennonites into the market economy society, especially if it results in individual Mennonites changing their reference groups. This process has been identified and documented in the experience of religious–ethnic groups adapting to North American individualistic culture,[73] and evidence would suggest that a similar dynamic is at work among the Mennonites.

Cosmopolitanism has two dimensions: (1) the degree to which a specific community or congregation is cosmopolitan in its value system— that is, the degree to which a given congregation or community has rejected the traditional agrarian Anabaptist-Mennonite value system or ideology in favor of those of the prevailing culture; and (2) the degree to which Mennonite individuals have become cosmopolitan in their orientation regardless of congregational encouragement of or hostility to this trend. Although there is undoubtedly some correlation between the two types of cosmopolitanism, the collective viewpoint may be different from that of the total of its members. It is, however, easier to speak to the second type of cosmopolitanism because extant studies provide, for the most part, individual level data.

Up until now we have been discussing the whole of the Anabaptist-Mennonite tradition. As we have alluded, there are important differences within this tradition as well as between it and the non-Mennonite world. These differences are situational as well as theological. The Hutterites, for example, live on large acreages of communally owned land.[74] The Amish live in rural areas, and, although cottage industries do operate within their communities, farming and agricultural work remain their primary occupations.[75] The Old Colony Mennonites, again predominantly farmers, have major settlements in Canada and Mexico with additional communities in Belize and Bolivia.[76] All three of these groups lie outside the urban environment of North America.

What of the bulk of Mennonites? The Hutterites, Amish, and Old Colony Mennonites represent only a small fraction of the total Mennonite population in North America. The four largest denominations— the Mennonite Church, The General Conference Mennonite Church, the Mennonite Brethren Church, and the Brethren in Christ Church— together make up about two thirds of all Anabaptist-Mennonites in North America.[77] The situation of people belonging to these denominations is quite different from that of the Hutterites, Amish, and Old Colony Mennonites.

We are fortunate to have a fairly comprehensive profile of these mainstream Anabaptist-Mennonites, thanks to two studies that monitored changes in their beliefs, attitudes, and behaviors. Howard Kauffman and Leland Harder conducted the first of these studies in 1972, dubbed Church Member Profile I (hereafter CMP1). The second study, Church Member Profile II (hereafter CMP2), was conducted seventeen years later by Howard Kauffman and Leo Driedger. Using large samples, these researchers conducted interviews with members of the four largest Anabaptist-Mennonite groups and smaller groups of Evangelical Mennonites. The two studies described these groups and provide means by which changes over nearly two decades could be measured.

In contrast to the more rural controlled environments of the Hutterites, Amish, and Old Colony Mennonites, a third of the mainstream Mennonites already lived in towns and cities of 2,500 or more by 1972. Of the five groups studied, the Mennonite Brethren were the most urbanized. Seventeen years later, urbanization had increased substantially. By 1989, half of the CMP2 respondents lived in towns and cities of 2,500 or more.[78]

The CMP1 and CMP2 studies also revealed that across denominations, mainstream Mennonites were relatively orthodox in terms of adherence to Anabaptist beliefs (see Table 2-1). Using an Anabaptist scale

TABLE 2-1
Responses to Items on Anabaptism

Anabaptism Items	1989					Totals	
	GC*a*	MC	BIC	MB	EMC	1972	1989
	% agreeing						
Baptism is unnecessary for infants and children.	81	85	79	89	85	82	84
Should follow the lordship of Christ even if persecuted.	62	63	67	75	75	72	66
Church discipline is necessary for the unfaithful.	55	55	66	78	60	60	60
Christians should take no part in war.	65	78	39	56	11	73	66
Christians cannot perform in some government offices.	52	71	48	49	31	74	59
It is against God's will to swear civil oaths.	64	59	32	54	31	66	57
Must follow Jesus in evangelism and deeds of mercy.	47	46	39	47	37	52	45
Should not take a person to court even if justified.	31	41	30	32	28	36	35

SOURCE: Kauffman and Driedger (1991).
a Abbreviations refer to the following groups: GC, General Conference Mennonites; MC, Mennonite Church; BIC, Brethren in Christ; MB, Mennonite Brethren; and EMC, Evangelical Mennonite Church.

to measure church members' adherence to sixteenth-century Anabaptist principles, the researchers were able to show that assent to Anabaptist principles remained a potent influence among mainstream Anabaptist-Mennonites.[79]

Table 2-1 indicates erosion in the commitment to some of the traditional Anabaptist positions. Given the modernizing role of urbanization in the theoretical literature, this falling away might result from the increasingly urban quality of Anabaptist-Mennonite life. Interestingly, however, the degree of urbanization had only a moderate effect on Anabaptist-Mennonite orthodoxy.[80] In fact, the variable proved a far less powerful predictor overall than the researchers had expected. According to Kauffman and Harder, among fifteen independent variables including age, education, income, socioeconomic status, and then faith variables, rural-urban residence ranked only thirteenth in its effect on other variables.[81] The replicated study by Kauffman and Driedger concluded that "rural and urban respondents showed no significant differences. . . . These findings were essentially the same as those in 1972."[82] Regarding the Anabaptist scale specifically, Kauffman and Harder concluded that "rural and urban Mennonites are very similar in their acceptance of sixteenth-century principles" and suggested that the so-called "urban life hypothesis" (i.e., that the urban environment, with all its social heterogeneity, provided a more congenial setting for vital Anabaptism) could not be supported by the data.[83]

Kauffman and Driedger noted, however, that Mennonites living in large cities did score differently on a number of scales than did Mennonites living in small cities or living in rural/nonfarm and rural/farm environments. For example, Mennonites in large cities differed from the other three residence categories by scoring lower on beliefs, church participation, and moral scales and higher on ethical issues, ecumenism, and political action scales. This led Kauffman and Driedger to conclude "that the urbanization process among Mennonites leads to diminished orthodoxy of beliefs, diminished support for traditional moral standards, greater support for liberal ethical principles, and greater acceptance of ecumenical programs and participation in political affairs."[84] Thus, it would seem most accurate to conclude that urbanization, to a point (to the point of leaving the farm and living in small cities), does not necessarily have the corrosive effect one might expect. To a point, the Anabaptist-Mennonite ethic derived from an agrarian tradition persisted even though Mennonites operated increasingly in an alien urban environment. Large cities may, however, pose somewhat different problems and obstacles for this ethic.

It is also clear that Anabaptist-Mennonites are obtaining more education (see Table 2-2). Berger would certainly expect that such developments would lead to increased openness to the world—a certain cosmopolitanism among Mennonites (a worry that many Mennonite leaders had earlier in this century). Whereas about a third of respondents to the CMP1 study had received post–high school education, half reported the same in 1989. Kauffman and Driedger noted, with some concern, that attendance at non-Mennonite colleges and universities grew during this time as well, from 21 to 43 percent.[85] The generally held belief that Mennonite schooling helps inform people of as well as cement their commitment to Anabaptist beliefs was confirmed empirically in the CMP2 study.[86]

Occupationally, Anabaptist-Mennonites moved far from the stereotype of the rural farmer. Although about a quarter of the males participating in CMP1 reported being farmers, that figure dropped to 15 percent in 1989 (see Table 2-3). This was more than offset by increases in the professions and in the business proprietor/manager category. In part, the increased interest in the professions led young Mennonites to seek educational opportunities at non-Mennonite schools, since Mennonite schools do not offer the required program of study.

TABLE 2-2
Educational Attainment by Denomination, 1972 and 1989

| Level Attained | 1972 | | | | | |
	MB[a]	GC	EMC	MC	BIC	Total
	% attained					
Elementary (grades 1–8)	24	19	15	28	20	24
Secondary (grades 9–12)	41	42	49	46	49	44
College (grades 13–16)	20	22	24	17	19	19
Graduate school (1+ years)	16	17	12	9	12	13
Total percentages	101	100	100	100	100	100
	1989					
Elementary (grades 1–8)	8	10	4	15	8	11
Secondary (grades 9–12)	32	37	39	41	48	39
College (grades 13–16)	33	32	37	24	28	29
Graduate school (1+ years)	27	21	20	20	16	21
Total percentages	100	100	100	100	100	100

SOURCES: 1972 data are from Kauffman and Harder (1975); 1989 data are from Kauffman and Driedger (1991).
[a] Abbreviations are as in Table 2-1.

The Kauffman and Harder and Kauffman and Driedger studies suggested that mainstream Anabaptist-Mennonites do live in an environment conducive to a cosmopolitan orientation. Yet certain questions went unanswered in the CMP1 and CMP2 studies. What is the place of entrepreneurs relative to the population overall? Are they, as we suspect, importers of the cosmopolitan motif? Are they the advance people, confronting the issues that will undoubtedly face others in the future?

What are the differences between ideology and practice? How do people maintain an Anabaptist-Mennonite ideology in the face of a worldview at odds with premises rooted in *Gelassenheit*? The discrepancies between ideology and actual practice, as are predicted by the sociology of knowledge,[87] become another variation of that ancient theme recorded for the history of philosophy by Parmenedes' denial of motion and Heraclitus's eternal flux. The paradox of identity and difference, of stasis and flux, is a durable element of the sociological reason and the rational foundation of how Mennonites find innovative ways to give entrepreneurial expression to their faith.

This then is the stepping-off point for our own empirical studies. Our contention is that Mennonite entrepreneurs embody the contradiction that is the affliction of most modern North American Anabaptist-

TABLE 2-3
Occupation by Sex, 1972 and 1989

Occupational Class	1972			1989		
	Male $N = 1,589$	Female $N = 1,858$	Total $N = 3,447$	Male $N = 1,401$	Female $N = 1,613$	Total $N = 3,014$
			%			
Professionals	23	10	16	36	21	28
Business proprietors or managers	8	1	5	16	4	9
Sales/clerical workers	5	8	7	6	15	11
Craftspeople	11	0	5	10	1	5
Machine operators	8	2	5	6	1	4
Service workers	2	4	3	3	5	4
Farmers	23	0	11	15	1	7
Laborers	5	1	2	2	1	1
Housewives/husbands	0	60	32	1	45	25
Students	14	14	14	5	7	6
Total percentages	100	100	100	100	101	100

SOURCE: Kauffman and Driedger (1991).

Mennonites. Anabaptist-Mennonites generally have been slow to face this contradiction. Although normative or traditional entrepreneurial practice has been commonplace in the Mennonite experience, such activity has been denied and agrarian life idealized. What cannot be denied, in view of mounting empirical evidence, is that the Mennonite social structure has entered a climate that is conducive to the emergence of the cosmopolitan entrepreneur in spite of its *Gelassenheit* ideology.

More than simply embodying the contradiction of Mennonite life, Mennonite entrepreneurs are a sort of archetypal character. Just as the entrepreneurial character is central to the discussion by Bellah and co-workers of the tensions between individualism and commitment in North American society more generally, the Mennonite entrepreneur serves a similar purpose for those who want to understand the tensions operating in the contemporary Mennonite world.

PART II

The Ethos and Experience of the Mennonite Entrepreneur

CHAPTER THREE

The Ethos of the North American Mennonite Enterprise

MENNONITES: AN AGRICULTURAL PEOPLE?

Although many Mennonites have long been involved in entrepreneurial activities, they have been better known as a rural agricultural people—the "quiet in the land." Even today, the Amish Old Order and Old Colony Mennonites seem to represent the Mennonite community in the North American popular imagination. What should be clear already is that this image, even though partially correct, does an injustice to contemporary entrepreneurs as well as to the early Anabaptists.

The self-image held by most Mennonites until quite recently supported this notion of the Mennonites. Michael Yoder noted that Mennonites operated with a "rural bias" and observed that "most Mennonites of European origin, until well into the twentieth century, have assumed that the Christian life is best lived in a rural community."[1] This assumption was grounded in both theological concern (Mennonites believed that rural life offered protection from persecutors and exposure to worldly forces) and historical understanding. Harold Bender, architect of the modern Anabaptist vision, commented that "the Mennonites of history, in all places but [the Netherlands] and northwest Germany, have been farmers and have almost universally produced outstanding achievements in agriculture."[2] The rural bias has even been confirmed for most people through the aesthetic arts, including poems and paintings that depict the idealized Mennonite rural/agrarian life.[3]

Scholarship in recent decades has tried to provide some correctives to this peasant image. Historical work has documented that the original Anabaptist movement was neither rural nor urban, but reflected the society of middle Europe of the sixteenth century.[4] Various writers have demonstrated convincingly that the movement was originally composed of a fair cross-section of society, including noblemen, teachers, lawyers, and other professionals, a goodly number of artisans, and—of course—it attracted the peasants, who made up ninety percent of the population. Driven out of the cities and towns by persecution, the movement became one of rural peasants, with artisans and craftsman providing the leadership and accomplishments to allow for toleration of the persecuted sect.[5] Calvin Redekop cited evidence indicating that Anabaptists-Mennonites became identified with the land by default, as the result of persecution, and that the retreat to the land produced a "marriage of convenience" which could not last.[6]

These scholarly contributions to the understanding of Mennonite life have been matched by a changing outlook in the Mennonite worldview. As Michael Yoder said, the rural bias "is losing its grip on Mennonites in the late twentieth century, as many Mennonites no longer are or want to be rural residents."[7] In Yoder's analysis, "Some in the church are embarrassed by the traditional Mennonite rural bias and see it as an impediment to the growth and witness of the church in the city and the larger world today."

How has this change come about? In part, it is the result of demographic changes; but it also is a product of the changing occupational structure of the Mennonite world and a shifting ethos. In north Germany and the Netherlands early Mennonites moved from strictly agricultural pursuits into commercial and industrial activities. The same happened in Prussia, Russia, and Canada, the United States, and Latin America.[8] Furthermore, many European Mennonite peasants ultimately became entrepreneurs when they immigrated to North America.

The biblical economic ethics that emerged as Mennonites retreated to the land and which may have fit European peasant society fairly well (and thereby providing its ideological *troika*) was an inadequate guide for the Mennonite experience of life in North America. The critical difference between the traditional peasant culture, or village mentality, and the North American situation was aptly captured by Max Weber, who noted that in Europe the farmer asks how many souls can be supported with a given piece of land; in America the farmer asks, "How much can I produce for the market from a given piece of land?"

Although ill suited to the North American experience, the primacy of rural life in the prevailing Mennonite ideology persisted and gave rise to a "rural life movement" among North American Mennonites during the 1930s and 1940s, illustrating the depth of the rural orientation that was transplanted.[9] During this period, Mennonites were still rural, with 82 percent living in rural areas compared with 53 percent of North Americans as a whole.[10] But many worried about the urban encroachment into their world. They worried about the intrusion of such modern innovations as the telephone, automobile, and radio, which gave people living in rural areas too much access to cities and urban culture. Among other publications aimed at assisting Mennonites was a book entitled *Mennonite Community Sourcebook*, edited by Esko Loewen. Loewen's book tried to help Mennonites become aware of the resources for preserving and fostering rural life. A chapter by Ralph Hernley, "Community Life," pointed to the trends causing disintegration of community life: materialism, urbanization, industrialization, secularization, modern education, communication, and transportation.[11]

Most North American Mennonite families were involved in farming at the beginning of the twentieth century. As late as 1940, many of them were engaged in farm-related occupations, a situation that began to change around the middle of the century, especially among the more progressive Mennonite groups. In 1950, 40.7 percent of the (Old) Mennonites, the largest of the Mennonite bodies in North America, were engaged in farming, but by 1963 only 38.9 percent still farmed.[12] The percentage for the General Conference of Mennonites for the period 1950–60 was 32 percent.[13] In his 1964 study of economic trends among Mennonites in the central United States, Howard Raid reported that 28.5 percent of the family heads were farmers.[14] Predominantly agricultural in the early years, North American Mennonites rapidly became diversified in occupational activities and industrialized in economic affairs.[15]

FROM FARM/VILLAGE TO TOWN/CITY OCCUPATIONS

As the proportion of Mennonites involved in farm and rural occupations decreased, occupations more suited to town and city life became more commonplace. The Mennonite Family Census of 1963 indicated that among the (Old) Mennonites, "sales, managers, and business" persons

TABLE 3-1
Mennonite Occupations, 1963

Occupation	No. of Men	Percent
Farmer	1,611	38.9
Craftsmen, skilled	591	14.3
Operatives, semiskilled	445	10.8
Factory laborers	260	6.3
Sales	236	5.7
Service workers	197	4.8
Managers	196	4.7
Teachers	117	2.8
Laborers, unskilled	110	2.8
Clergymen	80	1.9
Business	63	1.5
Clerical/secretaries	62	1.5
Medical	22	0.5
Bookkeepers	17	0.4
All others	132	3.1

SOURCE: Gingerich (1963), 12.

TABLE 3-2
Occupational Distribution, 1982

Occupation	Male	Female	Total
		%	
Professional and technical	16.2	27.7	21.0
Managers and administrators (except farm)	15.0	4.9	10.8
Sales workers	4.1	3.7	3.9
Clerical workers	1.9	22.2	10.3
Craftsmen/foremen	11.9	2.5	12.7
Semiskilled, except transportation	7.8	6.9	7.4
Transport equipment	6.0	1.5	4.1
Laborers, except farm	7.3	2.6	5.3
Farmers and farm managers	15.7	0.8	9.5
Service workers except private household	2.8	18.4	9.3
Private household work	0.2	8.1	3.4

SOURCE: Yoder (1985).

totaled 11.9 percent. Although not synonymous with these categories, entrepreneurs would be included in that percentage (see Table 3-1).

The agricultural character of Mennonite life had changed dramatically by 1982, when another census was taken of the (Old) Mennonites. Using the standard U.S. census categories, the 1982 census reported that only 11.6 percent were farmers and farm managers or farm laborers, and 35.7 percent were classified as professional and technical managers and administrators and sales workers (see Table 3-2).

TABLE 3-3

Occupational Distribution, General Conference Mennonites, 1960 and 1970

Occupation	United States		Canada		Total	
	1960	1970	1960	1970	1960	1970
			%			
Professional and technical	16.8	24.4	13.4	21.8	15.9	23.7
Farmers	30.7	21.6	30.5	32.5	30.7	22.1
Proprietors and managers	6.3	6.5	3.5	5.7	5.5	6.3
Clerical workers	7.1	9.1	6.7	7.9	7.0	8.8
Sales workers	4.2	4.4	2.8	3.2	3.8	4.1
Skilled craftsmen/foremen	10.4	10.5	12.8	14.1	11.1	11.5
Semiskilled operatives	12.9	9.1	13.8	10.0	13.2	9.3
Service workers	7.5	9.5	9.9	7.5	8.2	9.0
Farm laborers	1.3	1.4	1.2	1.0	1.3	1.0
Other laborers	2.7	3.4	5.3	4.1	3.4	5.3

SOURCE: Harder (1970).

Surveys of the General Conference Mennonite Church, the second largest Mennonite Group in North America, revealed similar occupational changes between 1960 and 1970. Table 3-3 shows a sharp decline in the farming occupation and an increase in the professional, technical, proprietary, and manager categories. In 1960 farmers comprised 30.7 percent of the population; in 1970 the number had fallen to 22.1 percent. Proprietors and managers had not increased so dramatically (from 5.5 to 6.3 percent), but the professional and technical occupations grew from 15.9 to 23.7 percent.[16]

More comprehensive data, documenting occupational shifts among the largest Mennonite groups, have been provided by the Church Membership Profile studies (for a discussion of the studies, see Chapter Two). The first of these (CMP1), completed in 1972, indicated that farmers constituted 11 percent of the population (see Table 3-4), whereas professional and technical workers (16 percent), business owners and managers (5 percent), and sales and clerical workers (7 percent) together amounted to 28 percent of the population.[17]

The second Church Member Profile survey (CMP2) revealed important occupational shifts between 1972 and 1989. By 1989, farmers and farm laborers constituted 7 percent of the occupations reported; professional and technical, 28 percent; proprietors and managers, 9 percent; and sales and clerical, 11 percent. It is clear from these figures that the proportion of town/city occupations (e.g., business owners and managers, professional and technical workers) grew considerably.[18]

TABLE 3-4
Occupation Classification, Five Mennonite and Brethren in
Christ Denominations, 1972 and 1989

Occupational Classification	1972 CMP	1989 CMP
	%	
Farmer or farm management	11	7
Proprietor, manager	5	9
Professional/technical (minister, physician, social worker)	16	28
Clerical/sales	7	11
Craftsmen/foremen	5	5
Operatives, machine (truck drivers, seamstresses)	5	4
Service workers	3	4
Laborers (farm, construction, car washer)	3	1
Housewife/husband	32	25
Student	14	6

SOURCE: Kauffman and Driedger (1991).

THE RESURGENCE OF THE MENNONITE ENTREPRENEUR

The few research studies and articles available on Mennonite industry and business generally support what most Mennonites know from their personal experience, namely that since World War II, Mennonites in North America have produced an astounding number of entrepreneurs, business managers, and tycoons. Vancouver and the Fraser Valley in British Columbia, Calgary in Alberta, Winnipeg in Manitoba, Lancaster County in Pennsylvania, Elkhart County in Indiana, Fresno County in California, Harvey County in Kansas, and many less populated Mennonite areas have all produced many substantial Mennonite businesses.

There are two basic streams of Mennonite entrepreneurs. The first is those derived from old North American Mennonite families. These were families who had immigrated to the United States as early as the eighteenth century. The second stream is the colony begun by the post–World War I refugees from Russia. These families settled mainly in Canada, but also on the West Coast.[19]

The old family businesses in the United States (with a few in Canada, mostly in Ontario) range from chicken processors and shoe manufacturers to sophisticated farm machinery manufacturers, most of which have been in existence for many decades, some going all the way back to the mid to late 1800s. These businesses normally evolved slowly alongside the main occupation of farming until either a son took the business over, or it became so big that it overtook the agricultural activities.[20] For example, oftentimes an engine or auto repair shop would slowly evolve into an auto/truck dealership, branching into leasing facilities or developing into a trucking firm. Mennonite entrepreneurs have taken advantage of many other opportunities, such as turning small chicken processing shops into major chicken processing plants.[21]

American Case in Point

Henry Gingerich grew up in a semiurban Mennonite community in an eastern state.[22] Because Henry's father had not been very good at farming, his family helped him start a little grocery store in the middle of a Mennonite farming community. When Henry's father retired, the business was prospering modestly and had a good reputation. Henry inherited the business upon his father's death. Eager to expand, Henry remodeled the original store, enlarged it, and launched a supermarket. Simultaneously, the demographic trend of suburbanization created a population that, made mobile by the automobile, spilled over into the previously rural and relatively isolated Mennonite community.[23] This fact greatly helped Henry's supermarket to prosper. With the increased market, his own growing experience in the business, and considerable new capital, the business thrived.

Some of the success of Henry's supermarket, and that of Mennonite business more generally, was the result of historically determined factors. First, Mennonite business success in the 1950s and 1960s was preceded by the transition of North America from a frontier culture, as Weber described it during his visit, to the urban culture it has become today. Second, Mennonite business benefited from the general surge of prosperity at the end of World War II. Joseph Goulden, in a book that documents these "best years" immediately following the war, noted that people in the United States experienced a new sense of optimism which was matched by new economic opportunities.[24] Whereas the average industrial worker in the prewar period had earned twenty-five dollars weekly, the same worker earned forty-four dollars weekly by V-J Day. Unemployment was less than 2 percent. At the end of the war, Americans had 140 billion dollars in liquid savings, about three times the national income in 1932. Mennonite business expansion was caught up in this wave of optimism and opportunity.

Another factor that contributed to a generation of Mennonite wealth was the phenomenal rise in the price of land, since it also was thrown onto the market as a commodity (as material capital for producing wealth, i.e., crops for the market). In Henry's case, this meant that selling land from the family estate made it possible for him to expand into other areas, such as real estate and automobiles. Henry then sold some of his business interests at a substantial profit and engaged in other investment opportunities. Interestingly, his new-found flexibility in terms of time enabled him to volunteer for church work.

Henry became a classical "Pharisee" according to Max Weber's socioeconomic definition of the same as a class that required a business income to practice their religion.[25] That such a pharisaical class should emerge in the Mennonite society once it adapted to the individualistic cultural soil of North America was anticipated by Weber, working with his concept of the *routinization of charisma*. The temptation to become part of such an "aristocracy of wealth" was created by the material conditions of life in postwar America.

Canadian Case in Point

Additional historical factors affected the development of Mennonite businesses in Canada (see Table 3-5 for a recent survey of Mennonite occupations, in Winnipeg, Manitoba, Canada, conducted in 1981 based on a random sampling of Mennonite Church members). The economic advance of post–World War II refugees who settled there was, for example, accelerated by the fact that some received interest-free loans from Germany as part of war reparations. Some of these refugees have become members of the economic elite, although their lifestyles in many cases would not seem to indicate this.

Beginning penniless (literally) in many cases, incipient entrepreneurs lifted themselves into wealth and power by virtue of hard work, careful management of resources and capital, and, above all, sheer determination. They forged empires in the front yards of many denizens who had lived there for generations and who gradually began to resent these aggressive interlopers.

Again, the case of one such person may prove helpful. Frank Friesen came from the Mennonite settlement in Russia but was inducted into the German army after the Germans overran the Ukraine in 1942. When the German army retreated, he returned with it to Germany and escaped repatriation back to Russia, the fate of many others who were less for-

TABLE 3-5
Occupational Study, Mennonites of Winnipeg

Factor	Percent
Marital status	
Single	17.5
Married	72.7
Widowed	8.1
Divorced	0.8
Education	
Eighth grade	31.6
High school	55.7
Some college	20.4
Employment	
Retired	20.0
Housewife	20.0
Student	5.0
Workforce	55.0
Workforce	
Professional	16.5
Managers	10.0
Clerical	7.0
Crafts/labor	17.7
Professional	
Teachers	32.8
Technology[a]	23.2
Nurses	12.3
Social workers	7.0

SOURCE: Rempel (1981).
[a] Includes medical, dental, etc.

tunate. He immigrated to Canada in 1952 and worked as an apprentice for a builder in a large city of western Canada. By 1961 he had learned the building trade well enough and scraped together sufficient money to build a house for his family. Before he moved into the house, he received an offer to buy it—an offer he could not resist. He built another house and again sold it before it was finished, making a fine profit on the sale. Thus began Frank's building business. He employed fellow Mennonite refugees, involved some of them in his business, and, over the next fifteen years, transformed his business into one of the major development/construction companies in the region. The recession of the 1980s caught him in an overextended financial position, forcing him into bankruptcy. But several years later he was back in business.[26]

DYNAMICS IN THE EMERGENCE
OF THE ENTREPRENEUR

In an attempt to understand better the nature and causes for increased entrepreneurialism among Mennonites, Calvin Redekop conducted one hundred interviews over a two-year period (1985–86) with entrepreneurs selected randomly from various Mennonite community centers in Canada and the United States. Redekop's Entrepreneurial Research (hereafter referred to as RER) provides important (and what proves to be rare) statistical and descriptive data on entrepreneurs in the Mennonite community and reveals something of the dynamics of the changes that have occurred over the course of one generation.[27]

As reported in Table 3-6, responses to the question, "What was your father's occupation?" confirm the fact that most (69 percent) Mennonite entrepreneurs came from farming and rural backgrounds. 21.1 percent were from homes that were arguably entrepreneurial in orientation (6 percent managerial and 15 percent professional). Referring back to Tables 3-1, 3-2, and 3-4, we are reminded that the decline in those involved in farming occupations has been accompanied by increased involvement in the managerial/professional sectors. Obviously, the changing occupational outlook for Mennonites would predict that the portion of entrepreneurs who had farming parents will decrease (as it has in the last several decades) while the percentage of entrepreneurs with managerial, professional technical, and highly educated parents will increase dramatically.

None of this is meant to suggest that the entrepreneurial impulse is necessarily absent among farmers. In fact, most farmers in America might well be considered entrepreneurs—according to Weber's usage of the classical definition of the entrepreneur. Mennonite peasants (except for the groups that deliberately resisted) who migrated to America became entrepreneurs whether they liked it or not. Family farms become hothouses and nurseries of enterprise, where the rewards for virtues such as diligence in carrying out mundane chores, paying attention to detail, creativity in improving productivity all pay tangible dividends. The neoclassical definition further expands *entrepreneur* beyond farmers to include managers, professionals, and artists as well as the traditional business categories. Generally, it can be argued that increasing urbanization/industrialization created the opportunity idea among a variety of occupational categories, and entrepreneurially oriented parents likely encouraged it among their children.

TABLE 3-6
Occupation of Entrepreneur's Father

Occupation	Percent
Professional	15
Farmer	69
Managerial	6
Clerical	0
Manual	10

SOURCE: RER.

Redekop's study also provides insights into intergenerational changes in education. His data reveal that the fathers of present-day entrepreneurs were rural in educational achievements. Referring to Table 3-7, 68 percent of the entrepreneurs had fathers who did not complete high school, whereas the entrepreneurs themselves had completed considerably more years of formal education. In research focused specifically on religious ethnic groups, Featherman argued that educational achievement best predicts the likelihood of a person from a recognizable religioethnic group to enter and succeed in entrepreneurial activity.[28] No other factor, not even personal motivation, is as influential or as crucial. Presumably, the critical role of education applies to Mennonites as well. If succeeding generations of Mennonites are more educated, they too will be more entrepreneurially inclined, becoming more upwardly mobile in terms of income, status, and power.

The rising educational attainment of Mennonite entrepreneurs must be understood in terms of a traditional peasant culture adapting to the North American market economy environment. Growing populations of young people in these communities have been confronted by a shortage of land and agricultural opportunities. New enterprises and industries that provide alternative forms of employment hold different educational expectations. The role and function of education in social mobility have come to be understood as an important variable within minority populations and other marginal groups.[29] Many scholars have argued that education has been especially significant for the social advancement of ethnic groups. As Joseph Kahl noted, "We have emphasized in many places that in the long run education is one of the main routes to high occupation, income, and prestige."[30]

TABLE 3-7
Educational Attainment of Entrepreneurs and Their Fathers

Level of Education	Entrepreneur	Father
%		
Postgraduate	14	3
University graduate	16	4
Some university	7	4
High school	20	11
Some high school	11	9
Less than high school	27	68

SOURCE: RER.

ENTREPRENEURS: PROTOTYPICAL MENNONITES

The most clearly sociological interpretation of the emergence of entrepreneurialism among Mennonites is a structural one—Mennonites will become entrepreneurs as the Mennonite community becomes increasingly integrated into the larger, entrepreneurial society.[31] In other words, as Mennonites become educated, they leave their rural enclaves and find a place in the general occupational/business structure of the society at large. Correspondingly, more entrepreneurs emerge, and entrepreneurship becomes a more accepted part of Mennonite life. In this sense, Mennonite entrepreneurs may, in fact, be prototypical of the Mennonite-to-come if not the Mennonite-that-has-been.

In part, what has compelled Mennonites to leave their rural enclaves has been the closing of the frontier. In the 1950s it was possible for the immigrant from Europe to do well through hard labor. But by the time the generation that opened the frontier was ready to pass on the hard-won family farm to the next generation, it had ceased to exist as an economically viable operation. The increasing economic difficulties of maintaining a rural community forced Mennonites to become urbanized, commercialized, and industrialized, consequently becoming inconspicuous in the general occupational distribution. In response, the more progressive Mennonite groups have opted to socialize their young into the urban culture.

In the wake of this increased urbanization, industrialization, and commercialization, many (Mennonites themselves as well as scholars of Mennonite life) find themselves asking whether Mennonites will find sufficient spiritual nourishment in their Anabaptism to survive these changes with their unique cultural/religious identity intact, or whether they will experience the assimilation of other uprooted peoples?

Sociologists have been interested in this question for a long time, as applied to Mennonites as well as other immigrant groups. They have crafted numerous models for tracing the paths these groups have followed into the cultural and occupational structure of North American society.[32] Although many groups, such as the Mennonites, initially resisted the entrepreneurial draw of their new-found host society, they often discovered that such resistance was difficult if not futile. Aldrich, Jones, and McEvoy declared that "the opportunity structure of the receiving society outweighs any cultural predispositions [against] entrepreneurship [in the ethnic community]."[33]

This situation is not new, of course, in that cultural and ethnic groups have long moved from place to place whether by choice or coercion. In ancient days, for example, the Jewish people were held captive in Egypt and faced problems of assimilation. But in that situation, an entire people was taken into exile and forced to come to terms with a novel understanding of peoplehood (which Nietzsche both despised and respected). The modern Mennonite experience is that their group is experiencing a gradual inner erosion of the traditional lived meaning of their peoplehood while retaining the rhetoric and aspects of that tradition in the urban setting.

FACTORS INFLUENCING THE MOVE
TOWARD ENTREPRENEURIALISM

The Receptivity Hypothesis

The move of any uprooted group toward accepting the prevailing economic orientation of what we might term the receiving society will be accelerated if the receiving society accepts or welcomes the ethnic entrepreneur.[34] There are two dimensions to this receptivity: (1) the actual economic opportunity that it provides to societal newcomers, and (2) the perceptions of discrimination or rejection of ethnic business (on the part of the receiving society) which the enterpriser may harbor. Both dimensions are factors in the success of the Mennonite entrepreneur.

Redekop's interviews with entrepreneurs (RER) again provide insight into the development of Mennonite business ventures. Entrepre-

TABLE 3-8
Reasons for Business Success

Reason	Percent
Persons outside the organization	32
Hard work	31
Persons inside the organization	10
Taking serious risks	9
Working with people	6
My faith	6
My need to achieve	6
Plain luck	3
Good products and service	3

SOURCE: RER.

neurs were asked, "What factors would you say were chiefly responsible for your economic (business) success?" Table 3-8 reports the responses to this question, the most frequent of which was, "Persons outside the organization." When asked, more specifically, "Who were the people most helpful in starting your business?" entrepreneurs pointed to a number of people. As Table 3-9 reveals, 36 percent identified family and relatives, 33 percent friends, and 29 percent noted the role of business partners and miscellaneous persons—many of whom were members of the receiving society, as Ward and Jenkins define it.

What is even more clear from the Redekop interviews is that few Mennonite entrepreneurs felt that the receiving society had discriminated against them. Redekop posed the question, "Do you recall any personal experiences of discrimination in hiring or promotion practices?" Five percent of the entrepreneurs said yes, and 92 percent said no. Perceived discrimination is obviously very low, and this suggests that the response of the host society to Mennonite businesspeople is benign or even friendly. In fact, many of the entrepreneurs with whom Redekop spoke felt that being Mennonite was probably an advantage in their business dealings. They were asked, "Do you feel that being a Mennonite has in any way proved advantageous to your business success?" Eighty-six percent said yes, while only 14 percent said no. Listed as reasons for the positive perceptions were honesty, trustworthiness, quality work or products, integrity, and "Mennonites have a good reputation"—the largest single response. Consistent with Weber's depiction of the North American Baptist sects, it would seem then that those in North American society share his positive view of them. This provides a good opportunity structure for

TABLE 3-9
Most Helpful Persons

Person	Percent
Close friends	33
Non-nuclear family relatives	17
Parents	15
Miscellaneous (Bankers, competitors, etc.)	16
Business partners	13
Spouse	4

SOURCE: RER.

Mennonite entrepreneurs—a structure that is perhaps more encouraging than that available to other, less positively viewed, societal newcomers.

There is reason to believe that the receptivity of the receiving society is only going to improve as Mennonite youth become more exposed to secular education by going to secular institutions and through the influence of secular curriculum in Mennonite schools.[35] Those Mennonites who become more educated will find the prevailing worldview less threatening and will begin to comprehend the receiving society's point of view, attitudes, and perceptions.

As the Mennonite youth are exposed to the values of the larger society, they will come to understand more fully its structural norms and the processes that support them. When today's Mennonite youth take on entrepreneurial roles, then, they will feel more at home in the business world and personally identify with it more than did their more traditional forebears. As their reference groups break open, their loyalties will shift.

Furthermore, education is likely to help the next generation of Mennonite entrepreneurs identify employment opportunities available in a modern society. Mennonites have long operated as a society in which traditional occupational skills and their supporting belief structure were passed on from generation to generation in the context of a relatively stable primary economy. To survive in the modern world, Mennonites are learning that they must prepare their young to participate in a relatively unstable secondary economy, where primary production has become almost completely mechanized, and human labor begins at the level of secondary production (i.e., in designing machines to make machines to do the physical labor). Education puts the means of participating in the market economy in the hands of the individual and the community.

Public education has combined forces with the popular media to socialize individuals in American society, regardless of ethnic or religious background, into participation in the market economy and generation of revenue for the state's coffers. Since the more progressive Mennonite groups are accepting and supporting general and technical education, including graduate schools and specialties such as medicine, engineering, and law, it is clear that a basic shift in values is taking place, of which education is both the cause and effect.

None of this is without peril to traditional Mennonite religious and cultural understandings. Students of Mennonite life have argued that the unchecked disintegration of the Mennonite community by unconscious substitution of secular for traditional values must be countered with a specifically "Mennonite" approach to the economy which gives the Mennonite entrepreneur a viable identity and a constructive place in the community. This is a view that is shared by Mennonite businesspeople and business organizations (e.g., MEDA). Finding this approach while also finding the way through the complexities of modern experience is and will be no easy matter.

The Cultural Contradictions of Mennonite Entrepreneurialism

Mennonite entrepreneurs are, in some ways, trapped between the cultural expectations of the Mennonite and non-Mennonite worlds. The receiving society invites them to participate in the world of business through the opportunities it has made available. There is some sympathy among Mennonites toward those who chose to move into the world and business—a sympathy that has grown through the opening up of Mennonites to the ways of the modern world. However, in many circles the longstanding Mennonite suspicion or even hostility toward business and profit persists.

Traditionally a very strong ethos has condemned the business-entrepreneurial aegis. As recently as 1955, in a substantive article on Mennonites in business, J. Winfield Fretz spoke of this condemnation, noting that "Mennonites longer than any other religious group forbade their members to engage in profit making business. One does not find Mennonites engaged in business enterprises for profit. Among the Old Order Amish and other conservative groups this traditional antipathy to business as a way of making a living is still maintained."[36] The congregation and the church as religious community have tended to disapprove strongly of economic and business involvement in the world, claiming that this practice posed the threat of an "unequal yoke with unbelievers." By avoiding business partnerships with non-Christians, Mennonites thought they could maintain strict standards of honesty and integrity, remain content with a smaller business in order to have much time and energy left for the life and service of the church, and to avoid litigation for purposes of collecting debts.[37] This restriction on entering the world has certainly been an effective barrier as well, and it is hypothesized here that relinquishing the strict nonconformity ethic hastened by the entrepreneurial aggressiveness in the community has allowed and encouraged Mennonites to become businesspeople and even entrepreneurs.

It is precisely this attitude that has been changing rapidly in recent years. As Mennonite economist Roy Vogt said of the Canadian experience, "There is no question that in the past few decades Mennonites have entered the mainstream of economic life in Canada . . . it was [earlier] made quite clear to them that as Christians they were to live the life of farmers or craftsmen, avoiding the worldly life of commercial circles."[38]

Shifting cultural and economic circumstance has prompted a shift in theological beliefs. Although this shift is still in the making, and no final resolution to the tension between the traditional Mennonite antipathy toward business and the new-found openness to entrepreneurial activity has been found, some choices are becoming clear. Vogt suggested that two modern Anabaptist approaches are possible. One is a type of *radical perfectionism* and the other a form of *ethical responsibility*.[39] It is the latter approach that appears to have captured the imagination of most theological-ethical analysis, as expressed by some of the leading theologians and ethicists in the Mennonite community. This approach holds that Mennonites can and must take their comprehensive social ethics into the marketplace.[40] Carl Kreider, a leading Mennonite economist and churchperson who has authored a handbook for the Christian entrepreneur, took this position and argued for the compatibility of the Mennonite ethos and the world of business. "Christian entrepreneurs can 'please God' and can function as an integral part of the body of Christ."[41]

Mennonite businesspeople seem to accept Kreider's argument. In a survey conducted among businesspeople in a number of congregations in 1976, people were asked to rank ideas in terms of how they influenced their decision to enter the business world (see Table 3-10). The top two reasons for entering business—contribution to the community and service and witness to God—reflect ideas about work which are not inconsistent with the Mennonite sense of religious duty.

TABLE 3-10
Reasons for Entering the Particular Business

Reason	Weighted Value	Rank
Leading of the Holy Spirit	2.55	1
Better able to support God's work	2.85	2
Challenges of the work	3.22	3
Friends who were in business	3.44	4
Personal contribution to society	3.51	5
Personal profit	3.66	6
Service and witness to God	3.77	7
Contribution to the community	3.81	8
Improve my social standing	4.85	9

SOURCE: Congregational survey, conducted by Calvin Redekop in 1975, sponsored by MEDA. The study consisted of selecting ten Mennonite communities in Canada and the United States and then inviting ten businesspeople to come in for an evening of discussion, focusing on specific questions and filling out a CMP questionnaire. Respondents were asked to rank the importance of each reason for entering business. They ranked them from 1 (high importance) to 5 (low importance).

The most specific information regarding the influence of religious commitments of the Mennonite community on entrepreneurial development derives from the RER and specifically from the question, "How has your congregation related to you in your business activities?" About 80 percent of those Redekop interviewed indicated that their congregations had not raised serious objections; the remainder said that the congregations had been either neutral or in some way discouraging of their business involvements. Typical of the responses was the following: "In my community, the people were most eager to become socially mobile because we are such a small group and defensive of the larger society."[42] That the majority perceived the church or the congregation to be supportive, or at least not openly hostile to the entrepreneurial quest, gives substance to the argument that the Mennonite stance toward the unequal yoke or nonconformity with the world has been changing.

Models of Anabaptist-Mennonite Economic Adaptation

To contextualize these changes in the Mennonite view toward business, and by way of drawing this chapter to a close, it should be noted that Anabaptist-Mennonite attitudes toward economic activities have found expression in three basic models over the past four centuries.[43] These models continue to exist alongside one another, each prominent among certain members of the Mennonite family.

The first of these is the *community of goods model*, exemplified by the

Hutterites since 1528 and by other related communal groups that are basically Mennonite in origin.[44] This model rejects any type of economic integration with the receiving community and has organized itself into communistic societies characterized by total collectivism. Clearly, even though they have been indirectly related to the economic goals of the larger society and have produced economic goods for it, adherents of this model hold themselves at an arm's length from the world—which they perceive as selfish and self-gratifying—and they make sure that the world does not control their system. Outsiders can argue with the consistency of this orientation, but their ideology is clear even if inconsistently ordered.[45]

The second is the *radical confrontation model*, which is typical of the many "plain groups" such as the Amish and Old Colony Mennonites and Mennonite utopian groups. In this model, property is either owned by the community and then distributed to the membership, as among the Old Colony, or it is privately owned but severely controlled by community norms as in the Reba Place Fellowship.[46] The communities are almost totally rural agricultural, and what business and commerce exist are totally subservient to, or derived from, the agricultural activities and congregational authority. In the radical confrontation model, there is some entrepreneurialism, but it is controlled strictly by the religious mores of the group, and a remarkable self-governing process restricts the size and nature of the new businesses that emerge.[47] All surplus resources, as in the Hutterite model, are recirculated within the community to purchase more land or help a son get started in the local agriculturally related business. The goal of business activity is to propagate the Mennonite way of life.[48]

The third model has been termed the *conventional economics model*, referring to Mennonites living in heterogeneous communities in which the religious activities form the cohesion for community life in the congregation. Faith and its ethics and lifestyles are imposed on what could be termed the prevailing socioeconomic institutions. It is this model that has led to the dilemmas and contradictions that we have been discussing, and it is this model that is by far most typical of the largest and most dynamic sector of Mennonitism.

As long as Mennonites of the conventional economics model were basically rural, their external profile was not much different from those groups adhering to the first two models, though their values and commitments may have been increasingly secularized. But the unchecked assimilation into mainstream industrial North American society has presented Mennonites—as it has other religious ethnic groups who harbor a communal impulse—with an increasingly confusing and complex set of demands, values, and practices.

As we have argued, with the shift from predominantly village and rural occupations to town- and city-related economic activities, the norms, roles, and values that the Mennonites traditionally espoused changed dramatically, more and more resembling those of the host society. The mass of conflicting pressures, loyalties, demands, attractions, opportunities, and enticements coming from outside and from within have shaken the foundation of the Mennonite ethos.

Some Remaining Questions

Cataloging economic models is just one small part of the overall project that we have set for ourselves. We are left with a number of pressing questions. What do all of these changes mean for Mennonite life and faith? Is religion determinative of the economic forces, or is religion the victim and creator of socioeconomic forces? And finally, what may indeed be the central question of this study: How does entrepreneurialism in the Mennonite context help us to understand how a religious movement integrates and rationalizes its faith as it participates in the broad economic structures and processes of the host society?

CHAPTER FOUR

The Entrepreneur and Work
Community or Self-Advancement?

Richard Pfeiffer, in a provocative book entitled *Working for Capitalism*, stated that "if we understand the essential quality of work, we will better understand the essential nature and purposes of (society's) organization, and if we understand the essential nature and purposes of social organization, we will better understand the essential quality of work." Pfeiffer, a professor at the Johns Hopkins University, took a year off from his teaching to work in a factory and from it gained immense insight into the nature of work in industrial America. So closely does Pfeiffer see the connection between work and American social structure that he concluded that an analysis "about work in the United States, is then also about American society."[1] A similar observation can be made about work and Mennonite life. To the extent we better understand the Mennonite attitude toward work (and entrepreneurial work in particular), we will also better understand the contemporary Mennonite ethos and vice versa.

THE MEANING OF WORK

Anthony Giddens defined work as "the carrying out of tasks, which involves the expenditure of mental and physical effort, and has as its objective the production of goods and services that cater to human needs."[2] According to this definition, the necessity of work for human welfare and survival is self-evident. Furthermore, there is no doubt that the consequences of work (or, more accurately, the organization of work) are all pervasive. But the *meaning* of work to those who engage in it and the values and norms that surround it are not so clear.

The different understandings of work which people hold are not just because of variations in personal opinion. Rather, the understandings emerges from cultural heritage as well as each person's unique biographical experiences. There are numerous—sometimes seemingly contradictory—interpretations and ideologies regarding work from which interpretations of work can be drawn. Greek philosophy, for example, tended to downgrade certain types of work, especially the menial. Jewish tradition, by way of another example, has placed a great deal of importance on work, as a part of God's creation activity, and as a continuing necessity in its maintenance. Often attitudes within a cultural tradition will vacillate. For instance, biblical writers sometimes shared Tom Sawyer's definition of work as something you have to do; work—or the drudgery associated with it—is seen as a curse.[3] At other times, work was to be celebrated, as in Proverbs (22:29): "Seest thou a man diligent in his business? He shall stand before kings."

Social scientists note that the meaning of work has been complicated by the "division of labor." As Marx pointed out, as time passes the means of production tend to become concentrated in the hands of one class in society. At the same time, political authority becomes concentrated in a similar manner. And it does not take long until a hierarchy has crept into the division of labor. Those with power, whether economic or political, force those without to accept a larger proportion of the drudgery associated with doing the business of society and assume for themselves a larger proportion of the creative roles. Thus, an idealized beginning in which all were equal in a perfectly egalitarian society, whether as in a Hobbesian "war of all against all" or in the Edenic garden of the Rousseauian "natural man," reveals itself everywhere to have become inequality, hierarchy, and the exploitation of human by human.

In any case, to understand the meaning of work, we must examine the cultural context in which that meaning is embedded and out of which it emerges. To understand the meaning of work for Mennonites we must first consider the broader Christian cultural context and then explore the Anabaptist-Mennonite context in particular.

Work in Christian Thought

The theology of work is relatively undeveloped in Christian thinking as a whole. Nevertheless, Charles Avila felt that the early Christian Church adopted many of the Graeco-Roman attitudes toward work
and wealth, including the disparagement of menial labor.[4] Likewise, the
Roman Catholic and Protestant traditions developed substantial, if not
theologically well developed, views of work and its place within human
society. Whereas the former was much more positively inclined toward
work, the latter (especially those Protestant groups influenced by Lutheranism) tended to downplay the relationship between work and salvation.
In a classic dualistic response, Martin Luther presented a concept of a
spiritual and a secular vocation or calling, wherein both were important,
but the secular was not connected to salvation.

Calvinism developed this understanding of work further. In his classic work on the Protestant ethic, Max Weber proposed that it was the
complete discontinuity between work and salvation in Calvinism which
ushered in the idea of work for its own sake (seen as a duty to God and
as a sign of personal commitment and piety). He noted that "the elected
Christian is in the world only to increase this glory of God by fulfilling His
commandments to the best of his ability. This character is hence shared by
labor in a calling which serves the mundane life of the community."[5] The
Calvinist ethos, then, held that the accumulation of wealth was the end of
productive labor. Furthermore, it stripped away from traditional notions
of work the rewards of indulgence and excess—rewards that normally ensured that quickly gotten gain was quickly redistributed. This new notion
of the *calling*, which became the ideology of the classical entrepreneur,
was inner-worldly ascetic, deferring gratification out of a commitment to
manipulate the opportunities for accumulation, ownership, and success.[6]

In fact, the *summum bonum* of this ethic—the earning of more and
more money combined with the strict avoidance of all spontaneous enjoyment of life—meant that humans were to be preoccupied with the
making of money; its acquisition was to be their ultimate life purpose.
In the Calvinist Protestant ethic, work has intrinsic value. It atones for
sins (although this is never stated directly as a consequence of the back-
lash against Tetzel's sale of indulgences, or good works, as commodities
that could be exchanged for time in purgatory), and its creativity is the
legitimate reward for those who have atoned by enduring the drudgery
that was their appointed lot. It is worth noting here that the dichotomy

implicit in this approach to work has evolved into two understandings of it in recent research: work as *instrumental* activity, as a means to other ends (extrinsic, or utilitarian, value), and work as a *terminal* (intrinsic, or ultimate, value) activity.[7]

Work in Secular Culture

Some writers argue that we are living in a "post-Christian," secular cultural period. In contemporary culture, work is more utilitarian than was it was four centuries ago. The drudgery of labor is endured because experience has proved that this is the best way to maximize the amount of time to pursue pleasure after taking care of the business of society. *Leisure*, bought on the market like Tetzel's indulgences, is the secularized, inner-worldly hereafter that was the neoclassical entrepreneur's *intrinsic* or ultimate goal. Whether a *qualitative* devaluation of the concept of an ultimate goal has taken place because of this secularization is another question.

MENNONITES AND WORK

Unlike the secular view of work, Mennonites have long understood it in religious terms. For traditional Mennonites, drudgery is a punishment for sinfulness. In short, because all have sinned, all are obliged to participate in the redeeming drudgery. This theological (or, better, *pre-theological*) idea is that hard work is a means of realizing and promoting the Christian life within the norms and symbols of the religious community. In simplest terms, one must work to be able to support the work of the church—work that is largely seen as evangelism to a very narrow confession of faith.

The Anabaptist-Mennonite tradition, although it shared much with the Reformation perception of work (described by Weber), deviated sharply from the Reformation interpretation of salvation, work, and economics by stressing the communal nature of the Christian and the economic life as well as the importance of *Gelassenheit* in social and religious activities. Over the years, this resulted in various experiments with communal institutions, ranging from the Muensterite experiment to the social organization of contemporary Hutterites. Even less communally minded Mennonite groups have pursued mutual aid in their care of their aged, their sick, their handicapped, and their young in the forms of homes, hospitals, and schools.[8]

The Anabaptist-Mennonite View of Salvation and Work

With their emphasis on community, Anabaptist-Mennonites parted company with other streams of the Reformation in their interpretations of both salvation and the role of work. They rejected the individualism/subjectivity that so thoroughly imbued Calvinist and Lutheran understandings of salvation. According to Weber, these two traditions promoted a view of "unprecedented inner loneliness of the single individual. In what was for the man of the age of the Reformation the most important thing in life, his eternal salvation, he was forced to follow his path alone to meet a destiny which had been decreed for him from eternity."[9]

Anabaptism, by contrast, argued that the process of becoming a member of the kingdom of God—a covenanted community—through mature conversion was central to salvation. It is, in part, because of this understanding of salvation that individualism and even the concept of private property (which was understood as an expression of it), came to be questioned seriously by a large segment of the movement and was actually rejected by some groups.[10] Economic, social, and cultural life were submitted to the discernment of the religious fellowship so that all aspects could be sanctioned by the community.

In addition, Anabaptist-Mennonites saw a relationship between works and salvation which deviated somewhat from the Lutheran position.[11] The Anabaptists insisted that obedience to Christ inevitably had to result in action—works. Recent scholarship provides support for this understanding of the Anabaptist-Mennonite view of work and salvation. John Oyer's analysis of Michael Schneider, an early leader, is particularly instructive.[12] During interrogation by Protestant authorities, Schneider responded that good works must accompany faith, otherwise true faith does not exist. The true Christian will follow Christ in manner of life and therefore, obviously, do many good works. He confessed that his Anabaptist brothers and sisters still clung ardently to good works—obedience expressed itself in activities that Protestants would label good works.[13]

This is not to say that Anabaptist-Mennonites saw work as a way of buying salvation—akin to purchasing indulgences. Work was more a ritual sign of yieldedness than a means to an end or even a duty, according to Cronk.[14] Stated another way, for the Anabaptist-Mennonite, work was a response of obedience to God's invitation to participate in the life of His kingdom; practically, it was an expression of love for, and promotion of, the neighbor. In reference, then, to the Weberian and the more contemporary analysis of work as individualistic or communal, it could be said that the Anabaptist-Mennonite attitude toward work was more communal than individualistic, but insofar as there was an intrinsic value in work, it was symbolic of love for the neighbor and for the kingdom of God. There is no evidence that Anabaptist-Mennonites considered work to be a calling and hence as means to salvation, either theologically or in practice.

Gelassenheit *and Work*

Behind this uniquely Anabaptist understanding of work and salvation is the commitment to *Gelassenheit*. Sandra Cronk provided a thorough discussion of *Gelassenheit* and its importance to the Mennonite worldview and view of work.[15] "The early Anabaptists had a word which encompassed this understanding of yielding, '*Gelassenheit*.' The term is not commonly used among contemporary Amish and Mennonites. However its constituent meanings continue as a vital part—The Anabaptists agreed that yielding is the heart of Christian faith and life. But they used this idea in a unique way. Yielding structured their external relationships with one another as well as their internal relationship with God." Cronk continued, noting that *Gelassenheit* in the Anabaptist view has two closely related meanings. "First, it means that the Christian must yield to God's will—Yieldedness also refers to the interior meaning of God's plan for humankind. It is the principle by which the whole social order functions. Thus, yielding to God means living a life of yieldedness toward others."

Cronk insists that this "yieldedness" has implications for the economic realm as well. "By working hard a member shows he is more concerned with others than with his own comfort. . . . Work is thus transformed into a service of love for others. It is not primarily a way of gaining personal wealth, power and prestige." This view of work combines traits of the so-called Protestant work ethic (such as frugality, honesty, and diligence) with the Mennonite tradition of giving priority to the community over the individual. The consequence of this orientation is that "the economic system is transformed from a potentially competitive, self-aggrandizing process into a way of caring for others."

The implications of this view of socioeconomic life and institutions are discernible in the history and life of Mennonite communities. During the first several generations, the Mennonite movement was either totally communal in economic matters or subordinated private property and work to the welfare of the entire community. Early Anabaptists rarely discussed the communal nature of work since the emphasis in their defense against their accusers was their care for the community's welfare. However, one direct reference, in the negative, illustrates clearly the communal nature of the work ethic: "Now if, then, each member withholds assistance from the other, the whole thing must go to pieces. If the deacon of the community will never serve, the teacher will not teach, the young brother will not be obedient, *the strong will not work for the community but for himself,* and each one wishes to take care of himself. The whole body is divided. In brief, one, common, builds the Lord's house and is pure; but mine, thine, his, own divides the Lord's house and is impure."[16]

In a more intensive analysis of the meaning of work in the early Anabaptist-Mennonite society, Cronk concluded that "work was an extremely important element in the faith and experience of the second generation Amish and Mennonite communities. It not only provided the basic necessities of life, it also embodied deep religious values of yieldedness to Christ, service, discipleship, etc. The process of working created the interconnecting web of daily life within the church community. It also formed a link connecting the church community with the larger world. It helped upbuild the whole society."[17] She observed that "work and its underlying meanings are so deeply embedded in the Mennonite and Amish culture, they rarely rise to the level of conscious reflection."[18]

The Legacy of Gelassenheit in Contemporary Mennonite Life

As the Anabaptist-Mennonite movement began to experience some semblance of toleration and acceptance, the property and work ethic began to change somewhat, but the collective or communal orientation were never lost entirely. Even in recent times, working in either a defense plant or a liquor factory, for example, was reason enough for excommunication. Other occupations and jobs were clearly proscribed and held as illegitimate forms of employment for Mennonites. As J. Winfield Fretz noted, "The church also was opposed to young people entering certain types of business such as life insurance and casualty agencies. Pursuit of higher education and preparation for the traditional professions were also discouraged because of the fear of diversion from disciplined Christian living."[19]

Proactively, the Mennonite community continues to express—in myriad forms—the communal property and work ethic through its communal experiments, ministry of relief, sharing and service, and in limiting the types of work permitted. Communal societies and experiments continue to emerge in the Mennonite society, such as Reba Place Fellowship, Fellowship of Hope, and the New Creation Fellowship, which place great stress on communal sharing and subjecting work to the norms and ethics of the Gospel as the congregation or movement understands it.[20]

Entrepreneurs: A Threat to the Values of Gelassenheit?

Operating in a cultural context holding such a view of work, Mennonite entrepreneurs have often been perceived as threats. People who begin to see work as a means of self-expression rather than of furthering the community's interests, who demand the freedom for creative expression, who find life's purpose in addressing larger secular needs, and who chart their own work courses without regard to the religious community's authority/interests all pose a danger to the traditional expression of the Mennonite work ethos.

The nearing of the Mennonite and non-Mennonite worlds has opened doors of opportunity to Mennonites. Modern civil society has freed the individual who chooses to reject the restraints of the traditional society. The utilitarian values and norms of the market economy society offer the Mennonite entrepreneur the instrumental possibility of working to gain self-advancement and amass private possessions for personal power.[21] As opportunities outside the Mennonite community have expanded so too have suspicions of entrepreneurs. Thus, Mennonite entrepreneurs are seen by many as pursuing their objectives without the regard for traditional community structure, and they are judged to have abandoned the *Gelassenheit* ethic that bound the individual's interests and identity to that of the community. Mennonites who become entrepreneurs are viewed by many as having relinquished the center of their faith.

But how does this view square with the entrepreneurs' experiences, their understandings of themselves, and their relationship to the Anabaptist-Mennonite tradition? Is there, in fact, no way to reconcile the traditional Mennonite village economy and its understanding of work with the world of modern business? Is there any possibility of retaining the essence of *Gelassenheit* while operating in an arena that assumes individual self-interest as its defining metaphor?

THE MENNONITE ENTREPRENEUR'S VIEW OF WORK

Ultimately, the problem faced by Mennonite entrepreneurs is this: does leaving the local market to participate in the cosmopolitan market necessarily imply that the entrepreneur must abandon community as the *raison d'être* of his or her activity? Must Mennonite entrepreneurs necessarily be bent on the utilitarian pursuit of happiness, limited only by respect for others' equally unrestricted right to pursue their personal interests? Or is it possible that Mennonite entrepreneurs are able to expand the Mennonite understanding of work as redemptive/creative and oriented toward establishing an eschatological community?

The Extant Literature

Although there is relatively little prior literature to answer these questions, several research reports suggest that the communal nature of work which we have said is inherent in Anabaptist-Mennonite theology and practice is more resilient than one might imagine. Joseph Smucker, for example, conducted in-depth interviews with twenty-nine Mennonites in the London, Ontario, area in the mid-1980s to discover how important the congregation was in influencing the rituals, symbols (beliefs), and actions of the church membership. Smucker noted that "the most frequent reference to 'service' occurred when respondents spoke of their work. With one exception, none of the respondents born as Mennonites had any desire to be constantly upwardly mobile in their occupations. Regardless of their occupation, respondents tended to view their work as a form of providing service."[22] He interpreted the concepts of *community* and *service* as ritualized symbols within the traditional Mennonite community[23] and believed that his research indicated that "the concept of community demands service from the individual." It is the obligation of the individual to contribute to the viability of the group, to be more concerned for others than for self. "One's occupation, for example, is not to be pursued for personal gain but for the benefit of the community."[24]

In some equally suggestive and creative research, Laura Weaver interviewed twenty Mennonite women who were selected randomly to provide a cross-section regarding age, education, occupation, and family (married and single). Weaver speculated that Mennonite communities emphasize community building more than individual achievement, that women were taught diligence, not creativity, and that women defined success in terms of service rather than financial rewards.

Weaver's interview material strongly supported these hypotheses. She concluded, "According to this research, Mennonite women were apparently taught a double message concerning work. In their instruction, community building rather than individual achievement was emphasized, but the service emphasis was not related to success [the women achieved on their own]." [25]

The Church Member Profiles of Kauffman and Harder (CMP1) and Kauffman and Driedger (CMP2) included no references to work.[26] The studies did ask respondents to rank reasons that people often give for being in a particular business or occupation. Ranked third highest by respondents was "the challenges of this work are stimulating." This reason was, notably, superseded by the reasons "support for God's work" (ranked second by respondents) and "the leading of the Holy Spirit" (ranked first). It is obvious that the personal stimulation of work and the challenges it provides are crowding some very traditional and orthodox Mennonite ideas about the purpose of work. Of equal importance is the fact that they have not superseded the traditional ideas.

The Lure of Self-actualization

The extant literature, then, implies that Mennonites still believe that work is akin to service. Redekop's research on Mennonite entrepreneurs (RER) suggested that the matter is more complicated. According to data generated from the RER interviews, Mennonite entrepreneurs do retain a commitment to work as service, but they also feel the lure of self-actualization. To illustrate, Redekop asked his respondents to select the characteristics they would most prefer in a job. Table 4-1 reveals their priorities.

The entrepreneurs interviewed by Redekop indicated that the sense of accomplishment which work can provide is significantly more important in career choice than are personal ambitions and goals. This sense of accomplishment can, of course, be understood in a number of different

TABLE 4-1
Ranking of Preferred Characteristics of Job

Trait	Choices and Weights			Totals	Rank
	First (X2)	Second (X1)	Not Important (X0)		
Work is important and gives					
a sense of accomplishment	67% (134)	27% (27)	0% (0)	188	1
Chances for advancement	21% (42)	10% (10)	1% (0)	52	2
High income	7% (14)	9% (9)	16% (0)	23	3
Security	2% (4)	6% (6)	35% (0)	10	4
Short hours	0% (0)	0% (0)	0% (0)	0	

SOURCE: RER. Interviewees were asked to rank the five choices. The responses were weighted as follows: first place was given a weight of 2; second, a rank of 1; and third, a 0. These were then multiplied by the number of persons choosing the various categories to provide the scores. For a discussion of the RER, see the Appendix.

ways, for example, as highly individualistic (self-gratifying) or collective (group-gratifying), or, for that matter, as rooted in both.

The responses of entrepreneurs to other questions suggest that Mennonite entrepreneurs may prize the individual rewards of work more than the previous literature has indicated. Redekop asked his respondents to reflect on their careers up to the time of the interview and to verbalize what they found most challenging about their work. Fifty-eight percent said personal achievement was the greatest challenge, and 33 percent said that helping others (either in the community—which may include the religious community—or in the organization) was the greatest challenge. An argument can be made that the response category "learning from others, and from past mistakes" also pertains to self-actualization and growth. So interpreted, this means that although some Mennonite entrepreneurs do see service to community as an important element in what they do, a majority values more individualistic criteria.

As Mennonite entrepreneurs become more involved in the world of business outside the realm of the religious community, they begin to make decisions about work and the workplace which reflect general societal values and norms. Respondents were asked about priorities in hiring, and, as Table 4-2 reveals, they are now unlikely to give a job automatically to fellow Mennonites or even to members of their families. Today's entrepreneurs have clearly opted for competence and creativity and recognize that their criteria depart from those they believe their fathers would have used, which preserved the traditional and normative familial and religious

TABLE 4-2
Employment Attitudes and Practices of Father and Son

	Father	Son
	% agreeing	
One should hire/promote persons with most creativity.	37	69
One should hire and promote family or close members.	36	18
One should hire/promote members of one's own religious group.	17	11

SOURCE: RER.

loyalties. In sociological terms the sons' values are *universalistic*, whereas those of the fathers are *particularistic* or local.

Entrepreneurs, simply by participating in the anonymous and impersonal transactions of the market economy, no longer receive the traditional returns for investing in the community. As they move along the continuum from local to cosmopolitan, the social investment in the Mennonite community yields ever diminishing returns. The economy of the Mennonite society is based on a network of personal relationships; the market economy is based on impersonal cash transactions. The former always suffers devaluation when it enters into business with the latter,[27] and so by definition, investment in the Mennonite community is a bad business deal for the cosmopolitan entrepreneur. This tension became clear when Redekop asked his respondents about the importance of profit and the circumstances under which the profit motive should be held in check. From the data presented in Table 4-3, it would seem that the current generation of entrepreneurs is more willing to operate with a profit motive alone than their fathers (e.g., where 41 percent of the entrepreneurs said "one should realize some amount of profit regardless of the party involved," 29 percent of the entrepreneurs' fathers held this position).

The entrepreneurs were also asked, "What do you consider to be the most important principle to learn in order to prepare for life?" (see Table 4-4). "Helping others when they need help" was surprisingly low for both cohorts (entrepreneurs and their fathers), but it is possible that given the extensive institutionalized mutual assistance activities within the Mennonite community and service commitment to others outside the community, this emphasis is simply taken for granted. It is surprising that working hard is not as high a priority for the entrepreneurs as for the fathers, but again it is possible and probable that the entrepreneur believes that it is smart work that counts, not sheer effort. This speculation goes

TABLE 4-3
Attitudes toward Profits, Family, and Community

	Entrepreneur	Entrepreneur's Father
	% agreeing	
One should not make profits from immediate family and friends.	21	27
One should offer discounts to family and close friends.	20	27
One should offer discounts to members of religious communities.	9	8
One should realize some amount of profit regardless of party involved.	41	29
Other (depends on circumstances).	8	6

SOURCE: RER.

TABLE 4-4
Principles to Help in Life

	Entrepreneur	Entrepreneur's Father
	% agreeing	
To think for oneself and take responsibility for one's decisions	58	26
To obey	12	28
To work hard	10	24
To help others when they need help	9	9
To be well liked or popular	1	2
To obey word of God	1	1

SOURCE: RER.

well beyond the data and begs questions that demand further examination. The entrepreneurs reported that the most important principle in life was to "take responsibility for oneself and to think for oneself."

Finally, Redekop explored the entrepreneurs' reasons for choosing the nontraditional entrepreneurial track for their work life. This may itself be one of the best ways of determining how work is understood by Mennonites. Redekop queried, "There are a number of ways to achieve economic success. Which of the following ways do you prefer?" (see Table 4-5). Almost three-fourths of the sample said that starting their own business was their preferred route to success. We cannot assume that this choice simply reflected their success in business since many, if not most, of the entrepreneurs had lost heavily at one time or another, and all of them knew and understood the nature of risk. Included in "starting one's own

TABLE 4-5
Preferred Road to Success

Path	Percent
Starting own business	73
Attaining a professional degree	14
Seeking employment in a well-established business	7
Achieving high profit investments (financial wheeling and dealing)	7

SOURCE: RER.

business" is the fact that one must leave his or her traditional occupation and employment in the community to step out of the ranks of the local way of life. The first risk is the loss of the community's understanding of the work this person is doing and its integration into the normative rules and regulations. Consequently, the loss of community support accelerates the push of the entrepreneur from the local ranks.

The neoclassical entrepreneurial work ethic, with its built-in sense of advancement (i.e., thinking, scheming, planning, organizing, risking), seems to be the opposite of the traditional Anabaptist-Mennonite notion of *Gelassenheit*—an orientation that aims at maintaining a traditional level of consumption in a traditional manner through the course of generations. Redekop's quantitative data suggest that Mennonite enterprise is undertaken not only for the benefit of family, friends, and religious community, but for personal benefit and advancement as well. This is to say that Mennonite entrepreneurs operate with both communal and individualistic considerations in mind. They see themselves as faithful to the Mennonite ethos as they understand it; objectively, however, the community has lost some of its "traditional" claims on the entrepreneurs to the extent that it can no longer dictate a business ethos to them.

Exploring the Intricacies of the Entrepreneur's View of Work

That entrepreneurs experience a sort of conflict between the *ideal* of *Gelassenheit* and the demands of a market economy is perhaps even more evident when they speak for themselves. To get a sense of the general importance of work in their lives, the entrepreneurs were asked, "Some people tell us that they couldn't really be happy unless they were working. How do you feel about this?" Strategies for answering this question varied, but in all cases, the ubiquitous tension between community and self-advancement was evident. Rather than conceiving of community and self-advancement as two options in a dichotomy, it became evident that Mennonite entrepreneurs fall somewhere on a continuum between these positions. Some emphasized the personal gains and satisfaction of work, and others stressed a concern for others.

The views of seven entrepreneurs illustrate this. The first of these, Wayne Classen,[28] is a very successful immigrant who established a manufacturing plant that now employs more than one hundred people. Wayne Classen can probably be seen on the self-advancement side of the continuum. He is also known to be very independent and free ranging and contributes to causes beyond Mennonite horizons. Nevertheless, throughout his career, he has maintained a strong loyalty to the church and contributes financially to many Mennonite causes. As he discussed the importance of his work, he was asked if he would rather have pursued another occupational path. To this he replied that he liked what he was doing, in part, because of the flexibility that the job offered him. When he was asked, "Would you be happy if you weren't working?" he responded,

I wouldn't say that I couldn't be happy, but I believe in working and also enjoying free time. I wouldn't want to work all the time, but you have to work. You have to have a balance. I have always enjoyed inventing something or improving the work methods or seeing how things could be done more profitably. When I go through the plant I don't look at the things that are going well. I look at the things that could be improved.

I would say [work] provides security and advantages for my family. It does give me prominence in the business world. If you are successful, other business people are encouraged by it. I think it's also good for the employees once you have achieved a certain level. Once you have achieved a certain success you look for other interests because you have this prominence. My son feels quite good too that I have achieved.

Our second entrepreneur, Benjamin Epp, came from a very conservative Mennonite community but moved to a booming secular area and became a businessperson. He experienced some ambivalence about being in such a competitive system but managed to survive in this environment and even overcame some physical illnesses that caused difficulties for him. Speaking of his attitude toward work, he said,

The number one gratification I have gotten from all the work I've done would be all the good people I've met. There are some very fine people in this community, which I found very rewarding. I have no problem working with people. I can relate to them all. I enjoy helping people. I guess one of my pitfalls has been that I helped some probably more than I should have. One of the things I've learned in life is that if you help somebody too much they expect too much, and they take you for granted. And if you have a bad year and have to withhold support, they get ugly. I guess that if I hadn't gotten into [a certain business] I probably would have gone into church work. I don't like to work all the time. I like to play too. I like to hunt and fish. I've tapered off in the last few years. Up until ten years ago I worked probably seventy hours a week. I enjoy work, putting things together and making them work. I was very creative in the business. And the way you do it is to keep things simple. Work was never a means to make money. I worked because I enjoyed it. I never had the drive to become wealthy. You realize that's a part of what you have to do when you're in business. You have to. You can't take the attitude that you're not going to make money because if you don't, you don't make it. You have to do each day the best you know how. You've got to work hard and you've got to be compassionate to people. That'll work. In terms of my business and the church, I learned very early on that you don't bring your business into the Mennonite Church. My business relationships affected my children very much. My children were not really accepted in the church, because we could afford things most of them couldn't. So it must have been lifestyle, although I don't think we lived that differently. It possibly goes back to the very root of the attitude of the Mennonite Church toward business. The Mennonite Church is very skeptical toward businesspeople because farming was the traditional way of life.

Thomas Hartzler is an esteemed community leader and a committed church member but is also an innovator and entrepreneur, having initiated several major institutions such as a bank and an area cooperative organization. His work has required that he walk the line between the world and the Mennonite community.

I don't know that I've been all that successful. I wanted to be an engineer when I started out, but that was a little beyond my opportunities. I made my grades in college, but that was not my first love. I feel that I've been happy in all the work I've done, and that's something to be thankful for. I've always liked to see things grow. When I became mayor of [the city] I thought we needed to put [the city] on the map because we have a very unique situation here. I've had a lot of opportunities to add dignity to the city. I wanted to see the credit union grow, and it grew. And I saw no conflict in getting a bank here because a credit union has to use a bank. So I pushed for a bank. I have since been pushing both institutions. Yeah, I worked hard. But church came first. One thing I always kept in mind was that I'm going to sit in church with this person next Sunday, so how I treat him during the week is critical. A lot of times I have thought, go the legal way, but when you go to the same Sunday School class and pray with the same person, that's not so simple. This is especially pertinent when you collect bills. I didn't do enough, but I always tried to feel how the other person felt. Basically I work to achieve something. Discipline is very important. If you're not disciplined, who is going to respect you? If I can't discipline myself, why should I expect someone else to respect me? Recognition for work is good, but it has never bothered me.

Respect is more important. I wanted to do the right thing. Well, if you're going to be successful you have to think about the other person, that's what the Mennonite philosophy does.

The importance of the community's evaluation of the individual's motives and actions stands out in bold relief in Thomas Hartzler's case.

John Hershberger grew up in a very traditional and conservative community and became an entrepreneur almost by accident. But after he became successful and tasted the excitement of growth, innovation and creativity emerged in a rather unusual way.

A friend of ours wanted to quit [his business] and asked if we'd take it over. That was a real boost. We worked at that for a year or so, and then we opened up [another business] in [another town]. I quit my job and went into this full time. We kept on and just kept on adding more items. Then we opened up more markets, and now we have [several]. Then we went into wholesale, and we had never planned to go wholesale, but people came and wanted to buy from us so of course we sold to them, and that grew large. Our accountant said [he] wouldn't believe this if [he didn't know us] so well.

The strange part is that we had no salesmen at the beginning. My wife gets 95 percent of the credit for the success for she designed practically all the [products]. Selling was natural for her. It wasn't for me. I'm a poor salesman. I was so bashful I know the first time I went out to peddle that if the first lady hadn't bought [my product] from me, I would have come home and never set out again. My wife worked for her dad. Some said to a neighbor, "That girl is going to make a man rich someday." We also had some neighbors wanting to help. One said, "If you want to build up your route quickly, come along with me for a day." So I went along, and I followed his advice, and overnight the sales grew. Sometimes, you felt that people, at least some, thought that the businesspeople were far out somewhere.

The church just had a conference on faith and business, and we couldn't go, but I played the tapes, and what they brought made sense. You know there are two sides. There is the side for the rich, you know the temptations, and the other side is its blessings—you can give. We always tithe, and in the past few years I'm doing a lot more than tithing. So I started giving more every year, and it just seemed that every year got better and better. I think that as far as the church and its views of business go I have a good feeling. I don't know why, I guess I'd qualify for being wealthy but I never feel that way. We were so poor at home we often couldn't pay the bills and I guess I've just kept this feeling that I am a poor boy.

We put in long days and worked hard, but I never got to the place where I was proud of being president. We had a meeting several years ago of all the employees, and each said what his job was. An older man who had worked for a long time got up when everybody else had said what he did. "Well, [he said to me] you didn't get up and say what you do." I got up and said, "Today I hauled the garbage out." It was sort of a joke, but it was true. It's sort of a joke here in the office—I'm the one who runs the disposal. I feel quite good about my work, but sometimes I feel as though I never got anything accomplished that was worthwhile. But sometimes when people ask what you're doing and hear [the name of our company], nine times out of ten they say something like "They make a wonderful product." That is a wonderful feeling. One of the greatest blessings is to be able to work. It would he terrible not to have something to do. We liked to work in our business for a good goal and accomplish something.

My grandfather was my role model. I just appreciate him so much. He was a real religious man, but not what you would ever call over-religious. I appreciated him so much and can't even say exactly why.

People say they're seeking the Lord's will. Well, I say you should do that, but the main thing is that you should be willing to do what the Lord wants you to do. Sometimes we ask the Lord to show us, but we have our minds set on what we want to do.

Although not explicit about it, this entrepreneur's view of his work life and accomplishments reveals the influence of a traditional *Gelassenheit* community. The communal context, both in terms of what he had received by way of help (e.g., when friends helped him learn how to sell) and what he gave back in return, is clear.

The next case departs from the ordinary pattern. It is really a story of more than one entrepreneur. Paul Landis (the husband), vice president of a large corporation, was contemplating an early retirement so he could pursue personal interests when his wife Evelyn developed a unique product that proved to be in demand. Their sons became involved, and when the business became substantial, the husband quit the corporation where he had been working and joined the family in their corporate venture. The two entrepreneurs described their work in the following manner:

Evelyn Landis: I worked for MCC for a while. Otherwise I was just a housewife. Then my husband got the idea that I sell a product that I occasionally made, and I started making a few, and he would take them and see if there was a market and then he started getting orders. So as time went on we were selling to market people, to other stores. So we rented a shop to produce them.

Paul Landis: We incorporated a few years ago, and our two sons and we two are the ownership and management. Each has his area of responsibility. My wife is the secretary of the corporation, and the two sons are vice presidents. I look after the marketing.

Evelyn Landis: We worked hard to start. We just kept persevering and just built up from there. You start out with an idea that you pick up somewhere, and after that it is one big learning experience. We grew slowly, we didn't want to jump into it too fast. I like to sleep at night. I think it's very important to do things better than other people, and to do things well. Quality and price—those are lasting benefits. I would say God opened doors for us, but He also gave us minds.

Paul Landis: Along that line as far as your relationship with God and His doing things for you, I think the business is an extension of your faith and life. I think that kind of affects all your life. You know if you're following him, and we've tried to do this. As far as our relationship to the church goes, for one thing we are rather small. If there has been anything, it would be a positive attitude from the church people. We have not been that close to the church in terms of organization, but from people in the church we know, I think that they've been very supportive and positive, so it has not caused many problems. People watch you as you get large, and they think you make bigger waves. And then you would be open for more criticism just because you are large, you affect them in a different way. A fellow told me one time that when you're in business for yourself the highs are higher and the lows are lower. In other words, the positives are more positive and the same with the negatives, and I imagine as you get bigger that sort of thing shows up.

Evelyn Landis: The biggest gratification for me has been the family working together, everybody getting along as well as we have. We have a certain camaraderie, and yet everybody does their thing and does it well. Our parents too were very ethical and assumed you could only stay in business if you were ethical . . . honest dealings, truthfulness treating people right. . . . . I enjoy working. It's part disciplining of your life.

Paul Landis: And helping other people, including our children, and being constructive. My mother and father taught me how to live properly, be honest, ethical and just how to live.

Evelyn Landis: My dad was just very ethical.

Although this couple did not explicitly speak of *Gelassenheit* or yieldedness, they expressed considerable awareness of their moral and communal responsibility and church obligation, even though they had not been very active in the organizational life of the church. Work for them was not aggressively exploited so they could get ahead and surpass the Jones's.

The final case is that of David Yoder, a minister who moved from preaching to religious enterprises to normal economic enterprises.

I always sort of wanted to be self-employed and use my own creativity, willing to work with more risk [than in ministry]. I began with trying to sell and produce toys that were more Christian than what you can buy. It was very difficult to succeed because I later discovered that the field was controlled by a certain group that had a very firm grip, and I couldn't break in at all. Earlier, my wife, who has a knack for interior design, and I would buy an older home, borrow some money, and fix it up. We started with sweat equity. We did all the work, and when we were finished, we would take the profit from it and buy another house. We did it in the evenings and got a great deal of satisfaction. As we went along we accumulated a little, and so we could begin to talk about buying a retail building and improving that.

So we worked into the commercial field. I used my ability in finding locations and options, and my wife used her gifts in saying what design blends with the architecture, etc. I'm the dreamer who sort of sees a project and says "Now this will work." People will say, "You're nuts, that will never work." But I have thought it through by then, and I say "It will work." There have been things where there was no profit, but I received great satisfaction in them anyhow. I get excited when I see something that is not moving, so you change it and it functions.

We've had little encouragement from the church community because I don't think people basically like entrepreneurs very much. One church friend did encourage me, and I think he sort of lived through what I did, living his dreams through me, and I think I have succeeded by taking risks at the right time. I've enjoyed being an entrepreneur, and I've taken some heavy financial losses, but entrepreneurs don't think about those things very long. They go into something else and forget it. I have never thought of going back to preaching. I have nothing against preaching, but the committee work and all that bore me. I am too restless for that.

I do not feel the religious community can expect any favors from us. I personally have a distaste for religious community members always asking us for a way of getting ahead.

As far as work is concerned, I have never been a workaholic, my objective has always been to give my family high priority. I have rarely worked evenings after the early years when my wife and I had to. I've sometimes brought a little work home and worked on it after the kids are sleeping. I think I was saddled with a guilt complex about work from my mother. Often my wife says, "Why don't you go out with the guys or go to a ball game or something?" and I've always had difficulty doing it because of that guilt feeling that I'm leaving the family alone. I will spend a lot of evenings thinking or planning or figuring, but it's not really work to me. I enjoy it; I will do projections while I'm listening to music or something. I can't do this kind of work during the day because of the phones.

I am not concerned about security, but I'd have to admit that community recognition for success is a motivator. There's the feeling of having power which is very important to most businessmen. In the beginning recognition from friends and relatives was more important than it is now. Although some of my employees are from the religious community, none of my associates or advisors are from the church.

The reference to the church community was surprisingly sparse in the interview with David Yoder. At times it almost seemed as if it was not really important. His earlier ministerial role and working for the church seemed to have been rather fully forsaken and unimportant. Work appeared to be a means for expressing his creative impulse and achieving security for his family and for prestige and respect in the community. In other words, in the terminology we developed earlier, this ex-preacher appeared to be cosmopolitan, and he fell on the work-as-self-fulfilling side of the continuum despite his earlier institutional leadership position.

ORIENTATION: COMMUNAL OR SELF?

Stories of these entrepreneurs and their attempts to find a ground between market and community provoke questions about who controls their work and for what purposes their work is carried out. Some are very concerned about benefiting the community and about how community members see and judge their activities. Others experience more individual control and have a personally driven motive for working.

Communally Oriented Work

Work that is communally oriented is subject to community norms and surveillance. It is most apparent when the interviewees speak of the religious community and its concerns about the ethic of work, how success is articulated, and how people are helped to see their work fitting into the religious scheme. In all these instances, the entrepreneurs *refer to* the community as they evaluate their work experiences, goals, and accomplishments. This orientation toward work is apparent in the quantitative data. When entrepreneurs give family and religious co-members special consideration in their business dealings, for example, they are addressing this issue (see Table 4-3). It is even clearer in the interview material. The communal dimension comes through in the continual and strong allusions to the role of people in work and business and how they have been central to the gratification derived from work. When entrepreneurs attribute their success to other people and acknowledge that they feel a need to be recognized, they are indicating a sort of communal consciousness, an orientation toward others (although many of the references to people are not to fellow members of the entrepreneur's congregation). The entrepreneur who had a fellow church member help him learn how to meet customers and sell reveals a willingness to rely on others.

A communal orientation to work is comprised of more than references to others. It also involves a deference to community values and an acknowledgment that these values transcend individual goals and objectives. References to the ethical and moral aspects of business life and management, even if limited to references of an ethical mother or father, point to a communal orientation, since work and its rewards are hemmed in by the claims of fair play, honesty, and integrity.

The importance of a goal for work and that the goal be helping others, as stated by the husband and wife team (Paul and Evelyn Landis), is at the heart of the communal ethic. Although the *Gelassenheit* ethic would say it differently, namely that work should be for mutual benefit of the community, there is still something of this tone in the more communal entrepreneurs. The residue of this orientation is found in the attitudes of most Mennonite entrepreneurs, but it has clearly receded among those who are in transition to a more individualistic orientation.

Self-orientation

Referring again to the quantitative data, it is remarkable that helping others and obeying God are given such a low priority among those important principles by which to live (see Table 4-4). These data suggest that the *Gelassenheit* theme—which emphasized a yieldedness to God's will and a concern for fellow members of the community—is not the central organizing principle for many entrepreneurs.

Has the triad of creativity, production, and satisfaction come to motivate the Mennonite entrepreneur, especially in reference to work? Some of the interview material would suggest that this is so. Again, the quantitative data also point in this direction (see Table 4-1, for example). For many, the easy life and security are not valued as highly as the opportunity for self-advancement and the sense of accomplishment which characterizes the neoclassical entrepreneur. The data summarized in Table 4-2 suggest that the maximization of profit has become more important to today's entrepreneurs and that family and community loyalties are becoming less salient. Table 4-4 demonstrates that thinking for oneself and taking responsibility for one's decisions are now the guiding principles. Table 4-5 corroborates the evidence of an individualistic tendency among our entrepreneurs, as 73 percent indicated that the best way to achieve economic success was to start one's own business (as was indicated earlier, the entrepreneur is one who steps out of the ranks of the laboring system as traditionally interpreted).

The qualitative data confirm the exhilaration that people find in the entrepreneurial experience. The joy of tackling something that is simply out there and needs doing appeals to the entrepreneurs. Putting the pieces together so the puzzle is solved is deeply rewarding. It is apparent that it does not make much difference what type of work it is. Above all, it must be a challenge. Whether in the joy of inventing as Wayne Classen stated, or in putting things together and making them work, in the words of Benjamin Epp, or in liking to see things grow as Thomas Hartzler expressed it, all go to the heart of expressing the entrepreneurial challenge. The important corollary is that work has lost some of its traditional (traditional Mennonite) meaning. It is no longer an onerous debt but a joy. It is certainly not a punishment as the traditional interpretation of the Old Testament teaching would have it.

The Changing Reference Structure of the Entrepreneur

It is also clear that many entrepreneurs welcome the sense of accomplishment which they derive from their work and the recognition they receive for their successes (see Table 4-1). Of course *accomplishment* is itself a social value, not solely an individual possession. Both the *definition* of accomplishment and the feeling of having it come from a community of peers implicate others. Thus, the difference between communal versus individual orientation does not turn on the influence of others; it turns on just who the others are.

Who are the others? Some are probably from the Mennonite community. However, a generally disparaging attitude among traditional Mennonites toward business activities suggests that the entrepreneurs have transferred at least some of their reference to the secular society in which they function.

This discussion begs a more thorough analysis of human motive which moves us beyond the goals of our project. However, we do not wish to leave the impression that the entrepreneur's sense of achievement is a social creation in its entirety. There is undoubtedly a subjective and innate human urge to create (Weber's *charisma*) and to make a difference in the world. In traditional society, this urge has been expressed through participation in group activities and is recognized through group esteem. Modernity is different in that we have become infected with cultural guilt according to the subjective social psychological approach.[29]

Perhaps a factor in Mennonite entrepreneurs not succumbing to this cultural guilt is its strong emphasis on the ethical and behavioral aspect of the Christian life as opposed to the doctrinal and theological separation of the individualistic spirituality which essentially distinguishes the other Protestant denominations. The guilt under which Protestants labor is that their efforts are inadequate to the enormity of their consciousness of their tasks. This may be alleviated for the Mennonite by the traditional emphasis on the significance of the practical and ethical expression of the faith and on the importance of faithfulness in exercise of the most mundane duties, as judged by the community.

One thing is relatively clear, both from the perspective of Mennonite theology and from that of agnostic sociology: personal success and personal achievement are much more likely to be approved by the larger secular cosmopolitan society than by the Mennonite in-group, whether because of jealousy or legitimate disapproval of the entrepreneur's lifestyle. *Ressentiment*, as analyzed by Nietzsche and Scheler, is certainly a factor in maintaining group cohesion. We must keep in mind as well, however, that membership in the Mennonite community is based on an adult confession of faith which includes a covenanting to a community as one of its aspects.

Neoclassical market economy strategy has taken advantage of the psychology of *ressentiment* to use jealousy to motivate greater entrepreneurial activity and increased commodity production. This response to the very human emotion of envy is in direct contradiction to the *Gelassenheit* ethos and its spirit of mutual discernment of how the individual can best serve corporate ends. Thus the effect of *ressentiment* as a defense mechanism in the face of the traditional ethos may have become a factor in the cosmopolitan entrepreneur not remaining part of the community and functioning as a role model for the young people in the congregations.

This problem is aggravated by the fact that the entrepreneur does not usually participate directly in community work but supports the communal goals of the religious community financially. The entrepreneur is more concerned about time than about physical labor value; the meaning of work has been changed. It is no longer measured in terms of physical labor expended but rather by the amount of time required to establish the connections and developments essential to acquiring the power and status among business peers and friends and to manage a business profitably. The essential difference is that an element of education is introduced to entrepreneurial work. It is in the entrepreneur's interest to learn how to make profit, and his or her tractability will become a factor in his or her success.

We appear to have a situation, then, in which the traditional *Gelassen-*

heit ideal of work, which finds its place in "the organically prescribed cycle of [the community's] natural life"[30] for the sake of the community, has been superseded, at least in part. However, the classical Weberian ideal type of work as a calling (for its own sake) in an inner-worldly context has not taken precedence. The Calvinist work ethic that was to lead to the disenchantment of the world and to the meaninglessness of personal existence[31] has not replaced the traditional view. The theoretical significance of the Mennonite experience is, in part, that the transformation of the traditional work ethic (represented for Weber by Roman Catholicism and for the Mennonites by *Gelassenheit*) took another modern format that is different from the Protestant work ethic posited in Weber's thesis.

Weber complained that the Protestant work ethic made attainment of cultural goals into a holy task and that it plunged we moderns into "an ever more devastating senselessness" and a "senseless hustle in the service of worthless self-contradictory and mutually antagonistic ends."[32] Does Weber's description fit the experience and point of view of contemporary Mennonite entrepreneurs? We think not. Weber's vision of the disenchanted, modern world does not allow sufficiently for the personal expression and realization in work which seem to be part of the Mennonite experience. Does this mean that Mennonite entrepreneurs have been able to *transform* the Mennonite work ethic without losing its connection to the organically prescribed cycle of natural life which gave labor its meaning and dignity in the traditional village?

Are the experience of achievement and the search for more the indicators that the entrepreneur is becoming cosmopolitan? There are good reasons to conclude that they are. In a communally oriented religious society, the strength and direction of the individual are rooted in the group, and the individual receives his standing, affirmation, and criticism from fellow believers. In fact, his salvation is determined in the collective. As Cronk maintained, "They believe firmly that personal salvation takes place only in Christian community. Yieldedness is not just a personal experience. It structures the whole of society."[33] Work thus does enhance the individual's standing—not by what he himself achieves, but how well he conforms to the community's welfare and faith, in the traditional Anabaptist-Mennonite communal ethic, as the Smucker and Weaver research also indicates.

The work of the entrepreneur, on the other hand, is not oriented toward his or her own salvation within the community but is rather channeled so as to achieve the personal satisfaction of "making things work" and to acquire prestige and status in the marketplace, where the symbols are bar graphs with increasing sales, profits, and orders. Work becomes a scientific technique: rational management moving things around on the basis of "management" of resources, energies, people, and economic conditions to maximize the effectiveness of all effort. The *individualistic* Mennonite entrepreneurs are probably not very different from the secular, although they may carry around in their memories the awareness and possibly even the guilt of a communal work ethic. They have apparently chosen to dispense with it. The question, "What for?" is answered: "It feels good to see things happen." Or, "It is important to provide jobs for others." Or "If I wouldn't have undertaken it, someone else would have."

It is apparent that the Mennonite entrepreneur is moving, at least in the aspect of his work ethos, from a communal type of work orientation to a more individualistic one. We say moving, since as we shall see in later chapters, even the most secularized Mennonite entrepreneurs evidence more of the communal orientation to work than does the general population of entrepreneurs. As the Mennonite entrepreneur is relinquishing the communal understanding of work, he or she is creating in work a new alternative mode of ethical action which is determined by the prevailing utilitarian capitalistic culture.

CHAPTER FIVE

Entrepreneurial Upward Mobility
and the Dilemmas of Success

The Old and New Testaments contain numerous exhortations against succumbing to the seduction of wealth and power. The prophet Amos warned, "Woe to those who are at ease in Zion, and to those who feel secure on the mountain of Samaria. Woe to those who lie upon beds of ivory and stretch themselves upon their couches and eat lambs of the flock" (Amos 6:1–4). Jesus carried on this tradition by telling the rich young ruler to sell all he had and give it to the poor, thereby ensuring that he would have treasures in heaven (Luke 18:22). Prophetic voices have since echoed the theme; Saint Francis, Menno Simons, John Wesley, and Mother Teresa are among those who have warned against the dangers of wealth and "the comfortable life."

Yet the Judeo-Christian perspective on wealth is complicated by the fact that biblical teachings leave room for enterprise and accumulation. Jesus' dictum to "give unto Caesar what is Caesar's and to God what is God's" and Paul's teaching of respect for the state and its institutions as well as his emphasis on Christian liberty, for example, leave the believer a great deal of self-determination regarding property, the power it brings, and the role it will be permitted to play in the life of the community and individual.

Given seemingly competing messages, many people find themselves confused and ambivalent about issues of wealth. Witness the difficulty that Catholics had in developing a coherent response to the the Bishops' Letter on the U.S. economy in the mid-1980s.[1] Redmond Mullin began his comprehensive treatment of the topic of wealth by saying, "The majority of Christians have always possessed wealth, or have wanted to possess it, whether in humble or extravagant measure, and have recognized at least notionally its power to corrupt."[2] He continued, "Wealth was sly and unnatural and threatened everyone with corruption." Hence, he said, the Christian's challenge is no small one: "Most Christians today live in societies which have effectively ceased to be Christian, and which promote values subversive of Christianity."[3]

Mennonites have always been deeply concerned about the "sly and unnatural" threat of wealth and its attendant loss of perspective which results in abuse of power and lifestyle. Concerns about conspicuous living and consumption are a common theme in Mennonite literature. Pastors lament the apostasy and loss of fervor among Mennonites, conditions they attribute to affluence and upward mobility that have sapped Mennonite communities of their vitality. Guy F. Hershberger gave voice to these concerns:

What has happened when the sons of the Anabaptist tradition of sobriety, simplicity, and ministry to the needs of others expend $60,000 [1956 figures] and more for private residences while most of the people of the world remain ill-clothed, ill-fed, and ill-housed. . . . What has happened when others of the same tradition accept apparently without question, the symbols of power and prestige which our age provides and pursue them for their own sake without regard to their social usefulness and the principles of stewardship involved.[4]

Although these concerns remain, the accumulation of material possessions and acculturation to the values of North American society have become more commonplace in Mennonite life. Unable to continue holding the world at arm's length or to jettison completely the communal ethos on their past, a deep ambivalence regarding the affluent life now is at work in the Mennonite psyche.

The experiences of Mennonite entrepreneurs bring into sharp focus the issues of status consciousness and upward mobility. Feeling alienated from their religious and social communities, entrepreneurs (especially those of the cosmopolitan variety) often seek symbols and relationships that support their new-found circumstance and interests. Furthermore, many of them have taken to heart the goals and objectives of personal achievement, material acquisition, and affluence, supplementing in some cases and replacing in others the norms and values of the traditional religious community.

WHAT MOTIVATES UPWARD MOBILITY?

Since Weber, a central question in the study of the entrepreneur has been what motivates the struggle to achieve upward mobility. Are entrepreneurs motivated more by the *results* of their entrepreneurial efforts—the accouterments of wealth—or by the attractiveness of the *process* of getting there? Weber argued that greed and the lust for power alone were insufficient to generate "rational" capitalism. For him, the persistence of traditional attitudes and relationships greatly stifled capitalistic development wherever its authority exerted itself. In the Protestant Reformation he found the very changes in attitude which fostered modern capitalism.

Although Weber's thesis cleverly detailed the manner in which Protestantism provided the push that freed the Dutch and English entrepreneurs from traditional constraints, it failed to account adequately for the pull of enterprise in North America. The North American neoclassical entrepreneur found rewards in the very challenges of enterprise. As Peter Drucker noted, "Entrepreneurs see change as the norm and as healthy . . . the entrepreneur always searches for change, responds to it, and exploits it as an opportunity."[5] The main point Drucker made is that the entrepreneur is driven by the need to take initiative in organizing the proliferation of material culture because it poses a challenge rather than by the security and status traditionally associated with the psychology of wealth.

MENNONITE UPWARD MOBILITY

Results Versus Activity: Where Does Motivation Rest?

Mennonite entrepreneurs conform to Drucker's description, finding satisfaction in the process of entrepreneurialism. One indicator of this is that 88 percent of the respondents in the Redekop Entrepreneurial Research (RER) indicated that, had they to do it over again, they would follow the same pattern in starting their career. When they were asked, "What have you gotten out of your career?" the majority (58 percent) indicated that it was a sense of achievement (see Table 5-1). The end products of entrepreneurial success—namely, money, a high standard of living, power, and prestige of position—were not among their responses to this open-ended question.[6]

This is not to suggest that Mennonite entrepreneurs are impervious to the temptations of wealth or that they fail to recognize the comforts that

TABLE 5-1
Rewards for Entrepreneurial Career

Reward	Percent
Sense of achievement	58
Helping and employing others	18
Service to others	15
Other (learn to do new things, be own boss, etc.)	9

SOURCE: RER.

TABLE 5-2
Motivation for Economic Success Then and Now

Motivation	Then	Now
	%	
Provides security and advantage for my family	71	72
Gives me esteem in the eyes of friends and relatives	6	0
Gives me prominence in the business world	3	2
Gives me recognition in the community at large	2	3
Other	16	22

SOURCE: RER.

entrepreneurial success can bring. We have seen evidence of this already in Chapter Three. When respondents indicated why they entered business, personal profit ranked sixth and improved social standing ninth of nine choices. Similarly, in Table 4-1, Mennonite entrepreneurs indicated the job characteristics they valued most highly. Although most ranked a sense of accomplishment near the top, few of them (16 percent) said that income was unimportant. When asked why economic success was significant for them, three-quarters of the respondents indicated that security and advantage for their families had remained paramount from the start of their careers (see Table 5-2). Thus, the quantitative data suggest that entrepreneurs are concerned about economic well-being and social standing even though this may be difficult for them (or they may be reluctant) to verbalize.

In a sense, Mennonite entrepreneurs may have simply adopted some of the conflicts inherent in the value scheme of the dominant secular culture. Robin Williams summarized predominant American values[7]: achievement and success, activity and work, moral obligation, humanitarian mores, efficiency and practicality, progress, material comfort, equality, freedom, external conformity, science and secular rationality, national patriotism, democracy, and individual personality. Thus, Mennonites have paid a price for upward mobility. Like many other Americans, entrepreneurial Mennonites struggle with traditional commitments that transcend personal gain even while they internalize the individualistic values of the larger society. This tension, for Americans as a whole, was captured recently in *Habits of the Heart*. According to Bellah and his coauthors, Americans are caught between traditional values derived from biblical and republican origins and those of a contemporary world dominated by the entrepreneur and therapist. Stephen Ainlay noted that the increasingly bureaucratic quality of Mennonite organizations, therapeutic quality of people's understanding of the church's function, and drive toward professionalism have created a similar dilemma for Mennonites.[8]

Managing the Dilemmas of Success

Once again, qualitative interview data provide additional glimpses into the lived experience of the entrepreneurs who struggle with the dilemmas of success. As their stories make clear, the pulls of the entrepreneur lifestyle and the pushes from the community—which propel people out by isolating and then alienating them through disapproval—must both be considered in explaining the motivation toward upward (and sometime outward) mobility.

Myron Friesen may be characterized as rather closely involved in his religious community and family.[9] He comes from an established family farm in a rapidly urbanizing area. With considerable risk taking and family cooperation, he succeeded in establishing a number of flourishing businesses. And like many others, he struggles to balance the priorities of work and church.

My family and I were always interested in serving people. We liked to and still do . . . that is the name of this business. When my father died I was seventeen [the oldest]. Because we had to do things, we did them . . . that's been the reason for our success. . . . I'm not saying that the Lord hasn't blessed us, but he has also given us the brains and other qualities. . . . I feel much better today about the church and business than I did ten years ago. . . . I had been very frustrated with my church relationship . . . all the church wanted was my money. And I'm not willing to give just money, because I want to be involved.

Friesen, then, wanted to be involved but not exploited. Asked whether or not his wealth alienated him from the church, he responded,

I think it's lifestyle and it's attitude. And I think businesspeople have brought it on themselves. It's very hard not to be influenced [to become upwardly mobile]. Because I think your lifestyle does change. I know mine has. My wife and I often talk about it. Today we try to live simply, but it's not simple, compared to a lot of people. The businessperson has created some of the alienation himself, but I also think the church really has to work at it and make the businessperson feel a part, not just being moneybags. The businesspersons I know are pretty much out there on their own, and it's their own fault, but the church needs to work at that. I think they need to do that by not looking down their nose at a person just because he has some wealth, but trying to see how that person can also be involved in the church. The greatest reward I get from my business is the sense of accomplishing something. Especially since I don't have much education. I'm a community person, and I like to be part of the community, and I guess I like when the community feels good about me and what I'm doing. That is motivation.

Susan Gingerich is an interesting case because, even though she is only in her late twenties, she started a successful, dynamic business totally on her own, in a most unusual manner. Beginning as a salesperson—the first job offer she had—she moved quickly to take over the business, expand it, and purchase several other businesses. The daughter of very active and involved Mennonite Church parents, Gingerich has not formally become a member of the church. She has circulated at the edges of church life and now admits that, since her daughter is kindergarten age, she is considering taking her to church.

For Susan Gingerich, *both* the challenge of making the business better *and* the idea making money proved attractive.

I was working fifty-five to sixty hours a week and not getting paid anywhere near what I should have been, but I enjoyed the challenge of it. The very first day that the business was mine I gathered the employees together and told them I intended to make the business a whole lot better than it had been in the past. And in order to make money they had to help me make money and they would get it back. When Lucy was born in 1983, I said I wasn't going to work any more on Saturdays. I guess I'd have to say that my heart lies in management. I enjoy managing for productivity. It was pure accident that I took this job, but it was my own initiative that made me think I could run it when the opportunity finally came. I was quite hardheaded and thought that's what I wanted to do. I was anxious to get out in the world and make money, and everything turned out wonderfully.

Gingerich found pleasure in the risk taking itself. As she put it,

You have to be a risk taker. That's the difference between the former owner and me, and that's the reason why we're now more than five times bigger than he was. You have to be a risk taker. I have enjoyed it. The gratification is making something work. I'm always looking to the future to what we can do, what we can be, thinking about when our debts will be paid off and planning what changes need to be made next.

Yet she also clearly understood this risk taking to be a means to an end.

Of course it's nice to be your own boss, you can take off when you want to. Work is a means to an end, it's just making the business grow and earning money of course—everybody likes that. I just view the work as a job to do. Its a job to be done, and I'm going to do it the best way I can.

For Susan Gingerich, the church did not have a direct bearing on her entrepreneurial activities.

Well, I guess the church itself wasn't, but that was because I didn't attend. I guess it would have been there giving moral support. I never felt the church to be a hindrance. I've recently started attending more because of our little girl, and I'm enjoying it, but I don't really see it as a personal need. If a church helps you personally it's going to help your business.

Gingerich seemed driven to pursue upward mobility and attain success. Her interview contains no references to relationships to others in the religious community or family for that matter, except for the implied importance of others to the socialization of her child. Her alienation from the religious community and her sense that it was not *of any personal benefit* are rather evident.

Joseph and Sharon Kauffman are a sort of entrepreneurial team and represent another pattern. Unlike Susan Gingerich, this couple was deeply involved in the life of the church but became somewhat alienated as a result of their business activities. In spite of this, they worked at finding a synthesis through creative adaptations. Sharon Kauffman was a reluctant entrepreneur. She described the process by which she became involved.

Soon after we were married we entered voluntary service for the church. After that we worked at various things until my husband began working for a contractor. We were soon offered a share and bought in. Some of the employees believed in my husband's potential and urged him to buy the company out. I wasn't enthused about going into business. I was scared stiff, but he wasn't. I basically jumped in because he didn't know how to do bookkeeping. I saw him struggling through the books and said, "This is never going to work." So I got involved.

Joseph Kauffman found that his experience in early life on a farm and his subsequent business activities shared a common principle. As he put it, "I was raised on a farm and I had that motivation—you could do it yourself. 'The more you do the more you make'—that kind of thing."

His wife insisted that his success was due in part to the fact that people trusted him. He in turn emphasized his ethical approach to business.

I've tried to give good service, even though we weren't always lowest in price on projects. I guess we prayed a lot, and we agreed pretty much about how to operate the business, and I think that is really important for a couple. My greatest gratification is achieving, doing what we did and succeeding at it. And making lots of good friends—good people. I can honestly say there are very few people that I can't look in the eye. [If there is a problem] I'll go up and talk to [the person] and try to clear the situation up.

The Kauffmans work hard at balancing their priorities in business, which they described as "trying to make a profit," and those regarding family and church. They are quite aware of the potential for abusing relationships with fellow church members and neglecting the interests of the family. As Sharon Kauffman put it,

We had a really hard struggle trying to make a profit in the competitive world and keeping our priorities with family and church. You know, we like to be involved with people on a level that has nothing to do with the business. And we did not seek business clients through our friends or church people. We were not using these people for our business. I think our children suffered a bit because of the time we spent on the business. I can't say our church relationship suffered totally because we always remained pretty involved. But it was really hard, and we would have to stop and evaluate our relationship from time to time.

As they encountered business success, these entrepreneurs faced growing criticism from the church community. Joseph Kauffman described this as follows: "If I think back to when we first started I experienced some negative feelings from some people, and we thought they were mostly jealous. After a while they left us alone." Nevertheless, he felt the hurt of disapproval, noting, "I guess for me, it did bother me some, but I tried not to let it affect me." His wife added,

We tried to maintain our friendships among people who weren't in business partly because we could let our hair down. But we also have a lot of businesspeople as friends, and we joined business organizations because we needed that too. I think there were people who did stay away from us because they felt we were rich, which we weren't in those years. We went through some criticism that was not legitimate because people put us in a category without really learning to know us. It hurt me.

We had some people criticize us to our face and almost made us feel that because you're in business you're a sinner. If you were poor you would be in a better situation with the Lord, and that hurt. I am frustrated, but you have to know where a person is coming from before you can make a judgment about him or her. We tried to go out of our way to let people learn to know us, especially people who were critical, so that maybe we could dispel some of those judgments. We felt that at the point that we left the Mennonite Church we were struggling with the idea of being saved by works, the dos and don'ts; we were trying to find a little more freedom in our Christianity, more reason to base our faith on a relationship rather than dos and don'ts. I think the Mennonite Church has changed its perspective a lot.

A sense of alienation from the church, prompted by disapproval, pushed them from the church. (Actually, this couple felt this alienation even before their business became successful.) Joseph Kauffman believed that the situation would be quite different today. "I think the reason we left was the fact that we were living in an area where the Mennonite Church was very conservative, and they preached that. Today, I don't think we'd have such problems getting back to the Mennonite Church." This couple experienced pronounced conflict with the church. But the conflict did not *cause* them to seek affluent and worldly status. In fact, the evidence appears to point in the opposite direction, to a desire to stay in good standing with the community and its norms. These entrepreneurs only reluctantly left the community fold.

John Miller was raised on a farm, became a minister in an urban church, and then went into business. His case represents the process of moving from the traditional farming occupation to church service and then on to the business arena. As he made this journey, his use of interpersonal techniques—learned through his life in the church—shifted from relational to utilitarian purposes (a shift that he failed to see).

I left the farm because we were a large family, and the farm could not support us. I like talking with people, and that's how I got into the sales area. I still enjoy it today. If the product is good, I try to convince people to buy it. I have had management positions for the past twenty years and have a natural tension to want to take charge. That's my nature. We took lots of risks and are still taking a lot. We provide a place for the employees to work, but then we also expect that they produce. My dad was success oriented and taught us to get things done, so I came into this naturally. People either perform or they leave. We operate our business on Christian principles, and we spend a lot of time in prayer about what's going on. I get the highest satisfaction out of accomplishment, setting goals, achieving them, and moving further. The partners in our business are basically our family and several friends. Regarding doing business with church members, my feeling is that we are in business to make a fair profit. We need to be stewards for our stockholders. Economic success is not all that important to me, although we have more advantages; if we say that it means our family will become respected members in the community then we have advantages. I like to be a winner, but that is not such a big need any more [since he is rather successful]. My business activities have not been hindered by my Mennonite community. I've heard some people are, but that is not my experience. There is, however, an advantage of being a Mennonite if you talk about the big boys' club . . . the people in the community. It's hard to penetrate. We have chosen not to try to penetrate that group, which includes the bankers, the inner circle, the . . . Club and so on. There are certain areas of business life that are excluded unless you can rationalize it yourself. The expectation I have for my sons is that they run a good respectable business, and my biggest job right now is to help them to establish their business, and then I will just sit back and let them take over. I hope they follow the Christian way and lead respectable lives in the community. I believe everyone in the world who wants to be successful works for themselves even if they work for another company, but no one is totally independent. I am responsible to my banker, to the investors we have. I'm responsible to do good, honest, fair business in the community. I think I have a tremendous responsibility. I guess there's some parallel in what I'm doing here and what I'm doing in my church, to be the leader and help the workers there do the best job. I sometimes have a conflict that pertains to business activities, but I have come to grips with that on my own.

The nuances of Miller's comments imply a strong independence that is camouflaged by the concept of everyone being responsible to someone and, in his case, to business institutions (bankers, stockholders, and the community). Even though he has a religious moral ethic, he also evidently has considerable interest in moving up the social scale in the community and in the larger arena. His relationship with the church is unclear.

Walter Smucker is, according to all appearances, a "whiz kid." Things have gone remarkably well and are seemingly easy for him. He grew up in a conservative family, church, and community, and he has managed to keep good relationships with family, friends, and the church. His success is marred only by one area of unresolved tension in his life—his relationship to the family that ran the business in which he got his start and from which he left, seeking better opportunities. When he left, he took a good number of the staff to form his own company with his partner. This added to the tension. Had utilitarian business objectives led him to forsake community loyalties? He started the new business in another town, and he moved to another Mennonite Church, thereby avoiding some of the awkwardness of having to face the offended family. The fact that this produced a tension at all signals this entrepreneur's refusal to subscribe totally to the goals of self-advancement. He described his departure from the family-run company in the following manner:

I started working in a garage, then quit and went into manufacturing. Within a year I was working in the wholesale part of the company. I was selected to do that. Then I transferred to another company doing the same thing, and after the second year they brought me into the company as a stockholder. More than 50 percent was owned by [one man] and two of his sons. It became an unhealthy situation where it was family versus nonfamily. My present partner and I said it was a dead-end situation, so we quit, and that brings us to [where we are right now].

Once out of the company, he was able to follow his entrepreneurial impulse more freely.

We incorporated immediately. We got an acquaintance from my church [who also worked for our former boss] to put a prospectus together for us. He said, "We'll give you a prospectus to take to the bank which gives them twice what they want, and I'll guarantee they'll give you the money." We had absolutely no track record. We were young. We sold ourselves to the local bank, and they loaned us the money [and the two of us] became equal partners. I've always tended to be an entrepreneur. When I was a little tot on the parents' farm I would pick up the tobacco leaves that fell off the wagon, string them on a wire, and they were to sell. Our farms were a family group, and we got together to harvest; this brought the cousins together, and I managed these cousins, and they worked for me. I didn't take wild chances, and I've worked hard. I've always been successful, though. My father has always been the motivator and encouraged me when I needed to sort things out.

Smucker found that he was not alone in his church and that other businesspeople provide a sounding board for discussing the dilemma of wealth and success.

Our church is made up of successful businesses. [Fred] attended the church I married into. [Henry] is very successful. [Jake] operates a successful [business]. There are a lot of entrepreneurs at our church. [Arnold] is the head of personnel at [large company] in town. I've been able to talk to these men and say "All of a sudden I have all this success. What do I do with it?" I have this money to contribute. Do I give it all to the church? I how do I handle this?"

My own peer group has not achieved what I had, so I felt somewhat at a loss [because of] this success and wealth. I haven't been able to go to some of them for help too easily with the questions I've had. I've been able to relate to the older successful people in the church.

Walter Smucker found comfort in these relationships but worried about the church's ability to relate to the next generation of entrepreneurs.

The church has not been successful in keeping the children of successful businesspersons for some reason. My age group and younger tend to be more, I hate to say "white collar," not the professional or the successful entrepreneur. So I've had some difficulty [relating] to them. I tend to be very sensitive and hesitate to project myself on them. My business and my position in it project the most as far as what I have achieved. I can [relate better] to the older generation in the church.

For Smucker, distinctions between work life and religious experience and commitment are not as distinct as one might imagine. He remains involved in the church, and God's hand is evident in his work.

I've contributed quite heavily to church. I believe my first commitment should be to share the successes I have with our church and other local organizations. I would have to say that the church has not found it difficult to relate to me. My wife and I are very active in the church. I am the church treasurer. I started a musical group two years ago. My business ventures were all well planned. The major move we made eight years ago involved a lot of planning and problem solving with the Lord, and I really feel that this was God's will though I think Satan tried to stop it.

Smucker ultimately believes that it is important to let values inform work and to instill these values in his children.

My father was a successful farmer and church worker, and I've always wanted to prove to him that I can achieve as much as he did and more. My wife's parents also operated a successful manufacturing company, and they encouraged me too. I think some of the principles you learn through the Mennonite faith contribute to success. You're taught honesty, trustworthiness, high principles and morals, respect for people, and to work with people. I would hope that our children would achieve an above average career status, learning that they're not just an average blue-collar worker.

MATERIALISM AND UPWARD MOBILITY: A PUSH OR PULL PHENOMENON?

Why do some Mennonites become "secularized" while others remain in the bosom of the traditional community? Are they attracted to the values of the secular society because they are convenient for pursuing materialist interests (consistent with the pull argument)? Or do individual Mennonites and Mennonite families succumb to the lure of market society because they have been alienated by their church (the push argument)? Or does a dialectical understanding better address the data?

There is no doubt that the psychological dimensions of human action explain some of the motivations of Mennonite entrepreneurs. Unique aspects of socialization—such as having an aggressive and entrepreneurial father or mother—may affect the next generation's propensity to leave the traditional community to pursue upward mobility. Rejecting congregational and community norms and opting for the symbols of worldly status and prestige may reflect the individual's personality. This psychological approach to explaining the motivation of Mennonite entrepreneurs is not entirely adequate in that it does not really address the fact that persons can adhere to traditional, conservative, and restrictive community norms *and* still achieve entrepreneurial success. No clear correlation between personality traits and entrepreneurial secularization (the capitulation to the seduction of the symbols, activities, and relations of the larger secular society) or "cosmopolitanization" can be found in the qualitative interview material. For some entrepreneurs, cosmopolitan success coexists with loyalty to traditional values and commitments even if their support does not take the traditional form of personal community involvement. Others find a surrogate religion in entrepreneurial activities to the extent that they even speak of their activities in religious language. For still others, entrepreneurial activity is indeed part of a personality formation in which rebellion against rational authority structures is a normal expression of creative energy. If we learn nothing else from the entrepreneurs' life stories, it is that the picture of Mennonite entrepreneurship is complicated and cannot be handled by any reductionist accounting.

We are also forced to confront the overly simplistic belief—sometimes found in Mennonite circles—that the entrepreneurial spirit and secular worldliness can be more or less equated with one another. This belief underlies, in part, the push-pull theory—that individual Mennonites become cosmopolitan in orientation because they are disgruntled with the limitations of their communal way of life and because the secular values of individual achievement and personal acquisition appeal to those who perceive their opportunities for advancement to be blocked by traditional constraints of community norms. Certainly some entrepreneurs operate with a sense of alienation from their community. But entrepreneurship is such a ubiquitous feature of the Mennonite community that one must wonder about the explanatory power of this approach to understanding entrepreneurial motivation.

If secularization and the desire for upward mobility cannot be blamed merely on the psychological (or theological, which underlies the psychological) motivation alone and if secularization is not a necessary consequence of personal capitulation to cosmopolitan values, we obviously need to reexamine the relationship of entrepreneurship to secularization.

The Ubiquitous Quality of Secularization and the Entrepreneurial Spirit

European society initiated the forces that have produced the modern national state based on an ideology of individualism and a free market economy. This has produced a post-Christian culture in which the values of Christianity are secularized and sublimated into the civil religion of the market economy and state. This condition has not replaced the traditional forms of community on which it is based and out of which it grew; it has merely come to dominate and exploit the traditional forms for its own interests while claiming to be the only basis of legitimate authority. As a result, the moral authority of the family and church has become eroded, and a vacuum is left which is filled with the narcissistic and ultimately self-destructive values of the "me" generation—anomie, or normlessness, made into the highest norm.[10]

We suggest that entrepreneurs, along with most others in traditional communities such as the Mennonites, are being socialized into the norms of hedonism and self-gratification by the secular educational system and by the mass media. According to Anabaptist teaching, the attraction of worldly status and material-technological commodities is the cultural equivalent to the abominations of incest, temple prostitution, and child sacrifice by which the Israelis were tempted in Canaan. These practices were part of the universal pagan religion in which Judaism was an island of difference.[11] The Mennonite of today must not merely profess personal allegiance to the God of the Hebrew Bible but translate this allegiance into cultural-historical self-conscious practice. One of the first steps is recognizing the close relationship between unrestricted expression of the acquisitive impulse and the "abominable" practices of modern life. Viewed sociologically, those practices that the Hebrew law and prophets condemned were for the most part destructive to the community. Furthermore, sociologically we perceive the destruction of community and infer individual deviance as the result.

Thus, we propose that the upward striving alienation of the American Mennonite entrepreneurs is the result of the breakdown of the traditional nurturing community or, more exactly, of the loss of the traditional Mennonite community in America. The market economy, the principle of universal secular education, and the uncontrolled use of the mass media in service of the profit motive expose the impressionable young Mennonite minds to the notions of the accumulation of the commodities symbolizing success, achievement, power, and status for which all are invited to compete but very few are destined to gain. Many accept the rules that protect great inequality for the few because all hope to gain in the big lottery of life.

The pull of the secular society is not necessarily the total cause of the alienation of individuals from the communal norms. If the history of Mennonite experience in Russia is studied carefully, this alienation is seen as the result of inequality in wealth and status within the community.[12] As long as the community remained closed as in Czarist Russia, the alienated simply had to put up with their status or endure the rough justice of thugs. In America, universal secular education and the mass market economy ensure that the most slightly offended knows exactly where to take his or her grievances, where to go to improve his or her lot in life— namely, competing for the market's rewards. The only problem is to discern the genuine from among all the spurious offers that the unregulated market makes available.

This alienation syndrome is caused by the deterioration of the communal ethic, and it is only one anvil on which Mennonite entrepreneurs are forged. The interview data, however, suggest another pattern in the personality structure of Mennonite entrepreneurs in which alienation is not a factor at all. Many Mennonites have been attracted to the opportunities presented by the marketplace as a spontaneous response to *practical* and creative challenges. These entrepreneurs did not begin with calculated ambition but rather stumbled onto a good thing. The practical, hands-on, active life of the business entrepreneur is very attractive for the offspring of the practical, hard-working, frugal, honest Mennonite. But even more impressive is the challenge of the creativity which is available for the son or daughter of the Mennonite farmer, mechanic, carpenter, craftsman, human relations expert, church leader, or wheeler-dealer, which have all been wrapped up in one person in the Mennonite community.

The dedication to hard work, innovation, ingenuity, problem solving, and overcoming of odds and setbacks which most Mennonite children have seen in their parents have primed the pump for creative problem solving. Seeing something getting organized and seeing it work are dear to the psyche of Mennonites. Even though this practical and creative urge can be considered a universal trait, we submit that there is an almost unique historical component to the Mennonite drive for work. As Redekop has argued elsewhere, creative and productive work during the era of persecution provided the Anabaptist-Mennonite communities with the opportunity first to receive toleration and second to prosper and establish themselves socially and economically.[13] The Mennonite work ethic thus has existential-historical roots and explains to a large extent the universally acknowledged reputation of Mennonites for honesty and hard work. If Mennonites can now be described as exhibiting the Protestant work ethic, it is applicable only to those who have been totally acculturated to the contemporary, cosmopolitan ethic described earlier. The challenge of the future, however, is that the new frontier in which Mennonites must express their entrepreneurial skills is social and spiritual rather than geographical. It was in the opening of frontiers—whether in Prussia, Russia, or North America—that Mennonites learned how to survive and to achieve toleration.[14]

This independent practicality and creativity discerned in the Mennonite entrepreneur's personality is not unique to those pursuing the classical economic entrepreneurial goals. Sociologically speaking, the concept of entrepreneurship should not be limited to secular economic life but rather covers the gamut of people from all classes of social activity. There can, according to the neoclassical definition, be religious entrepreneurs of which the present wave of television evangelists are one recent example; and there are academic entrepreneurs, including intellectuals who start their publishing houses, research corporations, or consulting think tanks. The Mennonite community conforms to the neoclassical understanding of the entrepreneur. Many nonagrarian occupations pursued by Mennonites share the entrepreneurial ethos and spirit, including spiritual enterprise. The plethora of strong religious leaders promoting renewal, new movements, and divisions in the last century gives evidence of independent mindedness, willingness to take risks and endure hardships for future, possibly eternal gain in areas of life other than the economy.[15]

Weber's analysis, though inadequate, is foundational—Mennonite entrepreneurial spirituality is only possible because Luther and Calvin took the discipline of labor out of the monastery and imposed it on the ordinary man. Post-Christian liberal market capitalism has destroyed the redemptive meaning of work by tearing down the cosmological framework and personal relationships in the Mennonite community in which it was possible for the ordinary man to find his labor meaningful. The Mennonite neoclassical entrepreneur, regardless of the field in which he or she chooses to serve, has the cultural wherewithal to compete on the market but to resist succumbing to the vacuity of the market mentality. However, this cultural bulwark is a direct function of the solidarity of the Mennonite community. The weaker the solidarity, the more prone the entrepreneur will be to accept the cosmopolitan cosmology.

The high visibility of the economic entrepreneur's affluent lifestyle has made him or her the focus of attention and even the scapegoat in the Mennonite community. This *ressentiment* morality, as was indicated earlier, is not peculiar to Mennonite experience (even though it may seem so to the victim); any subculture with similar traits will, we predict, create scapegoats on which to take out its collective *ressentiment*. Jean-Paul Sartre considered the modern prison system exactly such a scapegoating mechanism (*St. Genet*). Secularization (alienation) will be the inevitable response of the successful entrepreneur to the resentment shown to him by his coreligionists and community members.

In Summary

Our position is that the Mennonite entrepreneur in business is not motivated by an unchecked desire for gratification of the acquisitive impulse any more than are Mennonites in other nonagrarian entrepreneurial pursuits. Nor are Mennonites in classical entrepreneurial roles more susceptible to seduction by secular norms and practices than are other Mennonites who have left the agrarian way of life. This does not mean that the agrarian way of life protects the individual from sin, only that the sources of temptation are different. The appearance that the classical entrepreneur is more secularized and materialistic is because his *practical creativity* usually (setbacks and bankruptcies notwithstanding) provides access to material power as well as the highly visible accouterments of success more profusely and readily than most other professions. Some other professional pursuits, such as medicine, are not far behind. Mennonite medical doctors are normally equally well ensconced in the symbols and artifacts of wealth even though the motivation has traditionally been service.

Our argument here is that the business entrepreneurs are the scapegoats for a general secularization process as is implied in the researchers' casual conversations with entrepreneurs and as is borne out by the research material. It is the gradual secularization of the entire Mennonite community from the communal status which is pushing the classical entrepreneurs to the margins. A few entrepreneurs *are* succumbing to the temptation of the status of worldly success, but this is by no means the case uniformly. The personality types of the majority are not greatly different from the rank and file of the congregation in commitment to the Mennonite tradition. The appearance of greater worldliness may be occasioned by the fact that the materialistic symbols accompanying the businesspersons' lifestyles threaten the Mennonite worldview because they do not fit the pattern of recognized social roles in the traditional community. Other roles also require personal initiative and are therefore entrepreneurial according to the neoclassical definition. These include religious roles (the revered preacher), educational roles (the honored role of teaching), and service roles (the biblically mandated servant).

We would argue that the entire Mennonite society is becoming secularized, and that one group, because of its high visibility and traditional vulnerability to popular resentment in the forms of the money lender and grain hoarder (to use traditional biblical terms), is becoming the scapegoat behind which everyone else's entrepreneurial attitudes and activities lie protected.

CHAPTER SIX

Heroic Conformity
and Community Alienation

Mennonite entrepreneurs may serve as congregational scapegoats, deflecting attention from the more general drift (to use a common Mennonite expression from the early part of the twentieth century) of Mennonites toward the modern world. Are they, however, more alienated than their non–business-oriented fellow members? Do they, more than others in the congregation, come to value less the community to which they belong? Certainly common wisdom among many Mennonites would hold that both are true.

Mennonites have had reservations about the accumulation of wealth and business dealings with others in the receiving societies they have joined. This would suggest that entrepreneurs face pressures that are different from those faced by other occupational groups. And yet, history teaches us that Mennonites have sometimes found ways of allowing business activities and religious community values to coexist. Dutch Mennonites, for example, who moved to the Vistula Delta area of west Prussia in the 1540s and 1550s, developed a prosperous society by heroic labor which gained toleration for them. And although some economic stratification emerged, congregational controls and circumstances prevented this difference from becoming too apparent.[1] Dutch Mennonites, in spite of extensive persecution, developed entrepreneurial enterprises by the end of the sixteenth century and soon became well known in the Netherlands as a leading economic force, especially in the seventeenth and eighteenth centuries.[2] This economic prosperity, including successful entrepreneurial efforts in shipping, ship building, trading, and manufacturing, it is said,

contributed to the decline of the Dutch Mennonite Church and encouraged resentment against wealth, success, and entrepreneurship.

Emerging status differences caused some congregational strife, as
illustrated by two sons of a Mennonite banker in Danzig. They refused to
remove their wigs, and thus their baptism in Amsterdam was not recognized.[3] The Dutch also had their critics of growing Mennonite affluence.
T. O. Hylkema, a leading Dutch Mennonite in the early twentieth century, was quoted as saying on numerous occasions: "After the devil failed
in his attempt to destroy Dutch Anabaptism by means of persecution he
almost succeeded when he changed his tactics and made them rich."[4] According to another Dutch Mennonite, writing in the 1930s, "Originally
the idea was in the world but not of the world; later it was 'free in and
of the world.' For such freedom of activity, as was desired, material prosperity was necessary. Now, riches are not always a blessing. Many, after
they have become rich, have both in a literal and figurative sense bade
farewell to the church which kept them separated from the world."[5]

And yet, while realizing economic success, the creation of mutual
fire insurance organizations and other forms of mutual aid including assistance in further settlements as early as 1622, indicated the extent to which
congregational communalism among the Dutch existed as well.[6] In short,
Dutch Mennonites were sensitive to the tension between the church and
world but became increasingly cautious about confrontation on the issue.

What of North American Mennonites? Were business and religious
communities allowed to coexist? From both quantitative and qualitative
data, there is reason to question the commonly held belief that entrepreneurs, more than others, are propelled from the community. And yet,
the existing literature, as scant as it is, seems to confirm the belief that
entrepreneurs are more prone to leave the church than are people in other
occupational groups. With reference to the Amish, for example, John A.
Hostetler said, "The decision to remain or leave the Amish Church is
related to economic problems of setting up a farm or Amish business."[7] In
Calvin Redekop's study of the Old Colony in Mexico, an Old Colony
bishop maintained that the greatest threat of membership loss was in the
economic sector, usually among those whose business was rather successful and which included almost unlimited interaction with outside and
non-Mennonite people.[8] So what are the nature and extent of community
alienation experienced by entrepreneurs?

In a study of General Conference Mennonites Leland Harder reported that when professional, technical, proprietors, and managers are

TABLE 6-1
Membership Terminations by Occupations, General Conference Mennonites,
1960 to 1970

Occupation[a]	Percent
Professional and technical	45.3
Farmers	10.9
Proprietors and managers	5.4
Clerical workers	7.3
Sales workers	4.4
Skilled craftsmen	10.9
Semiskilled operators	6.7
Service workers	4.4
Farm laborers	.9
Other laborers	3.8

SOURCE: Harder (1970).
[a] Number, 4,488.

TABLE 6-2
General Conference Membership Status

Profession	Active Member	Inactive Member	Ex-member
		%	
Professionals	19.3	49.4	54.3
Farmers	15.4	2.3	4.3
Proprietors and managers	17.0	4.5	7.9
Clerical	7.5	8.5	6.7
Sales workers	8.3	2.3	5.5
Skilled craftsmen	12.9	11.9	15.8
Semiskilled operators	7.7	6.8	4.3
Service workers	7.4	9.1	0.6
Farm laborers	1.9	0.0	0.0
Other laborers	2.6	5.1	0.6
Total number	684	176	164

SOURCE: Harder (1970).

all taken together, they represent 50.7 percent of all of the defections between 1950 and 1970 but only 30.4 percent of the total membership of
the General Conference.[9] Harder also found that when comparing professional and technical with proprietors and managers, it became clear that
entrepreneurs were less prone to defection than the technical and professional and even less than the overall average! Thus, although technical and
professional workers represent 23.9 percent of the General Conference
membership, they represent 45.3 percent of the defections. Proprietors
and managers represent 5.4 percent of the defectors; the weighted average
defection for the General Conference is 16.32 percent (see Table 6-1).

Another source of empirical data by the same author corroborated these statistics. In a survey of the Steinbach Mennonite Churches, which included eight different Mennonite groups, the total defection of proprietors and managers was 7.9 percent, although they constituted 17 percent of the total membership. This compares with a community weighted average of 10.5 defections over ten years[10] (see Table 6-2). On the basis of the Harder data, therefore, the commonly assumed notion that business success and wealth are escalators out of the church is clearly challenged.

THE COMMUNITY ALIENATION FACTOR

Are entrepreneurs more alienated from their church communities? If so, does this alienation propel them out of the church community at a higher rate than members in other occupational categories?

Look at the degree to which entrepreneurs fit into their church communities. To put it in the form of another question: do entrepreneurs feel at home in their churches? The Church Member Profile data collected by Kauffman, Harder, and Driedger begin to answer this question.[11] In their surveys, they asked respondents in five Mennonite and Brethren in Christ denominations "How important to you is your current participation in the life and work of the church?" Table 6-3 compares the answers given by a subsample of entrepreneurs (managers and proprietors, designated as CMP2 ENT) with those given Redekop's sample of entrepreneurs.[12] Ninety-two percent of the entrepreneurs in the CMP2 study said that participation in the church was fairly or very important to them. This compares with 90 percent of all those interviewed in the CMP2 study who gave these answers (statistically significant difference). The RER data are very similar to those for the CMP2 entrepreneurs. This is important information because not only are entrepreneurs no less likely to value participation in the church, but the findings point in the *opposite* direction than that of the commonly held assumption, that entrepreneurs should consider themselves more alienated from the traditional community than the members in general.

Another question from the CMP2 survey also tells us something about the at homeness of Mennonite entrepreneurs. When asked, "All in all, how well do you feel you fit in with the group of people who make up your congregation?" the percentage indicating that they fit in fairly or very well was the same for both the general population of Mennonites (CMP2) and the entrepreneurs interviewed by Redekop (RER): 80 percent

TABLE 6-3
Importance of Participation in Church

Response	CMP2	RER	CMP2 ENT
		%	
Very important	53	65	73
Fairly important	37	28	19
Of little importance	9	7	6
Of no importance	1	1	2

SOURCES: Kauffman and Driedger (1991), RER.

TABLE 6-4
How Well I Fit into the Congregation

Response	CMP2	RER	CMP2 ENT
		%	
I really don't fit in too well.	4	7	8
I fit in, but not too well.	12	14	14
I fit in fairly well.	52	58	53
I fit in very well.	32	22	24
Total	100	100	100

SOURCES: Kauffman and Driedger (1991), RER.

(see Table 6-4). Seventy-seven percent of the subsample of entrepreneurs in the CMP2 study reported that they fit well into their congregation.

The number of friends inside and outside the church may also be a key indicator of community alienation. Whom do Mennonites in general and Mennonite entrepreneurs more specifically count among their friends? The data from the CMP studies and the RER can again be compared, providing two ways of examining friendship patterns among Mennonites: friendships within the denomination (a somewhat broader definition of community) and friendships within the congregation (community more narrowly conceived). Table 6-5 presents friends in the denomination. Entrepreneurs report more friends within the denomination than does the general membership. Seventy-nine percent of entrepreneurs in the RER study report having three or more friends within their own denomination compared with 68 percent of the CMP2 respondents.

When friends in the local congregation are counted, the differences are smaller, with the general membership reporting more congregational friends. As Table 6-6 reveals, 40 percent of the entrepreneurs report having three or more friends within the congregation, compared with 44 percent in the general membership.

One interpretation of these data is that entrepreneurs are more

TABLE 6-5
Friends in Your Own Denomination

No. of Friends	CMP2	RER
	%	
None	9	0
One	8	7
Two	16	18
Three	22	22
Four	18	25
Five	28	32

SOURCES: Kauffman and Driedger (1991), RER.

TABLE 6-6
Friends in Your Own Congregation

No. of Friends	CMP2	RER
	%	
None	16	10
One	15	20
Two	22	31
Three	18	21
Four	12	6
Five	14	13

SOURCES: Kauffman and Driedger (1991), RER.

"entrepreneurial" in their approach to friendships as well as business, seeking out friends beyond their local congregation. Whatever the reason, it is clear that they are just as likely to seek out Mennonite friends (if not more in the case of denominational friendships)—whether in the congregation or not—than are people from other occupational groups.

Another way of looking at the community alienation factor is to consider how people perceive their long-term relationship to the church. As Table 6-7 demonstrates, the differences between the general population and entrepreneurs (both from the RER and the subsample of entrepreneurs from the CMP2 study) are relatively small.

The quantitative data thus far appear to indicate that the entrepreneurs are at least as well integrated (and some data would suggest better integrated) and no more alienated than most Mennonites. Do these data mean that commonly held assumptions about entrepreneurs leaving the church are wrong? The quantitative data are limited in some notable ways, which limits our ability to be conclusive here. Selectivity factors, for example, in both the CMP2 and RER studies are significant. In both studies, the sample includes those who were still active in the church. Thus, the

TABLE 6-7
Future Relationship to Denomination

Choice of Relationship	Rank	CMP1	CMP2	RER	CMP2 ENT
			%		
I will certainly always want to remain a member and could never feel right belonging to another denomination.	6	26	28	22	27
Although I prefer my own denomination, there are some other denominations I would not hesitate to join if the occasion arose.	5	51	50	57	46
I feel I could be just as happy in certain other denominations as in my own.	4	17	17	18	18
I have sometimes felt I could be happier in another denomination.	3	4	4	4	5
I have some definite thoughts about joining another denomination.	2	1	2	2	4
I am considering discontinuing my membership in my denomination.	1	1	0	2	0
Average rank[a]		4.93	5.43	4.95	4.89

SOURCES: Kauffman and Harder (1975), Kauffman and Driedger (1991), RER.
[a] In this case, the rank refers to the statement in the row closest to the rank number.

data systematically ignore people who have left the church—people who may have been the most alienated from the community.

However, the data do imply one very interesting fact that will serve us later: those entrepreneurs who are still in the church are as close to it as are their fellow nonentrepreneurial brethren. The quantitative data may therefore minimize the effects of community alienation. There may be a heroic conformity expended by the entrepreneurs and other congregation members which bridges the gaps caused by feelings of community alienation. In other words, it is not that entrepreneurs do not feel alienated but rather that they make gallant efforts to resist the fragmenting pressures of that alienation. These efforts make them appear integrated. However, when the pressure becomes too great, there is a sudden rupture of the relationship between the entrepreneur and the religious community. In such cases, the entrepreneur and family leave "suddenly" and without much explanation.

DYNAMICS OF ALIENATION

When the data appear to indicate the contrary, why does the general impression persist that successful businesspersons are more prone to leave the church than others? It is probably because of the high visibility and salience (power) of entrepreneurs, which means that more attention is paid to them and more significance attached to their lifestyle and church relationship. This intensified congregational awareness (and possibly envy) can, in turn, intensify the feeling of alienation from the community.

The appearance of a *ressentiment* morality within the context of a *Gelassenheit* ethos would appear to be contradictory. This contradiction is an existential possibility, however, in the modern context in which the solidarity and cohesion of the group based on the traditional values are breaking down, and families adopt the secular values while retaining their traditional roles and relationships. Under these circumstances, it would make sense for those who feel their way of life threatened to resort to a *ressentiment* ideology, as this is a defense mechanism of the weak.

The Mennonite tradition has created its own theological and ethical understanding of alienation (i.e., becoming worldly) of the business-people who have become wealthy and successful. This tradition, common to all world religions (Weber), is expressed by abhorrence to the corrosion of the faith which materialism brings. Mennonite faith is premised on the literal application of the teachings of Jesus on wealth and materialism: "How hard it will be for those who have riches to enter the kingdom of God!" (Mark 10:23). Contrast the Mennonite attitude with Luther's emphasis on grace. Every child that goes through the Mennonite catechism learns that Luther placed the epistle of James at the end because he suspected it of being a straw epistle, emphasizing works.

In the Mennonite cosmology, the epistle of James has taken on the opposite significance by underpinning the emphasis of economic accountability to the community. This peculiarly Anabaptist dogma was given the following expression by Peter Riedemann: "Therefore we say that as all the saints have community in spiritual gifts, still much more should they show this in material things." [13]

Even though most Mennonites would admit that the congregation is at fault to some extent when entrepreneurs leave the fold because of fellow members' jealousy, envy, and discomfort in the presence of wealth and affluence, they would still maintain that the source of conflict is the changed lifestyle that no longer expresses *Gelassenheit* toward God and fel-

TABLE 6-8
Ranking of Six Major Values in Parental Family

Variable	First Choice	Second Choice	Third Choice	Score	Rank[a]
Education	48	22	10	198	1
Family obligation	26	39	22	172	2
Good deeds	14	15	11	83	3
Religious faith	14	13	14	82	4
Money	12	9	10	64	5
Ethical life	3	3	3	18	6
High living standard	1	5	3	16	7

SOURCE: RER.
[a] The ranking was derived by giving the first choice a weight of 3, second choice a weight of 2, and third choice a weight of 1. Fewer respondents checked second and third choices than first.

low humans. It is the possession and use of power, prestige, authority, and freedom which economic success provides which estrange the persons from their fellow believers and bid them follow the attractions of "high society" or beckon them to succumb to blurred morals and flawed ethical behavior, according to conventional Mennonite wisdom.

Church discipline, including excommunication, was practiced in some congregations in earlier times in an effort to contain these tendencies. In recent centuries, however, disciplining has become relatively rare.[14] The value system that nurtures the Mennonite community clearly implants a negative orientation toward worldly lifestyles, and the entrepreneurs themselves have often internalized this background.

To understand community alienation better, it is necessary to go beneath the surface of community membership (e.g., friendships). Entrepreneurs in the RER were asked to rank in order of importance six values taught in their homes: religion, money, education, high standard of living, family, and social (good deeds) obligations. As Table 6-8 indicates, respondents reported that a clear hierarchy of values operated in their homes of origin, with education as the highest value and high living standard as the lowest. When asked about their own family life today, respondents said that there was no difference and that they adhered to the same values. Entrepreneurs apparently perceive little or no discrepancy between their values and the traditional Anabaptist-Mennonite teachings regarding business enterprise and success. Of course, that a discrepancy is not perceived does not mean that it does not exist, nor does the community's presumption that it exists mean that it does.

To double-check the entrepreneurs' perception of themselves, we looked at the desirability of success as a factor in the process of alienation.

TABLE 6-9
Importance of Economic Success

Reason	Percent agreeing
It provides security for family.	72
It gives me prominence in the business world.	2
It gives me esteem in the eyes of friends and relatives.	0
It gives me recognition in the community at large.	3
Other (specify).[a]	3

SOURCE: RER.
[a] This percentage included answers such as all of the above, none of the above, to serve God, to serve my fellow man, etc.

If success is valued highly by the entrepreneur but downplayed by the Mennonite ethos of *Gelassenheit,* the existence of a discrepancy between the entrepreneur's ideology and practice should become evident. Entrepreneurs were asked, "Why is economic success important to you?" Table 6-9 reports their responses.

One would assume that an alienated entrepreneur would place more emphasis on the recognition gained in the larger context if the congregation and religious community no longer played a role. In this sample of entrepreneurs, however, the traditional nonconformed Christian lifestyle was clearly stressed.[15] It is also noteworthy that when the entrepreneurs were asked about the relationship between congregation and community background and career success, 86 percent of them said that their background contributed to their success, and about 14 percent said that it did not.

When asked why being a Mennonite was helpful in business, responses included honesty, integrity, good reputation, hard work, dependability, quality products, helpfulness. As one respondent from the RER stated, "I think that Mennonites in general tend to be thought of as having a higher moral or ethical standard. But I don't want to exaggerate that because that's obviously been shown to be not totally true. I am almost never ashamed, when someone wants to know a little of my background, to say, I am a Mennonite."

If the entrepreneurs are not alienated from their congregations in terms of either beliefs and ideology or relationships, it is still possible that personal friendships and relationships are centrally important in determining whether their lifestyle and the increased power and influence have any impact. If the relationships changed over time, we would know that

TABLE 6-10
Friendships and Relations, Over a Generation

	None	A Few	Most
		%	
How many of your relatives live in the same area?	18	45	39
How many close friends live in the same area?	8	40	52
How many were your close friends when you were growing up?	38	53	9
How many friends are same religious background?	1	34	65
Averages	16	43	42

SOURCE: RER.

estrangement had taken place, even though we would probably not know why. The RER investigated the residence and incidence of friendships and relationships over the course of a generation.

There is a remarkable stability of friendships and residence for the entrepreneurs, as demonstrated by Table 6-10, but most interesting is that only 9 percent said they retained most of their childhood friends. This appears to indicate that the entrepreneurs' friendship patterns change as their careers progress. The fact that 65 percent indicate that most of their friends belong to the same denomination and that only 1 percent have no friends in the same religious community could indicate a strong affiliation to church and community; the figures could be turned around, however, and posed as follows: 35 percent have only a few or no friends in their own religious community, which begins to suggest some alienation from traditional communal ties.

One more useful bit of survey material from the CMP comes from responses to the following question: "Is your present attendance and participation in the life of the church primarily because you *want* to participate, because you feel you *ought* to participate, or because you feel you *have* to participate?" Comparison of CMP and RER materials reveals only minor differences (Table 6-11).

Using the CMP1 for purposes of comparison (we cannot use CMP2 because the question was not asked in the second survey), we see that 7 percent more entrepreneurs considered themselves to belong to the category of the most integrated—those who always enjoy their participation in church life. Entrepreneurs scored lower in the categories of those whose experience of church life is not an unmitigated blessing and those who participate because of external pressures (9 and 2 percent less, respectively).

TABLE 6-11
Motivation for Participation in Congregation

	CMP1	RER	Difference
		%	
I really want to participate and I enjoy it.	71	78	+7
I feel I ought to participate and don't always enjoy it.	26	17	−9
I feel I have to participate because of pressure from others.	3	5	−2

SOURCES: Kauffman and Harder (1975), RER.

According to this table, the entrepreneurs seem somewhat more integrated into the church and less ambivalent than the general membership regarding church participation.

ENDURING RESENTMENT: EXERCISES IN HEROIC CONFORMITY

Once again, the qualitative interviews with entrepreneurs add to our understanding of the issue of community alienation. The president of an enterprise that was developed from scratch by an entrepreneurial family articulated quite well the experience of building a business while remaining in the midst of a conservative Mennonite community. When asked, "How has the church, your religious community, supported, criticized, helped you?" this entrepreneur responded,

I could become very vocal on this one. Most of my family attends the —— Church. My parents came from the Whistler Mennonite Church, and they were excommunicated for who can say? They did not give reasons. A church brother was instrumental in encouraging us to do what we could do best [developing new products]. But we got no further support. I desperately wanted to go to some fellow businessmen or church people for some guidance, but frankly, I didn't come up with very much. [The reason] seemed to be the larger Mennonite thing. And I have wondered whether this same jealousy and same power centeredness that we sensed [that Dad experienced in the conservative church] was operating now. In Dad's church, there was never an acceptance of Dad's involvement in a variety of activities.

And I wondered sometimes, is it just the sense of the local ingrownness, namely the conservativeness, orthodoxy, and legalism in our own community, or is it maybe larger than just the local church? This jealousy was taken to the point that a local businessman [church member] took our products and shipped them to their suppliers' companies to check out and ultimately they used copies against us in the marketplace. I was very critical and angry at the time, but I am not any more. I think it is the insecurities and inferiority feelings that create this kind of actions. I just wish I had some access to an organization that could have given me some help. In hindsight, I think Dad could have cued me to a number of persons who might have helped. There would have been those we could have gone to and talked to if he maybe had a little broader feel about who we were and what we wanted to do.

When probed as to whether or not the seeming difficulty that Mennonites have accepting each other's success might be caused by concerns of control, this entrepreneur said,

I think you've put it into perspective. It's jealousy. My family was considered not to be successful, while relatives around my father were. We were not supposed to succeed in terms of private enterprise. There is something wrong with taking a dollar and coming out with a dollar and five cents. You can't make a profit. That is filthy. I got caught myself in the jealousy game, comparing our company with others: "Hey we're growing, they're laying off." It didn't take me long to realize that this is the stupidest thing you can do. The best thing you can do is wish for their success and help them achieve it. But I certainly didn't feel that acceptance in the larger Mennonite community. People told me, "Look, you're going to have to recognize that people don't believe that you can make a profit." But I can't accept that, because we are instrumental in putting fifty, seventy, eighty family heads to work. Our pay is average with the community. Where is our respect for each other? I have to check my attitudes toward others' achievements or lack of them. It's apparently a mistrust of success, and I think the economic situation even played against us at times.

Did any of this translate into increased feelings of community alienation?

No. I think we could have been [alienated] if we had been very sensitive and took offense at every point. But I think that we have done some growing, and we've been around the world enough to see a bit better. It's foolish to take offense. It's an imperfect church, but neither are we perfect. I would hope we are committed to the church, but we don't always accomplish its goals.

Halfway across the continent, another entrepreneur echoed some of the same concerns about jealousy in the church. Again, this entrepreneur was asked whether or not the church played a role in his becoming a successful businessperson. To this question, he responded,

Yes, I have had support, but not as far as the church is concerned.

The critical attitude is increasing all the time. I can only think that it is nothing less than jealousy. I don't know what else to say about it because we have had friends that are no longer friends and for what reason I don't really understand.

According to this entrepreneur, differences in lifestyle between entrepreneurs and nonentrepreneurs may have contributed to the jealousy, with some people feeling that businesspeople and their families have too many resources.

There is a certain amount of that [jealousy] because my wife and I do quite a bit of traveling. We're going here and there all the time, and we take quite a lot of vacations and see a lot of country, so there are many people who say, "Where are you going next, and what are you going to do next?" They say it jokingly, but down deep there's some resentment because they can't go. But we have a lot of friends who are glad for us too, so I can't say that they're all that way. But I guess we're all humans, and if someone says something negative about you, you take that and mull it over in your mind. But a dozen people saying something good about you doesn't do as much as one negative remark does.

It's [the source of other people's envy] the ability to see an opportunity and then to stick your neck out and take a risk in doing it. I make decisions most of the time pretty rapidly. If I see something that I feel is an opportunity, I don't spend a lot of time in thinking about it. I really feel that if it's a good opportunity somebody else is going to get it, if I wait too long.

Despite the jealousy he perceived on the part of fellow members of the congregation, this entrepreneur resisted feelings of alienation from them and worked at not alienating others.

I had no intention of ever alienating anybody. On the contrary, I have always been involved in the church. I have been either an usher or a Sunday School superintendent. I have also been a teacher in a Sunday School class, I've been an elder, on the building committee, pretty nearly every phase of the church. And through that your name is mentioned a lot, and some people don't go for that. They figure you are getting too much attention. For me, I feel that it was the Lord's leading all the way. I tried to ask for guidance as much as I could and take his leading. I really feel that this is why I have been successful.

Moving halfway across the continent to the West Coast, a very successful entrepreneur spoke of the dynamics of alienation and his attempts to recover some of the earlier relationships. When asked, "How has your success affected your relationship to the church, and you to them?" he responded,

My family was very much church and service oriented, with MCC and the like. And that's how I was raised. When I was in the midst of this upward movement, socially and materially, many times my family and even my grandfather would come and visit me, and they would take me by the arm and being of that generation, would say, "How are things with the Lord?" They wanted to know about your business dealings, but they were more interested in getting down to the important issues. And I'd sort of give them an answer, "You know, I haven't really paid that much attention to this." But the concern was within me, and I often said, "When I hit fifty, I think I'll take a year or two and give it to the community or MCC or something." So the easiest thing was to write a check. If the college or a church or someone needed a thousand bucks, no problem. I was always supportive. But the way I see it now, that's not what it's all about—I mean Christianity. The word I never liked was *discipleship*. I didn't want to get too close, so I had to be committed. Writing a check was easy—you keep everyone at a distance. Several years ago my wife and I rededicated our lives and devoted the time that we have now to doing something productive. So when I look at the things we've achieved, yeah they were great, they were good, and I'm delighted that I had the opportunity of doing it. But it doesn't have much lasting value.

Although people in the church may have been critical of this entrepreneur's success, he was reluctant to assign them blame, taking at least a major share of the responsibility himself.

I think it was my problem, I couldn't have cared less about what their criticisms were. I think upward movement was something sought after by everyone, most of the people in the church. And families were proud when there was a younger one in the family who was a rising star and doing well. I mean, everyone is proud of success. And there is a tendency, when someone becomes successful, to accept the fact that he has become less spiritual because he is so wrapped up in what he is doing, providing he signs a check for the conference and gives to the local church.

Asked point blank as to who was at fault for any tensions that emerged, he responded,

I don't think it was the church's fault. It was definitely my fault. When I was a kid, I'd hear my father's stories, the tough times he had and all that. I was, however, never driven as some of my Mennonite friends, who were going to hit the city, and they were going to make something big. I don't think I was ever driven with that sort of necessity or obsession. I wanted to go and achieve certain things on my own. But I didn't think of the church. There were some basic things like social drinking that I liked. And then I started smoking, which was a big no-no. All in all, I got what I wanted to have, but the criticisms were not that great. There were times when the younger generation wanted to get involved in this and that, and my grandfather was usually for it, but he always maintained that you could in no way cut back on commitments to the Lord. Us younger guys thought that at times he got carried to extremes with his concerns.

An entrepreneur who initiated a prosperous business with denominational institutions provided an interesting accent to these other voices. Asked again about the church community's response to his business, he said,

It's surprising how this business has grown. We started small, and I had a policy, as I said, that prayer meant very much to us. And I have always said to my boys, "If you ever find yourself in difficulty, stop right now and let's talk and pray about it; we'll see what can be done." I have never borrowed large sums of money, have never gone in debt heavily, and my church [congregation] has not been neglected in giving, but I haven't asked for much either.

When asked if the church resented his success, he answered that he had not felt this from his own congregation, but knew the feeling existed in some quarters.

One minister, however [not from his denomination], when he inquired whether I had a particular contract, said, "What's the matter with you? You're not happy with your first million, you want the second million from our congregation?" And I thought right away, "Did I do anything wrong?" So I asked him, "Was there something you didn't like about my presentation, or didn't I conduct myself as a gentleman? He wouldn't even shake hands with me, and I said to myself, "Fine, I can learn from this."

An entrepreneur who moved to a number of communities and is broadly familiar with the Mennonite landscape said the following when asked about the religious community's response to his business success:

Stop me if get long winded. I think the MB's [Mennonite Brethren] were most eager to become socially mobile because they were a small group and were defensive against the others [Mennonite groups]. In the MB community you could become a medical doctor, or a teacher, or successful in business and plow ahead. That was the value. It was meaningful to the mothers if their boys could join the church and then plow ahead. So actually the idea of making money and getting ahead was really pretty good. I remember sermons that actually urged people to make more money because God wanted people to make more money so they could give more. That was the rationale, and it covered a multitude of aggressive motives, I think. But my father had always taken a little different mode. That created a bit of ambiguity. [This entrepreneur later joined a different conference.] Now recently, when I ran out of steam in [the business] and we were thinking of doing other things, we got most of our affirmation from our colleagues. It wasn't, "Well, we hope you find something else you like," but rather, "We're not going to tell you how much we enjoyed your services because you might feel worse about leaving, since you are already feeling the separation pretty bad." They rather said, "Hey, go to it."

Now there are the fundamentalists in our midst, however, who believe that if you are in business you probably are suspect, and you probably aren't using enough of your capital for the Lord's good, and second, if you are in business you obviously have much more money to give to the church. They don't understand cash flow. I had to tell one fellow, "You know we have had losses for two years," and he still came back with a very pietistic mode and [asked], "Why wouldn't I hear the Lord's call?" and I said, "Where would you want me to go for the money and would he please go to the bank and sign so that we could borrow money for his cause?" He never understood because he still believed "you're in business, surely you have lots of money."

Asked if he found himself alone in the business world, he responded,

In [my] congregation I don't. I really have found a lot of people who are interested and are giving good affirmation and actually thank you for the kinds of things you are doing. When you move out a bit, however, like the MB Church, or in some rural congregations, I find things quite different.

It would be misleading to say that all entrepreneurs are successful in their attempts at heroic conformity. One entrepreneur, for example, who was a member of the Mennonite Church at the time of the interview but who has since joined another denomination, provided another perspective.

Q: Have you availed yourself of the church community for counseling and help in your business?
A: Yes I have, unfortunately. I wouldn't do that again because I have found that the people I have spoken to in each case were listening for something else; they would be listening for a weak point and then would zero in on it.
Q: Weak point?
A: My business activities, etc.
Q: So why were they critical?
A: Either they were trying to grab off a market that I was struggling with or hire away employees, which gave me problems, so I would never reveal myself to anybody in the church again.
Q: So the church has not been helpful?
A: When I have chosen to speak to businesspeople in the church, it has not been satisfying. So I have chosen to speak to nonbusinesspeople now. You can trust them and you know that they're not listening to you opportunistically.
Q: Are any of your business associates friends or relatives?
A: Not any longer, though they used to be. I now choose my friends from areas nonrelated to my work. Yes, I have lost my trust in people, to the point where I would no longer share with them my personal economic life.

This last entrepreneur's case proved the exception to the rule. His case is exceptional not because other entrepreneurs did not sense disapproval or resentment but rather because he gave up the struggle to remain within the community. The balance of the responses presented above came from entrepreneurs who represent the broad landscape of North American Mennonite communities and the major conferences in the study. Their stories attest to the extent to which most Mennonite entrepreneurs go to remain within the community and to continue their participation *as Mennonites*.

ANALYSIS OF COMMUNITY ALIENATION

To understand the heroic conformity of Mennonite entrepreneurs in the face of sometimes pronounced community alienation, it is necessary to examine sociological, psychological, and theological aspects of the phenomenon.

Sociologically speaking, a number of changes affecting both North American society generally and Mennonite life more specifically must be taken into account if we are to frame the experience of entrepreneurs within their congregations accurately. From the interviews it is clear that there is a tension between entrepreneurs and their religious communities, resulting from a number of things. First, the differentiation in occupational status among members of the congregation has eroded whatever occupational homogeneity existed within Mennonite life.[16] The proliferation of occupational groups led to a proliferation of viewpoints within church life, accompanied by increasing individuation. In other words, the emergence of different professional, economic, and social categories (i.e., the shift from traditional to modern society, from the socially cohesive personal relationships of status groups to the socially particularistic relationships of classes based on common self-interest) increased the number of points of view from which the motivations, actions, and meanings of fellow congregation members' behavior could be observed. As self-interest replaced the common good as the primary frame of reference, the religious self-consciousness of congregations and individuals diminished.

Within this highly individuated context, resentment becomes a very real possibility. Consider the changing meaning of just one activity: travel. Today, when Mennonites travel to many parts of the world and experience an almost unlimited number of cultural/economic systems, it is not to search for new land for an emigration from a bursting colony, nor is it to spread the Gospel in a pagan land. It is most likely to enhance personal objectives. Inevitably, when private consumption of surplus wealth (luxury) of the free market economy replaces the corporate consumption (ministry) of the traditional economic ethos, the stay-at-homes begin to perceive a discrepancy between the common meanings and symbols and the travelers' practice of the long-held beliefs. This results in envy on the part of the *Schlechtweggekommene* (those who came off badly), as Nietzsche calls them and, in turn, an offended innocence on the part of the entrepreneurs who see themselves as committed to the church and furthering the interests of the community by creating jobs.

In North America, the linguistic, cultural, and economic peculiarities that made the individual psychically dependent on the community have, to a great extent, been lost. The result is that simplicity and nonconformity to the world are more difficult to understand, communicate, and accept when the members in the congregation, all adhering in principle to the traditional *Gelassenheit* ideology, have lifestyles that are so different and are informed by different (and proliferating) reference groups outside the Mennonite congregation and community.

The appeal of and recourse to religious terminology and ethical sanctions have also declined, and the old disciplines (methods of social control) can no longer be applied, since there are so many different and unique situations to which the principle must be applied. Each person or family will be prepared to rationalize and justify its own interpretation as being "no worse than so and so's" (another hallmark of individualism). In the agrarian ethic period, the ritual of excommunication and shunning brought wayward persons back into the fold. In more recent North American Mennonite experience, Bible references and revival meetings served to reinforce the norms. But with the secularization process, these traditional rites have lost their power.[17]

In short, Mennonites in North America have accommodated to modernism or materialistic culture.[18] This culture is perhaps best characterized by a scientific approach that often reduces the universe to discrete atoms, an anthropology that often reduces humanity to the animal kingdom, and an economics that often assumes that the law of the jungle will enable us to realize the common good most quickly and efficiently (as "smart" bombs illustrate perfectly). In Mennonite congregational life, this "disenchanted" (to use Weber's language) or individuated understanding of people and their relationship to the world has changed Mennonite congregational life. As Joseph Smucker observed, the modern (especially urban) Mennonite congregation no longer looks very much like the ethical community of early Anabaptism but more resembles a sort of "pit stop for emotional refueling and identity reinforcement."[19] The result is what sociologists would describe as *anomie*, in which symbols no longer mean the same thing for every member of a congregation or in which behavior can no longer be expected to conform to the assumed beliefs and commitments because the sacred canopy of beliefs and rituals no longer shelters the individual from the loss of identity which modern mass culture makes possible.[20]

The Mennonite entrepreneur appears to cope with this anomie by cultivating a sort of heroic conformity, which finds several significant means of expression. A major one is the desire of entrepreneurs to prove to their fellow believers that their "deviant" behavior is not resulting in apostasy, or value loss, as the common Mennonite understanding would have it. Entrepreneurs maintain that even though their lifestyles may be changing and their resources and power increasing, their solid grounding in the community is proven by their tenacious beliefs and support. It is possible that—as in the political sphere—the entrepreneurs may become religiously conservative to prove their loyalty and can be sociologically defined as overconforming to preserve an existing condition.

This tendency has already been documented with regard to increasing Mennonite affluence. Analyzing the relationship between income and religiosity among the Mennonite Brethren, using CMPI statistics, Peter Hamm said that "economic ascendancy does not necessarily mean increased secularization." He noted that "the middle range income group is the most orthodox, with the affluent possibly a little more so than the less affluent." However, he found that commitment to Anabaptist-Mennonite ideals was higher among the more affluent, which seems to be consistent with our position, with "the highest income [groups] responding most positively and the middle income group responding less favorably." He concluded that "in Anabaptism, the most affluent rank a little higher."[21]

Another significant expression of heroic conformity as applied to our study is what anthropologist Anthony Wallace called *rites of intensification*.[22] This mechanism has the effect of shoring up eroding beliefs or principles and explains the fact that in a number of indices the entrepreneurs were more conformed than the general sample, although there were also entrepreneurs who were less conformed to community norms. It also explains why entrepreneurs, who appear to be loyal members, might suddenly leave the church. Entrepreneurs who feel that their value commitments are becoming suspect to their fellow believers—whether they perceive this correctly or not—may attempt to compensate by intensifying their commitment to the traditional values. At a certain point, however, such compensations or the participation in mere rituals no longer suffices, and a fracture occurs.

That entrepreneurs conform does not mean that they do not experience community alienation. The change of friendships, for example (see Table 6-11), suggests that residential and/or geographical segregation may have occurred. When the entrepreneur emerges, either because of a geographical move or by socioeconomic upward mobility, the social relationships and possibly the religious are affected, so that the traditional relationships and expectations no longer apply.

Even more influential in the entrepreneur's alienation, however, are the role segregations that begin to assert themselves along with the entrepreneur's success. We noted that the substitution of financial donations for personal community involvement was an indicator of the entrepreneur's alienation. The substitution of market economy values (exchange value, measured in U.S. dollars) for traditional communal values sets in motion a dynamic that focuses the community's attention on the activities of the entrepreneur (biblical moneylender, grain hoarder).

Role segregation becomes very evident. The entrepreneur may need to postpone a tennis match, fishing trip, golf outing, for a church committee meeting, not only once, but many times, and finally call it off altogether. But the friends and congregation members feel that they are being taken for granted and slighted. The attendance of entrepreneurs at church committee meetings, likewise, may at first demand the adjustment of the time and place of meeting to accommodate their busy schedules, but even this may not be sufficient as the entrepreneurs miss more and more of the meetings to which they had committed themselves by accepting appointments at the annual church business meeting. Here, likewise, the enormous demand on the entrepreneur's time in getting a business started will be interpreted as a lack of interest in, and commitment to, the congregation and community.

Because there are no functional substitutes in congregation and community life for physical presence, the lessening of physical and social interaction brings growing questioning of the motivation and commitment of the person by those faithful members who are always present. This questioning acquires the judgmental overtones of *ressentiment* morality when the pattern of absence/presence of the entrepreneur (absence from recreational, informal, and intimate/presence at formal, festive, occasional events) is such as to create the appearance of class differences. The external signs of success (clothes, car, contribution) coupled with external alienation from the congregation and community provide the seedbed for *ressentiment* to germinate and eventually rule the congregation.

What appears at first to be a problem specific to the entrepreneur later reveals itself as endemic to the rationalization (in the Weber-Parsonian technical sense) of Mennonite society in North America. Entrepreneurs are not alienated and misunderstood because they are abandoning a viable communal society for individualistic culture (the popular perception) but because the entire congregation is probably comprised of equally *rationalized* (i.e., educated to their self-interest) individuals who misunderstand the cause of their own alienation and consequently blame the entrepreneur for their own guilt—lusting after the forbidden idols of Egypt, Canaan, or Babylon—contemporarily expressed by Rome, Venice, Amsterdam, London, New York, Vancouver. A certain congregational cohesion is achieved by all members of the group externalizing their own existential anomie on those in the congregation least able to defend themselves, who become ostracized and eventually excommunicated.

With the erosion of the cultural viability of practicing the *Gelassenheit* ethos, clear consensus on ideologically correct expression of what *Gelassenheit* in the modern market economy context ought to look like has broken down. As in premonarchial Israel, "Every man [does] what is right in his own eyes," and church discipline degenerates into judgment by gossip and rumor. Cultural anomie, economic individualism, and the growing role segregation of modern society—in which Mennonite groups in North America are increasingly being forced to participate— conspire to make it impossible for traditional authorities to enforce the communal norms.

As a result, when new entrepreneurs emerge, and their new tacks appear to indicate a weakening of the authority of the traditional norms on their behavior, they no longer receive the traditional visit by the elder admonishing them because they are getting too big and encouraging them to reconsider before they are called to account before the church. It is left up to the informal gossip network to inform them of their folly and the community's displeasure. But if their relatives and friends are also relinquishing their support of the traditional norms (if there is no longer a functioning elder, the social structure is breaking down, and the wayward entrepreneur is not an isolated incidence, but symptom of a malaise general to the congregation), the chances are further diminished that they will hear of the community's complaints from someone's friendly concern. The judgment of gossip, which is always *a priori*, will complete the alienation process by informally shunning the offender.

Hence, the willingness to participate in church affairs (refer back to Table 6-3) is high for the entrepreneur, but if the expectations of what

TABLE 6-12
My Denominational Bible Teachings Accurately Reflect the Word of God

Response	CMP2	RER	Difference
		%	
Yes, definitely	24	36	8
Yes, for the most part	46	44	−2
No	21	18	−2
Uncertain	9	2	6

SOURCES: Kauffman and Driedger (1991), RER.

it means and the basis of the entrepreneur's participation are misunderstood, the discrepancy between expectations and output breeds animosity and further misunderstanding. The entrepreneur may show strong commitment to the church (as evidenced in Table 6-7), but still be marching to a different drummer. The larger question is whether the faithfulness of orthodoxy is not, like the life of the master in Hegel's dialectic, dependent for its identity on the worldliness of heterodoxy, which—like Hegel's slave—must engage in a struggle to the death to acquire its life.

The cost of prosperity has been the breakdown of consensus or discipline in the language of the traditional Mennonite community. Table 6-12 addresses this issue directly. Only 24 percent of respondents in the CMP2 survey believed that the church's teachings accurately reflect the Word of God. The remaining 76 percent were either not sure or disagreed in many ways. Again, when these responses are compared with those of respondents in the RER study, it is apparent that entrepreneurs are more orthodox than the general membership. Most members of the Mennonite community are aware of the growing lack of consensus and are concerned about its effects on the religious life of the movement as well as its ethical and social expressions. It is undoubtedly true that the entrepreneur is caught in this growing alienation process and is in part a contributor to it. As the individual parts begin to loosen their bonds, alienation appears as its visible form. This alienation feeds on itself because abnormal effort and courage are required for congregation members to move toward another person who is moving to the periphery. This is the push factor. More tragic, however, is the situation where the person who is moving out does not want to be reconciled to the congregation. Some entrepreneurs find themselves in this latter situation, which expresses the pull of individualism, certainly a factor in the alienation of the entrepreneur.

In summary, Mennonite entrepreneurs are ideologically and socially as well integrated into the church as the general membership. They conform heroically to community values and continue to emphasize the importance of community membership. Thus, we propose that entrepreneurs are in an interesting (and instructive) position: the high visibility of their lifestyles and the cosmopolitan nature of their social relationships make them targets for popular resentment, even though they may be more conformist in doctrine. This situation results in conflicting pressures to stay and to leave, which are heightened to the point where the emotional tension becomes too great, and defection takes place. The pressures toward this parting of ways is *not* produced by the entrepreneur alone; the congregation, and the larger secular society both play their parts.

CHAPTER SEVEN

Rationalizing Faith and Business

FAITH AND ECONOMIC AFFAIRS

Faith and economic affairs are linked inextricably in Christian teachings. Western civilization and Christianity were deeply influenced by the Graeco-Roman heritage; hence the economic sphere and its independent influences on society have been widely addressed by the Christian tradition and are even anticipated by the Old Testament prophets.

Jesus told stories from the economic sphere to illustrate many of his teachings and to explain the meaning of religious salvation. Although His doing so has left many a minister and priest puzzled, other scriptural writings are unequivocal in their condemnation of business activities. The Christian Canon denounces and singles out for special judgment those profiting from merchandising in material production and profit, calling them "friends of Babylon" (metaphysical evil).[1]

This is a sentiment of many social critics and thinkers as diverse as Avilla, Calvin, Marx, Rauschenbusch, Simons, Tolstoy, and White. Rauschenbusch, for example, tersely stated that "business life is the unregenerate section of our social order."[2] Conversely, proponents of the economic enterprise have legitimized their worldview and way of life with arguments from the Greek sophists; Roman and modern apologists have produced an almost unlimited number of defenses of its social functions.[3] A. Friedrich Hayek affirmed, "It was men's submission to the impersonal forces of the market that in the past has made possible the growth of civilization without which this could not have developed."[4]

This conflict of views has resulted in a polarization that has persisted for many years between those who think that religion is noneconomic (i.e., not relevant for the real world of economics) and those who think it should dictate economic activity. According to Albert Rasmussen, "In the tragic separation between religion and daily life, no area has developed a wider gap than that between faith and economic affairs. The result of the split has been to make faith irrelevant and barren and economic life sterile and without higher purpose. So compartmentalized have the various concerns of human endeavor become in our time that even those people who are at the same time religiously active and business-oriented often embrace this split within themselves."[5] The conflict has become so wide and is supported by so much emotion that there has at times been little communication between the polar barricades.

A lack of communication is just one cause of the conflict in the Mennonite community between those critical of the acquisitiveness of economic life (*religious asceticism,* as Weber called it) and those supportive of and involved in it. The result is a great deal of mistrust and misunderstanding. Further, the lack of dialogue and meaningful interaction between the ministry (the carriers of spiritual values) and the businesspeople in the Mennonite congregations and communities reflects an underlying malaise.

Mennonite culture, perhaps more so now than ever before, faces an identity crisis.[6] And as the gap between the real and the ideal become blurred, further polarization may take place in the name of orthodoxy and mutual excommunication in a battle of church purity against Christian liberty. Contemporary North American Mennonites endorse a communal ethos, an individualistic ethos, or often a mixture of both. Those who feel strongly about one side accuse their opponents of not practicing what they preach. Thus, an unconscious ideological bias misleads the individual or community into giving absolute status to a one-sided interpretation of a text and tradition that embody both the communal and individualist elements. The individual and community are locked in a struggle to define Mennonite cultural values—a small-scale version of what James Davison Hunter called a *culture war.*[7] The extreme sides seem to talk past one another rather than confronting issues directly. The utopian element of the biblical message is pitted against the individual (personal) responsibility that it demands of us. Study conferences, position papers, and an almost unlimited number of personal statements have attempted to state the Mennonite Church's or a Christian position on economic behavior.[8] But the polarization continues.

In this chapter we shall explore the gap between the entrepreneurs' beliefs and those of the church community. We are interested in determining how diametrically opposite attitudes toward the modern market economy and the appropriate Mennonite attitude toward it can be defended and made to appear reasonable and consistent to their holders. Furthermore, we must determine why, if these arguments appear consistent and reasonable to one party, they cannot be communicated to the other. And how does the holder of the private (*idiotic* in the literal Greek sense) ideology come to terms with this failure to communicate?

THE CHURCH / CONGREGATION POSITION ON BUSINESS

The basic source of Anabaptism's critical stance toward the acquisitive impulse, expressed by business activities and the legitimation of self-interest which characterizes the liberal market mentality, is its position on the relationship to property. Historically, although Anabaptist-Mennonites have not been consistently communistic, property has always been considered a means to advance the common good. The individual's attitude to property was that property provided the means to enhance the common good rather than to drain from it. During times of persecution, property often had to be shared with refugees fleeing for their lives.

According to one Anabaptist document, "True, devout Christians hold all physical possessions in common, and no one among them should wish to be sole lord of his goods." The purpose of common ownership is of course, to ensure that "no one should be deprived of his due, neither in words nor with works." The utopian/eschatological ideal is that a community should become established in which all would be equally respected, loved, and accepted because "of a deep love and free, good will."[9] It is perhaps significant that this description matches, almost word for word, Hegel's description of the family.[10] Hegel's is not the nuclear family of modern society but rather the extended family, or tribe, of traditional societies which practically constituted a political entity.

The Anabaptist property ethic, it must be made clear, is neither *communistic* nor *capitalistic* but is rather a revision of the traditional peasant ethos (*Sittlichkeit*) on the basis of biblical interpretation. The assumption is that Jesus did not leave his disciples instructions to cope with success because he was much too preoccupied with his own imminent destruction and the persecution he foresaw for his followers. Adaptation of the Christian message to this life and this world was left for Paul and those who followed him. Logically then, Anabaptist censure would fall not on specific forms of organization, but on congregational norms of conduct within whatever political context the community of believers finds itself.

Thus, it appears reasonable that criticism and rejection of acquisition for the purpose of ostentatious consumption would be rationalized on the basis that luxury consumption is wrong when brethren and sisters are suffering persecution, war, or famine—and, in the modern worldly context—when war, famine, and natural disasters are wreaking havoc worldwide and the number of urban homeless in North America is reaching epidemic proportions. The Old Testament prophet Amos draws our attention very graphically to this abuse of property, targeting conspicuous consumption and luxury expenditures. Given that entrepreneurial activity is often seen as the route to the life of the idle rich, it is small wonder that holders of the communal ethic are deeply suspicious.

TENSIONS BETWEEN COMMUNALISM / INDIVIDUALISM

The more traditional Mennonite groups provide more pronounced examples of conflict between the normative and the innovative. Using the Old Colony community in Saskatchewan as a backdrop, for example, Leo Driedger studied the life history of an innovator and entrepreneur there.[11] Johann Driedger, a minister, crossed the boundaries of permissible behavior by purchasing a store, which necessitated obtaining insurance, forbidden by the church. His business prospered, and he expanded it to several locations. Mr. Driedger was building a modern new house in Osler, presumably to move into town and open another store. The situation seemed to be getting out of hand. Church leaders demanded that Driedger be reconciled with Heinrichs, the bishop. Within a year—in the spring of 1908—the frequent visits and discussions (arguments?) led to the excommunication of Driedger, with the intent "to bring him under control."

In evaluating the causes for the tensions and the ultimate rupture,

Leo Driedger said that "better reasons were needed why an articulate member, a former village mayor, a prominent community member, and a conscientious church-goer should be excommunicated. The autonomy of Driedger had gone too far; he was plotting against the community; he was emulating 'worldly' models instead of the Mennonite Community model."[12] The ensuing "boycotts of Driedger's businesses were as effective as their ban on church attendance."[13] After some acrimonious debates and tangles, Driedger was forced to leave the church and died without being reconciled with the church authorities and community.

This case study is representative of actions that have taken place in most if not in all of the more conservative Mennonite groups. A Mennonite group that was especially stern in its techniques to keep innovation in line was the Holdeman Mennonites. According to Hiebert,

The principle of the simple life still governs their choice, and by this token some occupations are automatically excluded. Another important guiding principle is the avoidance of high risk loans, speculation, or using money to make more money. The emphasis is on choosing a vocation which aids people and keeps one free from complex involvements.[14]

The extensive analyses of the Amish by Hostetler (1980) and Kraybill (1989) and the Old Colony by Redekop (1969) provide considerable data on this aspect. The disapproval of innovation and entrepreneurship is based on the desire to maintain the faithful community. It is part of the dynamic of the entrepreneur as the scapegoat for a communitywide malaise. Mennonites historically have consciously and unconsciously disapproved of innovation and entrepreneurship because of their threat to the community of love and mutuality. Unbridled individualism is assumed to break down communal relationships and life.

Traditional Mennonite groups point up in more exaggerated relief the same principle that operates in the more progressive groups, although among the latter the dynamics are much more subtle and intangible (i.e., less legalistic). Findings from various studies of contemporary Mennonite life reveal that the tension between the communal impulse and individual interest has become more complex among progressive groups.

The Church Member Profile (CMP1 and CMP2) studies provide some glimpses at the communalism-individualism tension as it pertains to matters of faith. According to these studies, most Mennonites are still committed to *mutual aid* and assistance, which expresses an aspect of the original Anabaptist-Mennonite concern. Respondents were asked, "The sixteenth-century Anabaptists took seriously their commitment to aid any

TABLE 7-1
Mutual Aid in the Church

Need for Mutual Aid	CMP1	CMP2
	%	
Mutual aid is no longer needed.	3	3
Mutual aid is needed, but it is not practical for the church to provide it.	11	9
Mutual aid is needed and can be best provided in the local congregation.	20	12
Mutual aid is needed at the local level and the churchwide sharing programs.	66	76

SOURCES: Kauffman and Harder (1975), Kauffman and Driedger (1991).

brethren in need. Given our affluent twentieth-century society and the availability of many commercial insurance companies, which statement best expresses your view on the need of mutual aid within the framework of the church?" Table 7-1 presents their answers.

Sociologist David Appavoo, in a rather extensive and intensive study of Canadian Mennonites, attempted to get at the awareness of community.[15] Appavoo asked respondents whether or not they agreed with two statements about Mennonite life. Seventy-seven percent of his respondents agreed with the first statement, "I cherish the Mennonite heritage as the model for my own life." Eighty-six percent agreed with the second, "Being part of the local Mennonite community gives me a sense of real satisfaction."

Open-ended responses confirmed the importance of community to many people:

I appreciate the strong sense of brotherhood of caring and sharing in the Mennonite Church and community.

I appreciate the openness and friendliness of my Mennonite friends and the feeling of acceptance and love in the community.

It is the closeness of the church, by helping each other out in the time of need.

I love the simplicity and humility. No amount of money or fame could make it better.

Appavoo recognized, however, that affluence may pose more difficult challenges to this sense of community than have the years of persecution and isolation. As he noted, the greatest threat is society's thrust toward

TABLE 7-2
My Investment Orientation

Opinion	Percent
I could invest my money in church-operated investments only if the financial yields were at least equal to what I could obtain elsewhere.	14
I would invest my money in such programs even if the yields were less than could be obtained elsewhere.	24
The Church should not operate investment programs.	20
No opinion.	42

SOURCE: Kauffman and Redekop study.

extreme individualism. The emphasis on the complete independence and self-sufficiency of the individual has left many North Americans unable to reach out, commit themselves, love, or be loved. This same influence is also found in the Mennonite Church. Also, affluence among Mennonites might push them further away from a conception of the brotherhood of man. He worried that in the end, congregations would become mere "pitstops" for "emotional refueling"—a conception of the church which is a far cry from the traditionally held views.[16]

Research conducted by Dan Kauffman and Calvin Redekop suggests that Appavoo's concerns are warranted.[17] Their research attempted to induce Mennonite understandings of *property* (material culture, in the anthropological sense, which incorporates private property in its modern form, as well as capital).[18] Kauffman and Redekop asked their respondents, "Which best expresses your opinion regarding investing your money (if you have some to invest) in a church-operated program?" As shown in Table 7-2, most respondents were not able to articulate an opinion on this issue. Nearly one-fourth of them were willing to invest in church programs even if it did not produce yields equal to those they could achieve on the open market. Of course, nearly as many said that the church should not be running investment programs. Notably, the fewest number of respondents took the purely individualistic option (14 percent indicating that yield was of primary concern). These findings are suggestive, more than anything else, of the ambivalence of Mennonites concerning issues of wealth and investment.

From the findings reported by Kauffman and Redekop it would seem that Mennonites are somewhat split in their views of what a "true Christian community of love" should look like. As shown in Table 7-3, the largest portion of Mennonites (42 percent) took a personal pietis-

TABLE 7-3
Nature of a True Christian Community

Characteristics	Percent agreeing
A group of people who share whatever resources for daily living they possess, whether food, or shelter, or worship, or admonition, prompted especially by a deep concern for the fallen brother.	33
A Christian neighborhood, town, or city in which citizens are prompted to live up to laws of God in their relationships with each other.	25
A spiritual kinship experienced whenever a brother meets a kindred brother beyond the boundaries of race, creed, denomination, or congregation; a very personal feeling of unity.	42

SOURCE: Kauffman and Redekop study.

tic view of the Christian community. A third of them, however, still operated with what might be called the Anabaptist approach, including a strong emphasis on mutual aid. Thus, although the strong communal stance is clearly diminished compared with that of the Old Order groups, it remains an understanding to which some adhere.

When Kauffman and Redekop explored commitments to congregational discipline, they found similar signs of an opening of the community to the styles of the broader culture. Respondents were asked to identify "important marks of the existence of the true church." Table 7-4 shows that although 40 percent still advocated an active disciplinary role for the church, 60 percent opted for a more individualistic or therapeutic approach (with an emphasis on counseling rather than reprimanding).

Findings from the CMP2 also indicate that Mennonites are split on the appropriate role of church discipline. Respondents were asked whether they agreed that "the Mennonite Church should practice a thorough church discipline so that faltering or unfaithful members can be built up and restored or in exceptional cases, excluded." Eleven percent strongly agreed, 44 percent agreed, 25 percent were uncertain, 12 percent disagreed, and 3 percent strongly disagreed. Hence, 55 percent were concerned about maintaining a strongly disciplined and relatively homogeneous church congregation. From these data, combined with those reported by Kauffman and Redekop, it would appear that contemporary (progressive) Mennonites are relinquishing the traditional communal property ethos.

A final question from the Kauffman and Redekop research required the completion of the statement, "The most essential requirement for raising the moral behavior of people is . . ."

TABLE 7-4
True Marks of the Church

Characteristics	Percent agreeing
The acceptance of members as persons, regardless of their style of life, and dealing with conflicts in a nondirective counseling way with tolerance and sensitivity.	60
The corporate discernment of right and wrong in the fellowship of believers and making binding decisions about disciplinary actions to be carried out by the congregation.	26
The practice of discipline toward certain members who fall into grave sin or error, which will also educate the other members with regard to the seriousness of sin and testify to the world of the holiness of God.	14

SOURCE: Kauffman and Redekop study.

As summarized in Table 7-5, the third response is clearly the orthodox answer for the consistent Anabaptist-oriented membership; the first and second are compromises or deviations. Slightly more than one-fourth of the Mennonite membership consciously adhered to the Anabaptist reasons for controlling lifestyles and types of behavior because they have a direct bearing on the communal nature of the Christian community. However, the majority took a more individualistic stance (the second possible response), and nearly one-fifth of the respondents (choosing the first response) removed the issue and placed it outside the realm of the church's responsibility entirely.

In spite of all of the indicators that point to declines in the communal impulse, there is still reason to believe that this decline has led to ambivalence more than outright endorsement of the capitalist worldview. The CMP1 research, for example, asked people to indicate their agreement/disagreement with the following statement: "Christianity and communism share in common some social and economic ideals and goals." Although 30 percent disagreed with this idea, 39 percent agreed, and another 32 percent were uncertain.[19] Minimally, this would indicate that the Mennonite community has some questions about accepting the free enterprise system as Gospel. This interpretation is consistent with responses to another question appearing in the CMP2 study: "The national government should take every opportunity to stamp out communism at home and abroad." Thirty-four percent agreed with this statement, 24 percent were uncertain, and 41 percent disagreed.[20]

TABLE 7-5
Requirements for Moral Behavior

Characteristics	Percent agreeing
To establish a society whose laws are just and enforced by leaders who are just, recognizing that the harmful behavior of immoral men needs to be controlled by moral society.	18
To encourage and teach traits of personal character, such as honesty, integrity, purity, and self-control, believing that there is a foundation of good in all men upon which one can build.	54
To call them out of immoral associations into a community of disciples in which high moral behavior is a distinct way of life and discipline.	28

SOURCE: Kauffman and Redekop study.

MENNONITE ENTREPRENEURS' UNDERSTANDINGS OF BUSINESS ACTIONS

To understand the responses of Mennonite entrepreneurs, we must place them into the Western industrial capitalism setting—one of the most formidable cultural systems of all time, having created the most colossal system of scientific and technical competencies resulting in the greatest productive capacity in the history of humankind.[21] Furthermore, although it has expressed very little concern for the lack of substantial social relations in North American secular life and ideology, modern industrial capitalism has produced an enormous infrastructure that interprets and disseminates these ideological views in the form of various foundations, study groups such as the American Manufacturers Association, the Chambers of Commerce, and promotional corporations, not to mention lobbying groups at the capitals of states, provinces, and federal governments. The average business manager/owner is normally a participant on various levels. In the end, one cannot help but be impressed with capitalism's system of research, organization, finance, production, distribution, and marketing.

Theoreticians from Adam Smith on have spawned theories and propositions that interpret and justify the modern industrial capitalist system. Adam Smith, the master architect, is well known for his reasoned treatment of the underlying social reasons and goals of the capitalist enterprise. And one only needs to note how much of Marx's material for *Das Kapital* came from the proceedings and activities of the British Parliament to appreciate the close relationship between knowledge and politics.

Milton Friedman, Ayn Rand, and Friedrich Hayek number among the American intellectual heirs of the British liberal capitalism inspired by Bentham, Locke, and Smith. They all championed an extreme form of laissez-faire capitalism. Hayek, for instance, maintained that social and economic planning by a society, especially its government, would lead to oppression and totalitarianism. "Economic control is not merely control of a sector of human life which can be separated from the rest; it is the control of the means for all our ends."[22] Hayek continues to believe that absolute individual freedom is the key to social happiness. "Our freedom of choice in a competitive society rests on the fact that, if one person refuses to satisfy our wishes we can turn to another."[23]

But the powerful ideology of classical capitalism deeply entrenched in the thinking and acting of the capitalist class is coming under attack. In a hard-hitting book on the ideology of managers, *The Ideology of Work*, P. D. Anthony said that the traditional belief of capitalists—that workers should accept the interpretation that they should work for the capitalist on his or her terms—no longer suffices.[24] An enlightened management has emerged in response to this situation which has been given the job of making submission more palatable.[25] "In business enterprises that depend upon the co-operative effort or at least upon avoidance of a withdrawal of effort of many thousands of people, some effective appeal is necessary. . . . It seems likely that management is inescapably committed to the pursuit of cooperation or to overcoming what it perceives as alienation."[26] Managers believe they can overcome this alienation by manipulating the workers to accept the legitimacy of their goals. According to Anthony, "The legitimacy function . . . is primarily directed at securing recognition and approval for managerial authority and the way in which it is used; it is concerned to achieve social approval and it is associated with claims advanced in management thought that it is based on socially acceptable values."[27]

To summarize, we have what Weber called *consumer capitalism*—a form of capitalism based on an ever-increasing level of consumption of commodities and in which a large urbanized industrial labor force produces these commodities in factories. Agriculture is mechanized, and we have a society of producers, distributors, and consumers of commodities administered by rational bureaucracies. The alienation Anthony documented is the modern worker's separation from the traditional peasant culture that was destroyed to create the English working class.[28] The United States and Canada have proved a fertile soil for this new form of capitalism and class organization in which individuals are administered as units from a central bureaucracy, producing, distributing, and consuming "commodities."

Enlightened management has become concerned about humanizing the workplace so the worker will also accept ideologically the individualism that is *de facto* reality. The problem of the working class is not with the ideology of individual initiative and private gratification—this is an Anabaptist concern—but with the *perceived* nonavailability of the rewards for individual initiative, private gratification.

Anabaptist-Mennonitism Versus Individualistic Liberal Ideology

Evelyn Kallen and Merrijoy Kelner studied Canadian ethnic entrepreneurs and reported in their book *Ethnicity, Opportunity, and Successful Entrepreneurship in Canada* that there are common characteristics of successful entrepreneurs among the ethnic groups. Their evidence showed the following traits or goals: dedication to hard work; a love of work; a high need for achievement; the challenge of risk taking; the confidence to persevere; emancipation from tradition and the courage to be innovative; and a drive for personal freedom and self-determination.[29] Do Mennonite entrepreneurs conform to these traits of the ethnic entrepreneur, or is there something distinctive about the Anabaptist-Mennonite ethos which channels their behavior and beliefs in a distinctive manner? Do they in fact reflect the ideology of modern industrial capitalism? How do they rationalize the management ideology of trying to convince workers to adopt the values so they too will work harder?

Our contention is that individualistic liberal ideology does not totally motivate Mennonite entrepreneurs. This is not to say that Mennonite entrepreneurs see a contradiction between their Anabaptist-Mennonite tradition and business. When entrepreneurs were asked, "Did your Mennonite tradition prove advantageous to your career or contribute to your success?" 86 percent replied yes, and only 14 percent said no.[30] Answers to the open-ended question, "How did your religious background help you in your career?" included honesty, integrity, dependability, practicality, and other similar qualities. This ethic is peculiarly compatible as well with the North American frontier ethic in which all of the material resources of a continent were made available to whoever had the initiative and the resources to exploit them. And this ethic has become the Mennonite pattern for success. The last frontier is closing rapidly, and the Mennonite community will have to learn to live in relation to its larger cultural context or continue to lose its brightest and best.

Anabaptism offers the hope of an alternative basis to individualism as a model for the larger society. The Mennonite community produces entrepreneurs as a function of its needs, much as the ancient *oikos* produced its merchant class to serve not only itself but a ruling community as well. Anabaptism thus challenges the individualistic and utilitarian ethos underlying capitalism as the only reasonable solution to the problem of the economy. The ethos of *Gelassenheit* locates capitalization in the larger context of a community mediating between the individual and the market economy and state.

Risk Taking with Community in Mind

The entrepreneurs interviewed by Redekop (RER) spoke to this possibility. A very successful developer and financier, for example, provided some good insights:

I was with a family firm—very conservative, very cautious. These are excellent attributes, and I think I've inherited a lot of them. But as a young man I looked about and saw all the opportunities that I felt our family business was not exploiting. I became restless, and consequently I started pushing for expansion. Then the company decided against it. I left the company. I looked around, went to [city] and [city], and wound up in [province]. I was fascinated by building, developing, and dreaming. There was no end of possibilities. You could be turning, loading, and unloading, and slowly start amassing and building something for yourself and your children. This gentleman came to [city] and started building for someone else. In very short order he became extremely successful and had a tremendous portfolio. This guy really struck me positively. He took me by the hand and he employed me to do several contracts for him. We became very close friends.

The basic reason for my drive and success was the values I learned at hone in the family business—being honest and doing your homework, knowing your product, or knowing what you are talking about. I really enjoyed people, and I think that is very important; but number one I think is to know your product and be confident. There was never a lack of confidence in my family. I think we had a type of pride in what we do. We held our heads up because we felt that the German language, culture, and music were good. I worked hard, but I was not a typical high roller type of salesman who would sort of bamboozle or fast talk people into doing business with me. I have been very happy with the work I have done. My family thought I would come back, but first of all I had my own pride in that I wanted to achieve something and do something on my own to prove to the whole clan back home that I can do it on my own. I'm the son of a Russian immigrant. When I came to [city] I said, "I'm going to get right in there and swim with the best of them. I can cut it as well as the next person." And we did it. [Upon reflecting upon my success] I thought that this effort was human egoism, but I thought [upon reflection] that this is one way of creating legitimate wealth so that I could endow the fantastic institutions that [the church] has. It is a kind of vision I have. I'll stay and die a Mennonite.

In this case the lofty goal of serving the church with the bulk of the proceeds of the entrepreneurial activity comes through very clearly. The personal gratification and consumption appear to be taking secondary status, even though the personal satisfaction of achieving success is expressed as well. The test of whether the largess to the church will actually happen lies in the future. Assuming that this individual follows through and shares extensively, it would be a conscious rationalization of entrepreneurialism which is generally consistent with the commitment to collective goals and needs.

Interestingly enough, the primary threat to this rationalization of personal risk taking with the community in mind came from the community itself, as was evident in the interview. The respondent was already partially disappointed with the church, and this cast doubts in his mind as to whether the community indeed deserved to benefit from his efforts. If not checked, this distrust of the deservingness of the community may begin a new rationalization that carries a greater emphasis on self-actualization and self-gratification.

A second entrepreneur joined a Mennonite Church through friends, but he might be described as an evangelical church member. Reflecting his evangelical orientation (more so than his Anabaptist-Mennonite perspective), he seemed bent on a personal lifestyle that was rather extravagant. Through his work he developed an insurance brokerage franchise and other partnerships.

I started selling furniture door to door. I felt the Lord was leading me into selling, but all the people in the church thought we were out of our minds to go from a good, safe job into selling. I worked my way up from a salesman to a sales manager in a year. I have built my businesses by hiring salesmen and keeping them a long time and then putting them in school. So now I have salesmen who are working for well over $—— with us, and we promote the feeling that it's an association—they don't work for me—we are associates, so they get a piece of the action. I always believed that the greatest gift a person can give is to develop people. And probably, since I became a Christian at thirteen and being in Bible clubs and things like that, it's more of a ministry, and that is what has directed me.

I feel like the hiring practices are what has given us the advantage over others—if we give our word to our people we do everything to live up to that word.

I get a lot of satisfaction out of seeing people grow. I think the success is basically because of God's blessing and leading us to the right people. I get a lot of personal satisfaction out of work, of designing programs that give people financial protection, and seeing people develop and grow. I tell every salesperson that I hire that I expect more from a Christian than I do from an unsaved person. I expect them to work harder than the average person in the community.

This second entrepreneur did not emphasize the role of wealth accumulation in his thinking and activity. Nor did he really discuss the purpose of wealth. The importance of supporting religious relationships and maintaining an evangelical atmosphere reflects this entrepreneur's origins. He did emphasize that his reason for being in business was his concern for developing and helping people. Critics might argue that his expectation of more effort from Christians sounds a little like what Nietzsche called the *priest-lie*—that is, the abuse of religious authority in relationships to exert power or exploit someone. However, there is little question that his emphasis on others departs from the ordinary rationalizations of economic enterprise.

A third respondent became an entrepreneur almost by accident. He was a development officer in several church institutions before he entered the business world. Over time, he discovered a strong entrepreneurial urge that was not satisfied in these institutions. Innovation and risk taking were not his paramount incentives. When asked, "What satisfaction has your career brought you?" he responded,

Well, a sense of accomplishment number one. Number two, I think that we changed from [state] when we were there, and that's my whole philosophy of stewardship. I think you should leave the place improved wherever you are. In fact, we got confirmation of this shortly before we announced we were leaving. We got the people thinking that they did have a part in determining their future and helping themselves out. I was director of the Industrial Development board. I headed up the Red Cross fund drive. I was trustee for [a college].

I guess if I'd be honest I would say that I am happy only if I'm working, but working in some worthwhile business. Work is part of my ethic. You need to be engaged in productive activity to feel good about yourself. Work is not a moral thing. Work gives you a sense of worth, for your own good. My rationale for being in business is self-employment to make myself a success and help make others successful too. I helped make [a church institution] successful. I helped make [a church member] successful, and I made myself successful. We belonged to [a non-Mennonite Church] for three years, and we were bothered that there wasn't the emphasis on the biblical teaching as a guide for daily living—they were acculturated.

Interestingly enough, this entrepreneur was self-consciously aware of the acculturation that threatens the traditional Mennonite community. More importantly, he was interested in social issues and in the welfare of the community. Having worked in church institutions for a considerable time, he was concerned about ethical issues beyond his own ventures (which included a newspaper business). To reiterate his rationalization for entrepreneurial enterprise, "My rationale for being in business is self-employment to make myself a success and help make others successful too."

A fourth illustrative case involved a young college-trained financier, intelligent and articulate, one of the new breed of businessmen. He began his career as part of a father-brother team but quickly branched out into his own activities as well.

I've always loved business and partly because my father and brothers were in it. I got a double major in economics and urban planning, which I thought were appropriate for development and construction type of work. Economics really got me involved in watching the markets, and hence I also became very involved in the markets. The basic motivators for my success have been the grace of God, putting my knowledge to use, and the work ethic. When I say *work*, I mean lots of hours of work. My work now is mainly meeting a lot of people, doing a lot of communication with them, strengthening relationships. On some days [one of the businesses I am involved in] does as much gross volume as a billion dollars a day, and that's all done on a verbal basis. There is not another business in the world where so much paper moves around based on so much trust. It's unbelievable.

When he was asked about the source of his gratification in work, he responded,

Meeting a lot of nice people, meeting a lot of interesting people, traveling, the opportunity to meet some people and learn more about this business. There is a certain risk element in my work, and the whole idea is to manage the risk in the most classic sense.

Business is our family hobby. We talk about business like a lot of people talk about hockey. We actually consider it a form of leisure activity, toss it around, and talk business. It's great! Last year, for example, I think we looked at about sixty business opportunities and decided on one of them which would be profitable. But the intention is never to make a big, big buck quickly, but simply to get into something that would be useful and productive and then bring it to completion. You want to go into business with people whose philosophy you can live with. If they're out to lunch on philosophy you probably won't even get down to first base. My greatest gratification is working. I like working, and I enjoy being with people who like to work. The gratification of work is just the simple accomplishment beginning something and seeing it through to completion. I don't care about prominence, esteem, or recognition, but I'm very interested in security and advantage for my family and myself. That's why I go to work every day.

This entrepreneur comes close to the classical entrepreneurial motivation of seeing something succeed but minimizing the risk as much as possible by effectively utilizing all the resources available, especially other people. Yet there is something about him too which departs from the commonplace rationalization of economic self-advancement. Part of this difference lies in the fact that for him, the relationships with business partners, customers, and clients are based on a common religious ethos regulating economic life and relationships. This modern-day, college-educated entrepreneur assumes such a primitive or face-to-face family of trust to be the basis of life's actions. Otherwise, consideration of his obligations to the society at large and to the religious community did not emerge in the interview even though leading questions were asked. His case raises a number of interesting questions such as what will happen to the basis of trust necessary for a capitalistic economy to operate when Christianity is no longer functioning as a viable cultural force integrating the individual into a larger community's interests.

One of the most fascinating entrepreneurs from the Redekop interviews was a woman who became involved in business when her husband, a former missionary, became incapacitated, and she turned a hobby into a very creative and productive business. Her community concerns and interests led her to include a lot of people in her business and also to become involved in a number of social welfare activities.

I have always loved the earth, I loved mud. I think that's basic. A Mennonite artist came through the area and stopped to visit us, look at my work and said, "I think you love clay." Since I began doing these things [clay animals] and taking them to craft fairs, people responded to the little animals. By 1977, it was obvious that I had to move to larger quarters. People were coming day and night. The people who now work for me are part owners of the business. Two of my women make more than I do. My accountant thinks this is absolutely horrible that they're making more than I am. We have staff meetings on Thursdays when we make our major decisions. People thought I was crazy, and sometimes I think I am.

I have to keep creating new forms because the strength of the business has been the new designs and I do the majority of that. And people come every year and see growth, they see new developments and new designs, and they buy. My commercialization of my art was sheer economic necessity. With a sick husband and our little boys there was no other way. I didn't have any other marketable skill.

Right now I feel some uneasiness because the business has demanded so much from me. I'm caught in the middle between the demands of the business and my interests in the church and community needs. Last June I was just over-whelmed by the demands on me, so I just set down a lot of my responsibilities in the church. I don't have any offices now, the first time in thirteen years. Well, I know some people have felt that I'm too busy and too involved in other things, but I made a basic commitment that the profits of [one part of the business] should go into the Hopi project [an Indian rehabilitation project]. We set up specifically as a nonprofit entity. So my time that I put in over there is a contribution to the church in a larger sense.

From the beginning I had been very much committed to producing what people want. It's interesting work, therefore, and has been very much from within, an interaction between people and my creativity.

My business has been tremendously rewarding. A lot of my art pieces are based on my years of experience before that. I think that the timing and all that are beautiful, and it has brought a richness to these years.

I guess I have a little touch of the work ethic in me. I've taken some time this spring to just sit and relax. And so I'm learning, I think, now, not to be as driven as I have been at times. My drivenness was a balance I would guess between the need to care for my husband and the creative need. But I go out and work sometimes just for the sake of creativity. I was working out here late the other night, purely energized to create.

My one hope is that they each [her children] will find a way to contrib-ute to society in a positive way. They all have very human concerns. That makes me happy.

This woman's general religious and economic philosophy is fairly self-evident and needs no interpretation. Driven into the entrepreneurial arena by circumstances, she managed her business and nurtured her gift with a strong sense of who she was and what her commitments were to herself, her family, and to the larger community, including the church.

DIFFERING INTERPRETATIONS
OF ENTREPRENEURSHIP

Differences in beliefs regarding business can best be understood as instances of rationalizing. To say that people rationalize themselves, their lives, and their worlds is to say that they develop different ways by which they understand and present the truth. Rationalizing can be conscious, semiconscious, and/or unconscious. Thus, people sometimes consciously attempt to make a statement, proposition, event, or social condition appear to be reasonable, understandable, and logical. Other times, they are only partially aware or unaware altogether that this shaping of reality is occurring.

Rationalizations are steeped in ideology; they are rooted in a particular life situation, and they make sense from a particular vantage point. As Karl Mannheim described *ideology*, "The ideas expressed by the subject are thus regarded as functions of his existence. This means that opinions, statements, propositions, and systems of ideas are not taken at their face value but are interpreted in the light of the life-situation of the one who expresses them."[31] Thus, when discussing the rationalizations of people in the workplace, we can say that both management and labor are bound to their respective motivations or life situations.

In this chapter, we have explored how Mennonite entrepreneurs make sense of their business activities. Their rationalizations derive, at least in part, from those of their Anabaptist-Mennonite ancestors, who self-consciously took up a position *contra* the ideology and social practices (including economic) of both the traditional (Roman Catholic) and modern legal-rational (Protestant) forms of religious oppression. But, although their rationalizing bears the mark of their sixteenth-century forebears, it certainly does not duplicate it. Their own rationalizing activities have been confounded by four and a half centuries of intervening history, which has left them sandwiched between the conflicting points of view of the dominant culture (individualistic values) and the religious subcultures (communal values). In addition, the entrepreneurs' views of life and work are shaped by their unique biographical circumstances.

Rationalization of the Mennonite Church General Membership

Why do Mennonites as a whole and Mennonite entrepreneurs in particular hold the views of business and entrepreneurial activity which they do? Are their rationalizations conscious, semiconscious, or altogether unconscious?

The evidence suggests that Mennonites are, on the whole, aware of the traditional Anabaptist-Mennonite stance and, however vaguely, accept it and defend it. At times, however, their position seems unclear, inconsistent, unconvincing, overly traditional, legalistic, and even contradictory. This is not surprising because many if not all Mennonites are being subtly influenced by the values of the dominant culture and especially the culture of affluence and the good life. Most Mennonites, not just entrepreneurs, have seized its values and its logic. The very goals that the entrepreneur is singled out for holding and pursuing—wealth, power, and personal liberty—are held by many Mennonites. Yet so uneasy are most Mennonites with their own transition that these traits become a source of suspicion and disapproval. Thus, entrepreneurs and entrepreneurial activity are perplexing. Entrepreneurs are viewed—by congregation members, church leadership, and intelligentsia—as people who have stepped over the traces, and yet they are simultaneously admired by those who lack the talent, courage, or opportunity to do the same.

This contradiction among the conscious, semiconscious, and unconscious rationalizations of most Mennonites has produced some seemingly hypocritical behaviors. It is not uncommon, for example, for people who were strongly outspoken about the deviance of entrepreneurs in the early stages in their lives to outdo those they criticized later on with their own aggressive entrepreneurship. They may have merely parroted the indoctrination of the subculture until they recognized the inadequacy of its perspective—a common occurrence in conservative groups, and it is usually rationalized as apostasy on the part of the person who has departed from the faith. All too often people operate with a cynical interpretation of the *Gelassenheit* ethos into its *ressentiment* similitude: simplicity is turned into sublimated envy. As long as one is poor, one believes that it is not good to be wealthy. The holder of this particular ideology does not curb his or her own acquisitive impulses but merely rationalizes the failure to use them effectively.

Many Mennonites today still live with the conviction that the road to entrepreneurial success is strewn with serious temptations of self-love and gratification and in turn leads to a loss of spiritual bearings and of the sense of obligations to the community of faith and the human community. However, Mennonite identity itself has become so fragmented and heterogeneous that a concerted unconscious attempt to impose ideological constraints on the entrepreneur's social practices (such as would have been the case a century ago) is no longer possible.

Rationalization of the Entrepreneur

Turning to the rationalizations of Mennonite entrepreneurs, we might ask why they are so aggressive in their defense of orthodox Anabaptism. This seems an especially curious position for them to hold in view of the commonly held belief that they are more assimilated into North American culture, a supposedly open society in which the individual is coerced by mass media into leaving his or her group and culture and adopting the values of whatever belief system fits.

In fact, the entrepreneurs appear to be generally as convinced of, and committed to, classical Anabaptist beliefs as their congregations as a whole. This may not say all that much, for both groups may be assimilating at the same rate. But it does suggest that the entrepreneur cannot be singled out as more corrupt or compromised, challenging the credibility of the popular Mennonite myth of the corrupt businessperson.

We propose that the entrepreneurs' unconscious ideology is forced to become conscious because they are forced to apply it to situations for which they have not been taught the appropriate responses. Semiconscious rationalizations appear when the entrepreneurs use their religious vocabulary (Protestant Latin) to sanctify their sometimes shady business dealings. Self-consciousness, as always, is a matter of degree; and judgments can only be made in a relationship and in a context of accountability, neither of which is provided by social science.

Rationalization is a two-way street. The traditional Mennonite is brought up with a profound awareness of the dangers of the marketplace. The abuse of Mennonite entrepreneurs at the hands of fellow members' good faith and their use of religious vocabulary to justify their activities and to maintain a good front in the community are grapevine proverbials, modern-day myths that function to socialize the young into the community's mores as effectively as do the myths of face-to-face societies.

The other side of this street leads back from the marketplace, and the Mennonite entrepreneurs on it need not (by definition) be unconscious defenders of the North American capitalistic system; nor are they blatantly extolling the virtues of the innovative and risk taking (heroic) role that appeals to the immature or rationalizing the good that capitalism has brought the world.

The semiconscious rationalizations of Mennonite entrepreneurs are, without a doubt, the most interesting in many ways. They live neither in the innocence of total identification with the Mennonite community nor in the transcendental clarity of the Mennonite saint who has weathered the storms of life and the temptations of the flesh to stand firm as a model to the Mennonite youth. The entrepreneurs live in that nebulous world in which Bible stories and Hollywood productions are used interchangeably and unconsciously to rationalize the vicissitudes of experience. It is a world in which relative conformity is achieved through the incentive to live up to the models of traditional Mennonite saintliness, on the one hand, and through fear of falling victim to the stereotyping of the grapevine, on the other.

From the interviews it seems that the strongest rational defenses of entrepreneurialism are creativity, self-development, and being able to help others become themselves. Risk taking and innovation were often mentioned, but with less conviction and confidence. The question is, Why? Consider the satisfaction that entrepreneurs gained from employing others, providing security for them and their families, and helping others develop and become free and full human beings. Is the Mennonite entrepreneur proud of helping others because of a commitment to the Mennonite ideology of *Gelassenheit*? Or does this reflect subtle defenses of the values and the individualistic striving which are at the heart of the secular justification of the entrepreneurial and capitalistic system of our society? We would argue that it is a most creative and subtle synthesis of both worldviews. The Anabaptist concern for communalism and *Gelassenheit* is, according to the rationalization of the entrepreneur, given concreteness by helping others find jobs and become better persons, and all this can be done in the name of the highest ethical Anabaptist principles! Who would want to contradict this?

For some time Mennonites wanted to extend their concern for mutual aid and love to persons beyond the separated community so that charity and entrepreneurship are not necessarily in conflict. This is the position taken by Carl Kreider, who believed that "biblical teachings can be applied to the problems of the modern [economic] world."[32] Their actions could also be seen as merely reflecting the prevailing ideology of secular business which attempts to justify its practices and profits by trotting out the age-old truisms that, "After all, we provide jobs, security and opportunity for the masses." Philosophers and scientists maintain that this is a classic case of a conscious attempt to delude the masses into forgetting about their oppression.[33] To put it somewhat differently, it is possible (and some would certainly argue) that Mennonite entrepreneurs are using the classic Anabaptist communal defense of their participation in the market economy unconsciously to sell their participation to themselves as well as to the brethren who are, in reality, being exploited.

How then can we best understand the rationalizations of the entrepreneur? Look at one recurrent theme in the interviews: the ability to be free and creative and to make things happen is the real motor that drives the entrepreneurs and is their defense for being one. We believe this is a subconscious rationalization. Remember that the Anabaptist-Mennonite ideology emphasizes the importance of the subordination of the individual's personal motives and goals to that of the welfare of the collective. Property is for the possession of all, and the welfare of the others always takes precedence. The personal gifts and energies of individuals (work) are to be subjected to the norms and goals of the community, so that even occupation and lifestyles fall under the eyes of the collective court.

The promotion of the self, in whatever form, so that one becomes more prestigious or esteemed than others, is at the heart of the profaning of *Gelassenheit*. Menno Simons' diatribes against the flesh and private will become almost monotonous in their clarity and thoroughgoingness: "All who do not believe the Lord's Word would rather have money, property, body, and life than Christ. These are earthly and carnally minded . . . if they were ready to forsake possessions and all they have and are for the glory of the Lord and if they were ready to give it for the needed service of the neighbors . . . then they would undoubtedly not murmur so and dispute against God." [34]

The stress on the personal achievement of seeing things happen, like the centurion of Jesus' parable who said, "When I say go, he goes" (Matthew 8:9), "When I envision something it actually comes to pass," appears to the outsider as a rather clear case of having adopted totally the ennoblement of the individual and his or her personal achievements and realization so prevalent in modern society. This position could not be taken by Mennonite entrepreneurs if they were conscious of the diametric opposition of this to the traditional view. The entrepreneur who is consciously aware of the conflict between the two paradigms does not stress the self-realization, and the interviews bore this out. It has become clear upon close reading of the interview transcripts that the entrepreneur who was more traditional and communal did not stress the dimension of personal creativity.

Interestingly, the issues of innovation, achievement, organizing people, and taking risks—trademarks of the entrepreneurial track—were often mentioned and discussed in the interviews but were not as central to the Mennonite entrepreneurial spirit as true entrepreneurialism would lead us to anticipate. Most tried to minimize risk and did not bask in the headlines of success. This reflects the sane and sober Mennonite tradition of not gambling and wasting God's resources. Innovation was given more positive status and was often referred to as coming out of the Mennonite tradition of making do with what there was or was believed to be part of the legacy of a father or uncle who was the real tinkerer or inventor.

It is probable, therefore, that the discussion and justification of innovation, risk, achievement, and organizing people were not defended semiconsciously but rather reflected a simultaneous familiarity with a communal responsibility originating in a tradition and a recognition that it became necessary for Mennonites to become successful in the market economy to survive in North America. In other words, since persecution had already made innovation, risk, achievement, and organizing people a necessity for the survival of the Mennonite community on a smaller scale in a hostile and frontier environment, it is conceivable that Mennonite entrepreneurs in North America have been able to rationalize their exploration of the secular (cosmopolitan) marketplace, both unconsciously and self-consciously, as being oriented to terminal ends other than personal gratification. Thus, entrepreneurs from a local background can quite unconsciously rationalize their cosmopolitan activities as continuous with what they were taught as children.

This unconscious model of reality was assumed by many people interviewed by Redekop when entrepreneurship was mentioned in reference to behavior in the church. It was usually assumed that the businessperson's work was for collective goals. When the church members criticized risk, self-assertion, acquisitiveness, and other unbiblical activities it was because they believed that the entrepreneur was interested in personal gain. This unconscious collective representation forms the basis of the Mennonite community's acceptance of its entrepreneurs, local and cosmopolitan. Its antithesis is its semiconscious collective representations of the entrepreneur as the source of all the community's ills.

We turn, finally, to the decision that confronts all Mennonite entrepreneurs: do they try to serve both God and mammon effectively, or do they abandon their traditional values and beliefs to participate in and give allegiance to the liberal market economy? This choice reveals an ideal type that fuels the myth sustaining the Mennonite community grapevine. Given the highly indoctrinated and socialized Mennonite matrix that eschews entrepreneurship (at least publicly), it is doubtful that a faithful member could become an unconscious promoter of the liberal market economy. Those who have lost all credibility and the trust of their communities almost always leave the church. They are condemned by the Mennonite community as mentally ill or as having renounced their spiritual and moral foundations.

The situation of the entrepreneurs is further complicated by what sociologists call *compartmentalization*. The (relatively) self-conscious entrepreneurs recognize that they must live in relationship to a community that is mostly composed of members whose rationalizations are either unconscious or less conscious than their own. These self-conscious entrepreneurs realize as well that the biblical ideology of their upbringing is profoundly at odds with the secular assumptions of North American civil religion.

Realizing that they must live in both worlds and with people who would be horrified to associate with anybody even remotely acquainted with the beliefs of the other world, the self-conscious neoclassical entrepreneurs (economic, political, legal, aesthetic, academic) must adopt several ideologies to function socially, rationalizing the hypocrisy of various personas to function psychically. But this is not entirely new. Speaking in Greek and demanding the rights of citizenship from the Romans and then turning to address fellow Hebrews in Aramaic shows that the apostle Paul embodied both ideologies as well. He assumed both the role of cosmopolitan entrepreneur addressing the Romans and that of the ethnic-religious (local) congregation member when he addressed the Jews in their own dialect.

This, however, is as far as the psychological insights of the sociology of knowledge takes us. But knowledge according to the Hebrew wisdom and understanding means relationship, and relationship implies responsibility. The entrepreneurs' compartmentalization is only part of the greater context which all commit, and in which denial of the transgression finds its visible form in the entrepreneur becoming the scapegoat ("He who is without sin, let him throw the first stone"). This unconscious (unconfessed) rationalization becomes the source of the alienation of the businesspeople from the Mennonite congregation.

Individuals and families on the business and entrepreneurial tracks are placed in a special box and are isolated by default from the general life of the church. The Mennonite Church has developed practically no infrastructure for organizing the business/entrepreneurial interests, not to mention relating them to the larger life of the church (i.e., making the reality of the business world and its impact on the believer's everyday life self-conscious) even though the business/entrepreneurial segment would like to see this happen.[35]

Compartmentalization of belief systems functioning differently in different contexts has brought about a crippling effect on the Anabaptist doctrine of the conformity of practice to the profession of faith. When the world of religious practice is in a different box from that of professional or business practice, it becomes impossible for the religious ethos to function socially. Such compartmentalization is only possible if both congregation and entrepreneurs are engaged in semiconscious rationalization, driven by motives only held consciously in part, and reflecting unconscious internalization of prevailing values espoused by the larger American value system.

Because both entrepreneurs and the congregation/community as a whole are unconscious of the larger forces shaping their social destiny, both are forced to act instinctively and rationalize their actions semiconsciously. One aspect of this level of existence (*Verstand*) is that someone needs to be blamed for the unexplained ills that befall the individual/community existing at this level of consciousness. Consequently, entrepreneurs develop an unhealthy resentment for the church, which they find judgmental and dogmatic. Likewise, the church is suspicious of the entrepreneur's innovations, especially in a context when it is losing its authority in the members' lives and having its jurisdiction reduced to sovereignty over a mere compartment as a result of assimilation to the modern world.

CHAPTER EIGHT

Mennonite Faith
and Economic Ideologies

Mennonites have developed a compulsion to rationalize (especially in moral terms) all actions to the tiniest detail and to engage in actions that will be defensible when the inevitable (and final) interrogation occurs. The result is a plethora of rationalizations running the gamut of economic action and causing ostracism and schism, bannings and hard feelings, sometimes for generations. The irony is that these rationalizations and the community's response to them are tied to discussions of ethics. It is, in fact, impossible to exaggerate the importance of ethics in the life and testimony of the Anabaptist-Mennonites. Throughout their history, Mennonites have sought above all to be holy, pure, and obedient to Christ. It was this condition that prompted J. Lawrence Burkholder to state that "examination of the Anabaptist vision with its almost exclusive preoccupation with ethics . . . would reinforce the conclusion that the Christian life is defined most basically in ethical terms."[1]

In spite of this, many Mennonites show little self-awareness. Our argument in this chapter will be that the mechanisms of Mennonite social control are so overpowering that people's understanding of the fundamental purposes, beliefs, and ideology of the Anabaptist-Mennonites must remain unarticulated and derivative. This is a problem in all traditional societies whose continued survival is premised on coping with a known environment (ecosystem, social, and spiritual as well as natural in the modern scientific sense) according to the accumulated experience of generations. Traditional beliefs expressed in traditional ways carry individuals through the cycle of their lives, and the meaning of those beliefs and people's consciousness of themselves in relation to them remain elusive.

For Mennonite cultural critics such as Burkholder, this is troublesome. As he said, "In view of the consuming desire of Anabaptists and Mennonites to live ethically . . . [it is] strange that no American has written to date a Mennonite ethic as a separate theological discipline."[2] As Burkholder implied, Mennonites take their ethics seriously but have no rationally operating system of ethics, no hermeneutic to contextualize their strict biblicism for the modern world. Therefore, they must respond to their situation instinctively, naively, and intuitively. Partly because of compartmentalization and partly because the Mennonite ethical framework is shaped by their church and community, the traditional ethic has found unconscious expression in the judgment of gossip that condemns the deviant in the absence of strict church discipline.[3]

In this chapter we propose to determine the Mennonite theology and ethic—the ideology that is expressed by the entrepreneurs who attempt to remain faithful to their Mennonite heritage while practicing their beliefs in the world. We can only approach the unconscious collective rationalizations held by the congregation as a whole by examining the semiconscious rationalizations the entrepreneurs devise to reconcile their beliefs and practices with their fellow Mennonites' expectations. This requires first an analysis of ideology and then the application of our general findings to Mennonite experience, for whether the Mennonites are naive biblicists or possess a theology, ethical aspects figure strongly in all the discussions.[4]

A DEFINITION OF IDEOLOGY

Ideology is one of those sociological terms that has found its way into the popular consciousness and popular discourse. In its commonsense usage, it is often associated with falsely held beliefs. Although some sociologists use the term in much the same fashion as the so-called person on the street, others have used it somewhat differently and with a more precise definition.

1. Ideology refers to a schematic image of the social order. In this definition, there is the possibility of conscious or unconscious distortion of reality, but it is only a secondary concern and almost irrelevant to the concept.[5] Stated another way, but conveying much the same idea, an ideology could be said to be "an attempt to develop a consistent and logical

understanding of the social order."[6] This definition is especially useful in situations that are inadequately expressed in traditional terms.

2. Ideology refers to a "comprehensive, closed system of ideas."[7] This definition comes closest to the one that people use in everyday parlance. *Ideology* in this sense is often associated with the views of the extremist and is reserved for descriptions of the ideas of utopian visionaries (such as Robert Owen) or despots (such as Adolf Hitler).

3. Ideology refers to "the distorted or selected ideas in defense of the status quo of a social system."[8] Associated with the work of Karl Marx, *ideology* in this sense is used as an instrument of reactionary warfare, to defend a system that is considered desirable and hence to oppose all attempts to change it. Marx referred to the capitalist system as an ideology of the powerful and wealthy to keep the proletariat in subjection.

4. Ideology refers to "selected or distorted ideas about a social system or a class of social systems when these ideas purport to be factual, and also carry a more or less explicit evaluation of these 'facts.'"[9] This fourth definition is more democratic than the others in that ideologies are available to and used by many rather than a few.

Our interest in ideology is to clarify Mennonite explanations of their participation in the economic order. In this analysis we rely heavily on the first definition of ideology, being aware that elements of the other three definitions, especially the notion of both conscious and unconscious distortion of ideas, certainly have a bearing on how people understand the world around them, their place in that world, and their relationship to others. This understanding of ideology is probably more closely related to structural anthropology's concept of *mythology* and the Jungian archetypes than it is to its usage in American political sociology.

Ideologies (there are obviously more than one operating at a time) ensure conflict because they are derived from differing commitments and differing social situations. Holders of any given ideological perspective can and will accuse holders of another of bias or of promoting false (which can mean *wrong* or *immoral*) ideas. In addition, disputes over ideology lead people to action. As Gary Schwartz observed, "Ideologies are ideas which move men to action. Religious ideologies tell men how to achieve salvation. . . . For the believer, then, religious ideologies accurately portray the forces which affect his spiritual welfare and, at the same time, point to a safe way through the diverse contingencies which might prevent him from reaching this goal."[10] Ideologies also function to reduce what the social psychologists call *dissonance*. As Schwartz put it, they function to "reduce the uncertainty which surrounds action undertaken in perplexing situations."[11] Finally, an ideology works in the present, and its credibility is grounded in its ability to demonstrate solutions to what at first appear as insurmountable problems. Ideologies, therefore, afford their adherents increased instrumental control over a hazardous natural or social environment.[12]

In *Communism in Central Europe* Kautsky moved from the superficially conventional Marxist definition of ideology to this deeper sense, touching on the essentially religious core of human culture.[13] He observed that "a class or community . . . hopelessly trodden down by others, will always oppose itself to the knowledge of truth. It will not use its intelligence to define clearly that which *is*, but will try to discover arguments by means of which it can pacify, console, and—deceive itself." Kautsky argued that because the knowledge of the Renaissance (Roman law, Greek mathematics, Italian bookkeeping) served the interests of the ruling classes, "the more the poor and oppressed thought they understood what was the truth, the more wretched must they have deemed it. . . . They began to detest the newly dawning culture, which did their tormentors such good service, quite as much as they hated the beliefs of the Papal Church, which they were attacking. They turned away from the miserable and comfortless reality, and . . . arrived at a belief in miracles which finally developed into a faith as firm as a rock."[14] The Anabaptists thus forged a new ideology—mythology, or cosmology (*ideology* is here used in a manner consistent with the first definition)—because they rejected the ideology (used in a manner more like that advanced by the third definition) of the ruling class, church and state alike.

Of course, the situation of Mennonites today has changed. Old Mennonite ideologies, which reflected a traditional communal ethos in a world that was a mosaic of such ethnic religious communities, no longer fit the modern individualistic society into which North American Mennonites have been thrust. Like many other ethnic religious communities, Mennonites have responded by creating ideologies that tend to rationalize their own problems in such a way as to treat the entrepreneur as a scapegoat. Such ideological responses do not, of course, directly deal with the challenge these communities face: to confront realistically their new circumstances and the new situations in which their members find themselves.

Participation in the mainstream economic sphere is one of the greatest accommodations the Mennonites have made to the modern world. This accommodation demanded that they adapt an economic ethos that once functioned in a closed, self-sufficient, agrarian village economy to a new situation in which its members must compete as individuals in an impersonal and secular market. The meaning of communal solidarity—when the community of faith is no longer the community of economic production and consumption—has therefore undergone a drastic devaluation. The entrepreneurs, who are on the cutting edge of this devaluation, are singled out to assume blame unjustifiably, since nobody can really be blamed given the impersonal nature of the money economy.

Our interest here is to discern how Mennonites in general, and their entrepreneurs in particular, rationalize their necessary involvement in the market economy when Mennonites historically have rejected any ethical responsibility to the larger world, or society. According to Burkholder, they "cannot accept the Responsible Society as a comprehensive ideal without denying their own presuppositions." [15]

THE ECONOMIC IDEOLOGIES
OF ENTREPRENEURS

The reasons people gave for choosing their careers (see Chapter Seven) tell us something about how people make sense of the string of decisions they have made. Their reasons, to return to the first definition of ideology reviewed above, reveal their schematic order.

When entrepreneurs were asked to elaborate their paths to business, their stories tended to cluster around four different thematic types. [16]

Taking Over the Family Business

Those who fell into the first of these thematic types spoke of taking over a fledgling family business (often with other siblings in the family). This was the most prevalent type of entrepreneurial venture in the Redekop sample (RER). One entrepreneur took over a small family-run cabinet shop and expanded to a larger market. Another discussed his reasons for pursuing entrepreneurial activities as follows:

My initial vision was to put together a team of people that I knew had very good mechanical skills. Dad always enjoyed making a new piece of equipment for our farm operation. But there was never a chance to move that invention to the public, to refine it, and make it a winner. The [number] of us brothers have responded very cohesively on what we want to do. We originally started the company doing repair business. Although we had a vision of building [a line of machines], we repaired machines and discovered, "Hey, we can do something about that problem, we can do it better." And so in the product area, that is how we moved to the present. Dad would have never started a business. We brothers and Dad obviously created strength and technical skill. There has been an intense desire to make it go, which means working many long hours, it means taking home less pay than our own employees have taken home sometimes. There have been failures. It has been fun, to see the business grow, and we've grown between 20 and 110 percent every year since we started. Our ability to meet community needs, like providing employment, has been very rewarding. I sometimes think people don't understand what it takes to employ people. When I see families that are making something of themselves, when an employee is learning something from us, and going on to greater things, I feel good about that.

Expanding and Differentiating a Family Enterprise

The second thematic type included people who developed a business either directly or indirectly related to the family economic life. One farming family began a small motor repair business and developed it into a manufacturing business. Another entrepreneur, representative of this second type, reported,

I started working in the family business. It was in product "x" and in the servicing of some of the products. The family business was facing some internal organizational problems so I bought part of the business from the family in 195 . We changed the course of the business from an —— product base to a North American and European market-oriented business developing, producing and marketing ——, ——, and ——. A series of events happened to allow the business to change so dramatically. Certain members of the family had different ideas and interests. And as the interests changed, I took more of it over. For reasons of capital and market, I sold the —— parts of the original business and got into —— and —— business. There are now still fragments of the old business, but very few. I think my unique contribution (to developing the business) was processing the changes that needed to be made, making adjustments for the coming changes before they happened, and being ready when the changes took place in the market and being ready with the products. I changed the business to what I thought was a trend and a needed area. Thus we also developed some offshoots. That was where my career started and developed. If I had had more education early in my career, I would say I would have made less mistakes. They were made because of my lack of perception of the total world of business and what it took to make a business work. I certainly would do the same thing again, though. The rewards I have gained out of this business are the satisfaction of being able to create, to develop new organizational relationships as well as products. It goes beyond the material satisfaction. The creation of jobs has not been a major source of satisfaction. I don't think I have the same sense of purpose my father had. His purpose was a strong commitment to help his friends, to help them achieve a higher level than he himself was. Maybe you could define that as religious community; in any case, he really believed in it.

Personal Initiative

A third type of career path was for individuals to work for someone else, gain experience, and then launch their own business. One such person worked for a cabinet shop and then left his employer and began a shop of his own. Another representative of this third entrepreneurial path said,

I started as a parts man, became manager in six months, and worked there until 197 , when I became a commissioned salesman for the —— division of the company. Even though selling was very difficult for me, I decided it was psychological, which indicates how stubborn I am. After three months, and without any income, I started writing deals, and I never looked back. Being on commission, I really did not have to answer to anybody, I was successful, and I think I was blessed. But when you have a position where you have to produce, you are always dependent upon somebody else's whims, ideas, and restrictions. If they don't like you, you may not be required. Then the company was sold to a larger company. I thought this was the time for me to go out on my own. While there were many rewards, there were very many concerns and difficulties as well. But we are in business now for ourselves and have just completed our —— year. The last years have been better than earlier, and we're looking forward with courage. There are very large operators in my field, and we have considerable competition. The problem is, when everybody thinks you are doing well, there are eleven others who then try to get into it. We have a new approach in that we try to work directly with the customer and try not to oversell. There is an awful lot of stuff being sold to people that they really don't need, and yet it costs them horrendous sums of money. If a man wants to get rid of his money, I'll be the first to help him; at the same time, you have to live with yourself. I guess I never consciously planned to go into the career I am in now. I guess I sometimes questioned the methods of my boss. Often the customer felt he had been had. That was one of the things that bothered me. That may be why I have not been as successful as some people feel I should be, but I like to have the customer satisfied so that he tells me he's happy he got a fair deal.

The Self-conscious Entrepreneur

The final thematic type, and the least prevalent of the four, includes those who self-consciously launched an enterprise without any previous experience or connections with the industry. This type is probably the most salient for our analysis. Representative of this thematic type, one entrepreneur recalled,

Oh, I was interested in doing business when I was twelve, selling —— made from salvaged —— . I had the whole neighborhood of kids working, and they were getting from three to five cents an hour. While I was in college I was already looking for an area in which I could work as a developer. I graduated *summa cum laude* with a BA degree supplemented with a BS degree. I am an overeducated entrepreneur, since I completed four majors in college and don't really need any of them to do what I am doing. My doctorate in [profession] allowed me to practice for —— years. I picked [state] for my scene of operations for several reasons. First, the economy was expanding there, with similar investment opportunities available in [where he started]. Further, there was an extensive Mennonite settlement; hence, I could stay close to the brotherhood.

I am the chairman of everything, the sole proprietor, the sole decision maker. I'm the president of [a list of companies spread over a half-dozen states]. We are dealing with pretty massive ventures. I was influenced a lot by people like my father, and Roy Vogt, editor of the *Mennonite Mirror*. They worked with the public welfare in mind. Well, I'm not quite that philanthropic or altruistic. I suddenly realized that I was very good at business, I was beating [businessmen in several business sectors] and all the assorted vultures at their own game, and I was doing it on the side [since in the beginning he was still working at a profession]. It was a hobby, and I realized all of a sudden, "Wait a minute, I can do it because I really think the deal through before I do it." And I thought that if you created wealth through legitimate means you could endow the wonderful institutions [church] that we do have. That dream has faded slightly because I have gotten so close to the principals in some of our institutions and I see so much infighting and backbiting that I don't know why I am supporting them. I am doing it because I have momentum. I still have my will ordered that if I die there are substantial endowments to five categories of institutions. But I think many entrepreneurs [Mennonite] are losing that sense because we are not as cohesive as we used to be. But I'll live and die a Mennonite. This joy of giving and the love of involvement in the economy and even a certain measure of risk are what motivate me. But also to build the kingdom. You can't get away from it. Kreider was right; your vision should be to build the kingdom because wealth is transitory, and you will leave it behind. Humanly speaking, there is no reason to amass wealth. I read all the biographies, starting very young in life, of the major successful philanthropic people, including the Eastern establishment, from the Rockefellers to the Zuckermans. I knew what they did, I knew the empires they built. I started out thinking negatively. And I have been challenged in Sunday School and at social events, and in general, about how much does a person need. That has never impressed me, because that is not the objective [goal], you go after the challenge. There is a big difference in motivation for the challenge of it and for greed. This is not understood by people in general, but the entrepreneur understands it. I'll tell you how it sorts out, the entrepreneurs who are motivated by greed are bankrupt, they all overreached, they all had to have the last dime.

PRINCIPLES OF MENNONITE IDEOLOGICAL TYPES

The above material provides us with a set of ideologies of the world of business. These, like all ideologies, should not be seen as organized or fixed. On the contrary, they are four emergent approaches to the creating or constructing of an ideology for business activity. In other words, they are works in progress.

Keeping in mind their emergent quality, Mennonite economic ideologies do reflect the gradations of Mennonite rationalizing with regard to the emergent economic ethic. They also reveal coherent principles which, in the minds of the entrepreneurs, govern their economic activities.

Principle 1: Doing Business Activity Because It Is Necessary

Mennonites engage in business—whether farming, blacksmithing, repairing, building, manufacturing, or whatever—for the same reasons most people have always been active: because it is obviously necessary. When Mennonites do business for this reason, there seems to be little criticism of it. In other words, from the most traditional to the most high-risk entrepreneur, there is little thought given to the legitimacy of producing food, building a house, or repairing or building a better and more advanced machine. The use of technology for the efficient pursuit of elemental needs is not questioned, and there is no need to defend it. In this respect, it is evident that Mennonites—or at least their entrepreneurs— have adopted the general societal value of goodness and the necessity of maintaining it.[17]

Anabaptist-Mennonite society has never really challenged the validity of natural existence and human life. Mennonite theology assumes that human existence is a consequence of God's will; therefore, consumption to exist is good, and as a consequence it is also good to produce things for the "good life." Early Anabaptists were involved in all types of occupations and industries, even though there was considerable control of material existence and the quantity and types of production and consumption. Agriculture, in recent centuries evaluated as the most sacred occupation,[18] was not theologically sanctioned per se but became so through the persecution of the Reformation period.[19] Although Mennonites have not questioned the business of living, there have been and still are stringent norms directing and controlling the specific types of economic behavior, and it has been expressed in Mennonite life in copious detail.

Principle 2: Business as a Form of Mission

Entrepreneurs of all types express this rationale. In this perspective, business is seen as a way of helping other people, in the form of providing jobs, which are assumed to be the basis for livelihood and sustenance, as discussed in Principle 1 (although there is rarely a direct allusion to the way in which jobs provide food and clothing, evidently because of its obvious connections). Business as a mission is expressed most often in terms of the ways in which business can help people develop their own abilities, their opportunities to move on to higher and better things, and their opportunities for greater fulfillment.

Because some Mennonites are so deeply indoctrinated in steward-ship, the idea that business allows them to support the work of the church and the building of the kingdom of God is even more important. By providing financial resources, they are helping in the mission of the church.[20]

The ideological principle of business as mission moves beyond the first principle by emphasizing that producing is good not only because it provides a livelihood but also because it contributes to the employment of others, to their development, and uses material gains for the collective and heavenly kingdom. This principle assigns a greater role for business in the design of society and in the sacred system, contributing to its fulfillment. Although entrepreneurs are not theologically sophisticated in articulating this principle, there is the tacit assumption that when business is done for the church, it has consecrated meaning.[21] Not all Mennonites share this ideology. To many, the mere suggestion of business as mission would represent the highest form of falsehood.

Principle 3: Doing Creative Things as Self-expression

In this third ideological principle, the focus is on subjective, personal, and internal elements. To varying degrees, this principle is evidenced in all four types of entrepreneurs. In all there is a motive of doing what one can do, likes to do, and has a special penchant and talent for doing. The type 1 entrepreneurs—those who take over a family business—do so because they think they can do a better job than others. Type 2 entrepreneurs—those who expand or differentiate a family enterprise—are stymied and start their own businesses, believing they can run them more effectively and more honestly. The third and fourth types sense their personal worth and want to express their personal resources and abilities.

For the entrepreneur who adheres closely to this third ideological principle, there is often less allusion to the religious dimensions of business. This is not to say that they fail to see God's hand at work. Success is an expression of God-given abilities and is not questioned. Those interviewed by Redekop offered no apology for their gift of doing business well, although the humility theology that runs through Mennonite life was almost always apparent in them.[22] Reports of success were accompanied by the proviso that "I did not really do it, rather it was a blessing of God."

"Doing what we were made to do," may be the best way of expressing this principle. Mennonite theology has always stressed the principle of the priesthood of believers, which teaches that all members of the body of Christ, not just the clergy or the ordained, are partners in the building of the kingdom of God. Hence all vocations (within the given ethical restrictions) are equally legitimate and important. To use God-given abilities is consistent with Mennonite and biblical teaching. The parable of the talents, even though not focusing on secular activities, is clearly an informal support for the expression of individual abilities and gifts and is often used in Mennonite discourse,[23] even though Mennonites have not often contemplated work and vocation outside the context of building their community.

Principle 4: The Challenge of Making It Happen

As with the previous three principles, this fourth one operates at some level in all four entrepreneurial types, but most often in the self-conscious entrepreneur. It focuses on the objective factors that need to be accomplished; terms and phrases such as *markets, products, future opportunities, outsmarting the competition, managing and organizing the personnel,* and *goal achievement* are paramount.

Notice that there is an external structure or reality "out there," and the entrepreneurial response is to accept and conquer it. The secular world sets the parameters, the justifications, and the criteria for responding.

There is little allusion to the religious elements or the churchly restraints on the way the situation is perceived and handled. When discussing how the church reacted to his pursuits, one self-conscious (type 4) entrepreneur said, "Mennonite communities generally don't understand it because the Mennonite entrepreneur is rather rare. Many people question what I do, but my defense is, if I don't do it, the other guy will, because I am competing against all the rest of the —— that are surely going to do it, and much more unethically."

Strong materialism, greed, and selfishness are not necessarily expressed in this principle, nor is there a great sense of personal ownership and worth. In this principle, what is important is the response to the external challenge, not the social status it will provide. The power incumbent with wealth and success may be enjoyed, but it is probably secondary and not expressed overtly, most likely because of the universal value of social concern, the Mennonite ethic that discourages personal egotism and boasting, and the importance of humility and piety. The universalistic values and Mennonite beliefs would doubly discourage them from a conscious gratification from power. We will discuss the subconscious aspects of this ideology below.

Remember that the self-conscious entrepreneur we quoted earlier mentioned the importance of the Mennonite beliefs and norms regarding business ethics. This and other apparent contradictions should not come as a surprise or as a challenge to the principle, since nowhere is there an assumption or requirement that ideologies are, or should be, totally consistent and coherent. Nevertheless, it is safe to say that considerable secularization of the Mennonite faith principles has taken place. As Burkholder said, "The Mennonite ideal, on the other hand, is the ideal of the separated few who despair of making the world Christian as a whole." [24]

One additional note regarding the purity of the entrepreneurial ideological types: we have been analyzing them as though they were fully represented by individuals in real life. They are not. All four principles are present to some degree in the various individuals. The constructed ideal type is a theoretical manipulation of data, not an empirical reality, but it is useful for isolating and examining each specific factor.

ECONOMIC IDEOLOGY AND THE MENNONITE COMMUNITY

Are the ideologies that Mennonite entrepreneurs hold merely distortions of reality which suit their vested interests? Or, are they field testing ideologies that will ultimately come to serve the schematic understanding of all Mennonites?

Entrepreneurial Ideologies as Vanguard

A strong case can be made for the latter position in that Mennonite entrepreneurs are developing/presenting a rationale for moving into a social field for which there is little precedent or experience. Of course, if Mennonites remained in the traditional economic activity, there would be no need to develop new rationalizations for economic life. Objectively speaking, there is little question that more and more Mennonites are moving into the entrepreneurial realm, and thus there is little question that those who have pioneered the business world have something to say to those who follow.

Anthropologists and sociologists have long been concerned with the disintegrating effects that cultural contact with modern capitalism has had on traditional belief systems. The experience of Mennonite entrepreneurs in North America gives us an opportunity to look at this cultural disintegration anew. Cosmopolitan capitalism is not endemic to Mennonite tradition, nor are the Mennonite entrepreneurs unconscious of the stress between their chosen professions and traditional perceptions and expectations. Rather than succumbing to the pressures toward anomie or any of the escapist solutions that many other North Americans have embraced, Mennonite entrepreneurs are struggling to build a synthesis that expresses *Gelassenheit* in the modern world.

Mennonites are experiencing a societal and cultural transition from an agrarian and communal tradition to an individualistic and capitalistic one. Going beyond the Mennonite ethos was unnecessary in a rural agricultural structure because its ritualistic embodiment was its own justification. But as Burkholder noted, "The Mennonite community is a partial approach to the problem of Christian culture since it has been limited to agrarianism." [25] That Mennonite life has changed and requires new ideological justifications is not really at issue. The only real question is whether or not Mennonite entrepreneurs are their vanguard and are the ones most clearly articulating the change.[26]

Entrepreneurial Ideologies as Distortions of the Mennonite Ethos

There is the distinct possibility that the entrepreneurs are expressing rationales that are at odds with the interests of Mennonites as a whole. One could certainly argue that their ideologies are conscious or unconscious expressions of systems of distorted ideas promulgated in defense of a status quo. Thus understood, Mennonite ideology would be defined as defending a new interest—Western capitalism—rather than updating traditional core values.

The Mennonite belief system has been informed by both communal and religious impulses. Any attempt to treat the free enterprise system (with its emphasis on individualism and secular rationality) as being in harmony with Mennonite tradition must deviate from orthodox interpretation and commitment. It is apparent that entrepreneurs of the second, third, and fourth types would support the proposition that Mennonites are seeing the larger secular economic system not as off-limits but as an open and legitimate area for exploration and conquest.

The apology of economic entrepreneurship in the face of the traditional Mennonite rejection can be defined as an ideology in which distortion or an attempt to legitimize a certain system is being promoted for the benefit or interests of a particular group of people. One need simply consider the cases of the representative entrepreneurs we presented above. The second, third, and fourth entrepreneurs—to an increasing degree—illustrate the plausibility of this proposition. In each of their cases, no questions are raised about the legitimacy of the values, norms, and institutions operating in the larger world, the main point or goal being to be able "to get into the fray and succeed." The argument offered by some entrepreneurs—"If I didn't move into this field, someone else would and do a worse job"—defends a situation based upon a strange and secular normative system. Their ideologies are not directed toward the world outside the Mennonite community, but rather at the orthodox inner community itself. If the rationalizations of Mennonite entrepreneurs are understood this way, there is a clash of worldviews which confronts Mennonite beliefs, ethical schemes, values, and symbols.

The Truth Lies Somewhere Between

The question of the source of this new ideology is of central importance. That the entrepreneurs are the pacesetters of the acculturation process is probably not exclusively so. Many other dimensions operate in the adoption of the secular value system by the general membership: education, creative arts, lifestyle, and religious fervor.[27] The Mennonite community is undergoing a socioeconomic and a value shift, and the entrepreneur is one of the most visible sectors. No doubt the Mennonite community is also increasingly infused with the values of the larger society, and ideologies—seen as representing distorted or vested interests—are observable everywhere, as entrepreneurs and others move into the economic mainstream. In this process it is also possible that the Mennonite ideology appears more in harmony with the host society than was previously assumed.

As we saw in the early chapters of this book, the economic actions of Mennonites are increasingly varied and disparate. The movement of Mennonites into the larger community is continuing apace. Although ideologies supporting entrepreneurship may have been necessary and more prevalent in the beginning of this acculturation, one would expect that there is less and less need for them as more community members become involved in the world. Simply put, an acculturated community no longer requires a justification for behavior or an accounting of deviance, since deviance is no longer as clear.

A word about the relationship between ideology and belief is probably in order. Here Schwartz is helpful: "From one perspective, we can see the potent effect theologically based models of social reality have on the believer's orientation to his mundane affairs. . . . On the other hand, it is equally true that religious ideologies are congruent with the status preoccupations and economic aspirations of their followers."[28] Schwartz directed his attention toward the Seventh Day Adventists and the Pentecostals and asked, "What psychological tendencies dispose some people to opt for belief systems which sustain either optimistic attitudes toward personal success in this world coupled with marked cosmological pessimism [Seventh Day Adventism] or pessimistic attitudes toward future success in this world coupled with marked cosmological optimism [Pentecostalism]?"

For the Mennonites, one might ask what psychological tendencies dispose some of them to select belief systems that sustain the communal authority over economic behavior and some to accept the values of the competitive society. The interaction of the belief system and mundane existence dictates which ideological type will develop. The critical psychology is probably that to which Weber referred. But Schwartz concluded that Mennonite psychology is unlike Weber's. "Commitment to a sect ideology not only reduces the sect member's uncertainty about his place in the social order but also delineates the praxis that decisively resolves it."

Although individual psychological idiosyncrasies might affect the sect member's receptivity to diverse ideological appeals, "nevertheless, it is important to remember that in the process of adopting a comprehensive religious ideology, the sect member acquires a vocabulary of motives that may be only tangentially related to the needs that initiated his quest for a sacred vision of reality." According to Schwartz, "Therefore, any explanation of ideological commitment that views sect affiliation as the product of the actor's needs alone will overlook the ability of sect ideologies to generate the psychological dispositions and motives that sustain their unique patterns of conduct."

In any search for the sources of ideology, then, we are confronting the issue of group cohesion and the maintenance and change of group identity. Group identity is defined here as the belief and symbol systems that have served as the basic cohesion of the Mennonite subculture and have long been maintained by geographical and social isolation, limited interaction with the larger environment, economic and cultural autonomy and self-sufficiency, and even persecution by the larger societies. "It has long been recognized that a social collectivity is held together not only by the basic premises to which its members adhere and the institutional arrangements these premises generate, but also by the manner in which these internal properties and outside forces impinge on one another."[29]

Research on attempts by religious or ethnic minority groups to retain their own faith and accompanying ideology in the midst of larger societal forces presents an almost uniformly dark picture. Ethnicity and modernity appear to be incompatible. "The fate of the Amerinds, the many immigrant groups, such as the Irish attest to this fact."[30]

Perhaps most instructive for an analysis of Mennonite self-conscious survival is the Jewish community, also a religious as well as an ethnic minority. Edgar Litt proposed that North American Jews have three alternatives before them: absorption, adaptation, and antagonism.[31] The acculturation of the Hebrew-Jewish community has been a history of self-conscious survival as well. This community has been remarkably involved in the economic life of the larger society, as Ezekiel's intimacy with commercial and nautical terms attests.[32] Although a mass of material is available on Jewish enclavic life in Western society, few studies contain material that is useful for our comparison. An exception is the study of Jews in Great Britain, reported by Harold Pollins.[33] The story of Jewish entrance into British business is very typical. The first Jewish entrepreneurs were merchants within the Jewish community, with peddling and shopkeeping as the major activities and the basic services directed toward Jewish community needs. Then Jewish merchants developed specialty services and products, which catered to outsiders, and slowly emerged in the unusual trades such as finance and trade.

Their ultimate entrance into the higher echelons of British trade and finance materialized by the beginning of the twentieth century. The most important factor, Pollins concluded, was the immigrants' motivations: "sobriety, temperance, frugality, willingness to defer gratification, and commitment to education. . . . Such ambitions did not necessarily include an escape from the Jewish world. In general they maintained their religious culture, however modified, while acquiring a British one."[34]

Pollins felt that the impact of the entry into the entrepreneurial world could not be fully assessed yet, as Jews begin to question whether there is a danger of the inner dissolution of Jewish solidarity. In a survey conducted of Redbridge Jewry in 1978, Pollins stated, "A large majority of parents, in answer to the question, 'What careers would you like your children to follow?' stated, 'Whatever they want.'" The authors of the survey commented, "Redbridge Jews do not want to push their sons into industry and commerce . . . there appears to be a concern with the quality of life of their children."[35]

The Jewish community has managed to survive the "destruction of most of the Jews of Europe, the end of the . . . distinctive community life of the Jews of the Soviet Union" through "the powerful and assertive Jewry in America."[36] Of course there have been enormous casualties along the way, but the core of Judaism has held.

Striking differences are evident among the Mennonites. First, Mennonite society has never been able to adapt to the urban centers, nor has an urban critical mass developed a strong cohesive core of tradition. Second, its religious and ethical centers, normally rural, require that the actions of the group be religiously based and justified. The Mennonite community "has been able to perpetuate itself only in agrarianism."[37]

The attractiveness of the secular world, especially the power it brings, seems too seductive, especially since the Mennonite community is so isolated and small that it cannot give individual members the recognition and security the Jewish community can give its members. Simply put, a Jewish entrepreneur would not need to accept an ideology that defends capitalism to become involved in it, since the concept of the *Goyim* justifies the dualistic concept of being in the world and benefiting from it, but not of it. A Mennonite, also steeped in a dualistic tradition, finds it much more difficult not to adopt the values of the world since the Mennonite community itself is not sufficiently strong and large to provide the security of an in-group retreat.

A Mennonite Case in Point

In summary, here is the experience of an entrepreneur who became deeply involved in a successful and growing manufacturing business.

I got into farming by helping Dad. I worked with Dad until [my wife and I] got married, then we rented a farm close by. We worked hard, rented more land, and finally bought all the land we farmed. Then in 1958 we moved to [city] to allow our children to go to college. I put my application in at the [company name] corporation and began as an assembler. Then I got involved in this small company which needed assemblers. The company needed reorganization, so they finally elected me as president, after a lot of turmoil. I could see better ways of making the whole process work, simply by trial and error. It was very interesting, it wasn't that I had any background in manufacturing or anything else. I really had no intention of getting deeply involved. Our farm was doing well. But you know, when you just come up [move in from the farm] and are working in a company, you put yourself and your money in as well. The only aim I had was to put some money in the company so I had some say in it. I did not have any experience with financing, and when the company started getting into the millions, it was nice to have some good bankers in the local community to work with. A lot of the reason for my success is the opportunities that came along and the timing. When we got into [company], we were just at the right time, and the personality conflicts at the plant were also influential. I think timing and opportunity just happened to come our way. I think I am a relatively conservative person, I don't like to take risks, but I don't look the other way when opportunity knocks, either. I never planned on getting into manufacturing. I didn't plan on doing anything other than farming. It is nice to be successful. I think I probably get the most satisfaction out of seeing new products develop. Something that you need, something that does a little better job out there for the customer, something that's really useful, a good product. I don't particularly like the power of being a president of a company. I feel rather the opposite, the feeling of responsibility for the livelihood of the people who work for the company. When you give them the kind of wages they need, it is more than a feeling of power, it's the responsibility.

This entrepreneur and his family left the farm in 1958 and never returned to it, although they continued to own it. The children have all left the farm and are either working at the company or are self-employed in businesses of their own. The family is actively involved in the Mennonite Church. The rural ethical ethos is still operative in the entrepreneur's ideology. But moving from a prairie farm to a manufacturing town so his children could have a college education set in motion factors that surprised him. There was little economic pressure to become an entrepreneur, and his desire was to provide advanced training for the children, which motivated the move to the college town. But economic forces were in the background. Only one of the five children could inherit the family farm, and the other four children would need an opportunity to grow on their own. The ideology of entrepreneurialism is somewhat vague in this case, but all of the factors of developing an apology for moving *into* the world and thus becoming *of* the world are there.

From the point of view of a sociology of knowledge, this family adopted an attitude toward the scarcity of land predicated on consumer capitalism, the dominant ideology of American society. That this entrepreneur could remain faithful to and a benefactor of the Mennonite Church while taking from it the determination (destiny) of his own life and that of his family presents a contradiction deserving sociological scrutiny.

PART III

Theoretical Reflections

CHAPTER NINE

Sociological Paradigms and Mennonite Economic Sociology

What are the implications of the portrait of Mennonite entrepreneurs which we have presented? What lessons are we to learn from their experience, their struggles, their ambivalence, and their accommodations? Addressing these questions will be the primary objective of the final two chapters. Reexamining the treatment of Mennonites in various theoretical paradigms, in the light of the historical experience of Mennonite entrepreneurs, will provide valuable insights for sociological theory and may well set new priorities for the sociology of religion.

THE WEBERIAN INTERPRETATION

Anabaptist-Mennonites and the Protestant Work Ethic

One of the most significant economic analyses of Protestantism and Mennonites is Max Weber's *Protestant Ethic and the Spirit of Capitalism*. Although the thesis is relatively simple, its qualifications and assumptions are so intricate and sometimes convoluted that simple characterizations become treacherous. Furthermore, *The Protestant Ethic* was written as an introduction to the studies of the world religions, making it both tentative and foundational. According to its thesis, a new form of capitalism was created by the events of the sixteenth century, beginning with the discovery of the New World, the translation of the Bible into the vernacular, the invention of the printing press, the Protestant Reformation, and the dawning of modern national states and economies.[1]

This new form of capitalism, characterized by Weber as *rational capitalism*, was unique in that it replaced religion as the organizing principle of social life. Economic activity was given an independent secular existence by the teachings of Calvinism, which stressed work for its own sake. Work was a sign of submission to, and glorification of God, whose sovereign will determined the fate of one's soul. Hence, total application of one's rational resources was an indication of faith in God. Because the accumulation of wealth was not the goal of work, and its enjoyment was condemned, the building of a surplus capital was an inevitable outcome; wealth not selfishly consumed thus became available for reinvestment.

Keep in mind Weber's insistence that there is no direct connection between Calvinism as described above and the encouragement of capitalism. Calvinism was not a theological (ideological) system that directly condoned (rationalized) capitalism. Weber knew full well that Calvin and his successors were as stringent as any others in the repudiation of avarice, accumulation, and indulgence. Weber rather maintained that it was the unconscious psychology created by the religious ethic of the Calvinist Reformation which set the ideological stage for the rise of capitalism. For Weber this sober bourgeois capitalism with its rational organization of free labor was the central problem of "a universal history of culture." Qualifying his interest as one in cultural history (a most significant qualification), Weber defined his problem as "that of the origin of the Western Bourgeois class and its peculiarities, a problem which is certainly closely connected with that of the origin of the capitalistic organization of labor, but not quite the same thing" and added that it is "a question of the specific and peculiar rationalism of Western culture."[2]

This submission to asceticism, with the Protestant Reformation, moved out of the cloister and subjected entire national populations to the discipline of work. More specifically, Weber observed that what God demands is not labor in itself but rational labor, in a calling.[3] The result was the production of profit as by-product rather than as a goal in itself, an understanding originating in the Hebrew worldview of inner-worldly asceticism.[4] Crucial to this materialistic development in the West was a suitable spirituality, different from that of the Eastern philosophies. Weber found one such distinction in the discipline of work emerging from Christian monasteries in the West. Replacing monotonous, repetitious, mind- and body-dulling forms of labor was a concept of creative labor emerging under the influence of the Hebrew world-affirming spirituality. Weber proposed that Protestantism, beginning with its Calvinistic expression, provided a "psychology" of capitalism.[5]

Rational capitalism—as opposed to its traditional counterpart that assumed a traditional rate of profit and traditional means of production of traditional quality and quantity of goods, employing traditional (i.e., patriarchal) forms of labor—required a new psychology/ideology because new opportunities made old conceptions and relationships obsolete. The result of the Protestant Reformation was a complete revolution in social ethics, carried to its logical conclusion by the development of Calvinist, Pietist, Methodist, and the Baptist sects. In Weber's estimation, Luther held fast to the traditional, communal values of medieval Europe, and with the Calvinist ethos began the modern spiritual individualism that lashed back into the heart of Lutheranism to create such a figure as Kierkegaard.

Enter the Mennonites. Weber noted that the closest connection between ethical religion and rational economic development—particularly capitalism—was effected by all the forms of ascetic Protestantism and sectarianism (such as the Mennonites).[6] For Weber, Mennonites should have been consummate capitalists. The paradox of Weber's dialectical analysis is that, except for the Dutch, the Mennonites became (and had already become by the time Weber wrote) the exact opposite of this depiction. But even here, the master of qualification equivocated: his interpretation of Calvin was that the believer best glorified God through service that was social, in the world. It was expressed by "labour in a calling which serves the mundane life of the community."[7] Our clue to resolving this paradox is that Weber wrote about *religious economic ethos* and its relationship to capitalism in India, China, and ancient Israel. He discussed capitalism in Mesopotamia, Egypt, Greece, and Rome in *The Agrarian Sociology of Ancient Civilizations*. Furthermore, Weber wrote from a pagan—Platonic—backward-looking perspective, and he considered the secularization of the Protestant religious ethos an accomplished fact. Weber really needed to explain why, given his broad world-historical brush strokes, he included in his sketch of human destiny a group that existed only as a world-historical curiosity.

Again, excluding the Dutch,[8] the only material basis of Anabaptist complicity in the destruction of traditional European culture was that they were willing to lay down their lives for the religious liberties enshrined in modern constitutions. The tragedy is that these liberties are not so enshrined on the basis of an enhanced spiritual consciousness, but on a secularism that has doled them out from the perspective of tolerant indifference to all religion. The excesses of North American culture and empire so foreign to the Hebrew spirit and culture are the obvious results that Weber did not live to see. But he would have recognized Mennonite participation in some of these excesses, sanctified as religious orthodoxy even though this individualism originated in fifth-century Greece, spread through the Mediterranean world, crept into the Bible (notably in Ezekiel and Ecclesiastes), and ultimately became a stone in the foundation of European Christendom.

Paradoxically, Weber attributed the liberation of the acquisitive impulse—whose importance for the emergence of modern capitalism he assumed—to the development of "the ascetic conventicles and sects . . . [that] formed one of the most important historical foundations of modern 'individualism.' " As if to clinch his argument he concluded that "only the methodical way of life of the ascetic sects could legitimate and put a halo around the economic individualistic impulses of the modern capitalist ethos."[9] Central to Weber's thesis was the individual calling in which the person faces God alone: "For everyone without exception God's Providence has prepared a calling, which he should profess and in which he should labour . . . a fate to which he must submit and which he must make the best of."[10] Fatalism and a personal confrontational attitude toward one's deity originated in the Greek tragedies, which shaped the pagan psyche. Biblical humans delighted in their God and in their calling together with the entire community.

The final element in Weber's assumption that the Baptist sects were the supreme bearers of the capitalist spirit was their voluntary nature. The motivation and the discipline to fulfill the goals were structured freely, whereas in the state churches—including Calvinism—they were externally imposed and "enforced a particular type of external conformity, [which] in some cases weakened the subjective motives of rational conduct." So important was this factor to Weber that he included the Mennonites among the foremost proponents of capitalism: "the connection of a religious way of life with the most intensive development of business acumen."[11] Weber believed that the Baptist sects "accomplished the religious rationalization of the world in its most extreme form."[12] By *rationalization* Weber meant the culmination of the disenchantment of the world which began with Hebrew religion.

The Critique of Weber

Most scholars have uncritically assumed Weber's description of the Mennonites and analysis of the sects. In fact, most researchers simply lumped the Baptist sects (including the Quakers, Church of the Brethren, Mennonites, and some Baptist groups) in with the other streams of Calvinist influence.[13] One notable exception was Estel Wayne Nafziger's article, "The Mennonite Ethic in the Weberian Framework." Nafziger analyzed the Weberian thesis as it applied to the Mennonites and suggested similarities between Mennonites and Calvinists in the areas of inner-worldly asceticism, attitudes toward wealth, the concept of the calling, and the rational pursuit of economic gain. In these areas Nafziger found Weber's description to be adequate.

However, discrepancies within the Weberian model concerned Nafziger. First was that Weber's thesis failed to explain how a group—supposedly capitalist and originally urban—should have become and remained agrarian and relatively modest in capitalistic accumulation. Nafziger proposed that this happened since the Mennonites consciously remained rural and resisted accumulation because of their Christian perfectionism and primitivism. By this, Nafziger meant that the absolutist view on love and nonresistance could be propagated in the urban setting, and therefore the Mennonites placed more emphasis on religious principles than on economic achievement. Christ's teachings on love and nonresistance are at the "heart of the Christian ethic."

Nafziger also criticized Weber's analysis for not recognizing adequately "that high religious and ethical standards of works and conduct may mean a withdrawal from some worldly activity, instead of a vigorous pursuit of worldly activity." Nafziger argued that although religious asceticism can make a strong contribution to capitalistic striving, some of the traits that entrepreneurs need, "such as shrewdness, emulation and a drive toward power, are less compatible with Christian perfectionism."[14] Our view is that this criticism of Weber fell short of the mark. It ignored the critical Weberian distinction between Hebrew inner-worldly and Eastern other-worldly asceticism. Weber argued that the biblical tradition was critical for modern *rational* European bourgeois capitalism because it provided the secular worldview that modern science needed and the world affirmation that modern acquisitiveness required to justify its project.

Nafziger addressed another weakness: the lack of an achievement motive among Mennonites. To bolster his position, Nafziger made the cogent point that the Mennonite low need for achievement derived from strong conformity to community and congregational norms. Why should Mennonites who feel they are the people of God accept the success standards of what they perceive as a wicked and perverse world? Although

Nafziger did not state it so directly, his implication is clear: the individual consciousness that Weber assumed to be present in ascetic sects is simply not there in Mennonite groups. A collective reality and goals are the operative norm for Mennonites; this is in direct opposition to the individualistic striving of capitalist Christians.

In fairness to Weber, it is possible that he understood some of the contradictions within Christianity (and Mennonite ideology) far better than we have been led to believe by his interpreters. As many students of sociology know, it was Talcott Parsons who presented Weber to the American readership and who suggested that Weber equated rationality with economic advantage.[15] Marianne Weber's biography of Max Weber disclosed a dimension of his thought which his published writings do not. She added a level of complexity of which English language scholarship is pretty well unaware and gave us a view of Weber's thought which is diametrically opposite that of Parsons. She noted,

Weber mercilessly illuminates what most modern Christians . . . do not want to see. The central ethical postulate of any religion of salvation is *brotherhood* [italics in original] as a force of selfless sacrificial community and of human solidarity generally. An increasing tension develops between it and all kinds of purposive and rational [*Zweckrational*] action concerned with the expanse of cultural values. And beyond this there is even more tension in relation to the irrational forces in life—the economy. . . . But the most basic and most conscious tension exists between the religions of salvation and the realm of *thinking cognition*.[16]

If Weber truly appreciated the tension between brotherhood and *zweckrational* action, then his understanding is particularly salient to our current project and proves helpful for understanding the ambivalence of Mennonite entrepreneurs concerning the capitalist impulse.

Perhaps a more fruitful way of looking at the issue—more, that is, than asking whether Weber was right or wrong—is to consider the Mennonite experience in North America in terms of whether the unique economic ethos Weber overlooked has found expression in post-Weberian North America or whether it has degenerated and polarized into a *ressentiment* ethos on one side and into capitulation to modern individualism on the other. Psychologically, this would mean addressing the question of whether the Mennonite self-consciousness has regressed from its attitude of *Gelassenheit* or whether Mennonite consciousness of individuality has also become consciousness of group relatedness.

Finally, before we leave Nafziger's critique of Weber, we must keep in mind that Weber's *Protestant Ethic and the Spirit of Capitalism* essentially lamented the loss of its religious ethos, whether pagan (Niezsche's pre-occupation) or Christian. And the bottom line as to whether Weber was correct is the point at which the Mennonite ethos no longer influences their economic activities. Mennonites can only prove Weber wrong existentially by living in the light of his projections, as a future to be avoided. And, at this level, we are convinced that Weber—unlike Jonah—would be happy to be proved wrong.

The Amish Case

It is interesting that Nafziger's article elicited little social scientific reaction, but research on the Amish reflects similar concerns with Weber's analysis (although Nafziger is not cited). Gregory Appling's careful study of the Amish society convinced him that Amish doctrines —like the potlatch societies of Benedict's *Patterns of Culture*—"generate anti-individualistic pressures, and provide justification for the periodic redistribution of accumulated wealth." Quoting Weber's thesis at length, Appling stated, "This general argument does not apply to the Amish case." He attacked the central idea of the voluntary motivation for asceticism by stating, "The doctrine of voluntaristic society of saints actively promotes homogeneity among the Amish." Since salvation is derived from the "suffering community" rather than individualistic striving, "they must work constantly to preserve their communal way of life and their individual orthodoxy within that lifestyle."

Appling proposed, contrary to Weber, that the Amish rejection of political activity does not direct their attention to economic accumulation. Rather, it focuses the energy and attention to the immediate community and its religious reality. "For them, as for other inner-worldly ascetic Protestant groups, religion permeates the political, economic, social, and even aesthetic spheres." [17] Separation from the world thus forms the basis for the nature of their entire life and forms a psychology different from that of the prevailing society.

It is not that the Amish are uninfluenced by the larger world but rather that the norms of the community are constantly applied to evaluate and reject those forces that are interpreted as inimical to the Amish way of life. Hence the importance of the *Ordnung* and the ban becomes understandable. The many internal tensions, excommunications, and schisms that have characterized Amish life attest to the profoundly important dynamic that is experienced. Thus, it has been argued that although the

Amish are one of the most conservative and traditional sectors of the Anabaptist-Mennonite society, they express in many ways the more "authentic" essence of the group.[18] But it is an authenticity that may be relatively antiquated and irrelevant—a historical curiosity in many ways. It is an authenticity still wrapped in the swaddling clothes of its European, sixteenth-century expression.

The Hutterite Case

The Hutterites, an Anabaptist-Mennonite group, have received considerable attention, especially regarding their economic activity. In the most intensive research to date, John W. Bennett provided an in-depth study of Hutterite life. Although he analyzed most of the Hutterite social institutions, he concentrated on economic issues, including production, labor, management, and technology. It is surprising that the Protestant work ethic idea received only one brief reference. "The Hutterian social order provides a fresh perspective on the key elements of the 'Protestant Ethic.' . . . The Hutterites seem to feel little need to achieve, but they certainly are given strong incentive to do well . . . for the good of the group they are taught to forego their desires for the good of all."[19] Bennett concluded that "the Hutterite case illustrates the fact that very strong incentives to produce, and, if not to 'achieve,' at least to perform well, can arise in a social system that negates individualism. . . . The Hutterites exemplify the theory that strong incentive can exist in social systems that suppress individualistic competition and aspiration."[20]

The conquest of individualism emerged constantly in Bennett's analysis, and it appears to be central to the Hutterite maintenance of a system at odds with the general society. According to Bennett, there is considerable suppression of individual desires, and a latent source of conflict is continually present. He concluded that the Hutterites handle individualistic drives by a system that includes "(1) a normative denial of differentiation and competition; (2) a latent belief that individualism will out, because of imperfect human nature; (3) an instrumental need for differentiation; and (4) an effective mechanism for eliminating or mitigating the effects of these needs."[21]

The General Conference Case

A study of the General Conference Mennonite Church, conducted by Leland Harder, also suggests some of the limitations of Weber's analysis when applied to Anabaptist-Mennonites. Based on figures collected by conferencewide research, Harder demonstrated that when compared with the U.S. population the General Conference Mennonites were under-represented in the proprietor, manager, and officer categories (5.4 to 8.8 percent) and overrepresented in the farmer and farm manager (31 to 4.1 percent) and professional and technical worker categories (15.9 to 11.8 percent). This overrepresentation in the service area is corroborated by the Kauffman and Harder study, in which Mennonites were overrepresented by 32.6 percent to 14.5 percent.[22]

Harder pointed out that as the Mennonites leave the farm, they do not choose entrepreneurial activities but rather embark on service and professional pursuits that are more compatible with the *Gelassenheit* ethos. This choice, as well as the fact that the Mennonites share "certain Calvinist traits of industry anti thrift," put them on a path that does not lead to the accumulation of wealth. Harder concluded therefore that "Max Weber's theory of the Protestant contribution to the rise of capitalism is at best only a partial explanation [for Mennonites]."

The best explanation for the Mennonite avoidance of the entrepreneurial and accumulative track, according to Harder, is that there must be a connection "between the Mennonite preference for the service professions and its value system."[23] Rempel's occupational study of Winnipeg Mennonites showed that of those entering professional careers, 32.8 percent chose teaching, 12.3 percent nursing, and 7 percent social work, with the remainder distributed among accounting (9.2 percent), managers, and the ministry (no percentage breakdowns for the last were given). The Mennonite emphasis on *Gelassenheit* and the ethic of love constrain the members to seek the welfare of others before their own, expressed in this context through the service professions.

The Applicability of the Weberian Thesis

In the end, we must conclude that Weber's analysis of the Protestant work ethic is applicable to the Anabaptist-Mennonites in its most general terms: they participated in the overthrow of the traditional authority structure and economy and could only flourish in a polity that practiced religious toleration. Whether they can be placed at the end of a continuum stretching from Calvinism to modern secularism is as tenuous a contention as it is serious. The diversity within the Mennonite family makes it difficult to draw any one conclusion about all Anabaptist-Mennonites. Also worth bearing in mind is that Weber only addressed the Baptist sects—of which the Mennonites formed one group—and to press his text for accuracy of detail or judgment reveals very quickly that he was expressing hunches. Recent scholarship has uncovered a sufficient number of empirical and theoretical peculiarities specific to the Mennonites to warrant a unique conceptual scheme for describing and understanding them.[24]

THE SECTARIAN SOCIAL DEPRIVATION/ DISINHERITANCE THESIS

Almost simultaneous with Weber's development of the Protestant ethic thesis, Ernst Troeltsch developed the church/sect typology. Troeltsch's theoretical understanding afforded a different interpretation of the sect type group's involvement in worldly affairs. Although Weber used this distinction, it has no bearing on the Protestant ethic thesis. The communal/individualistic economic ethos was not divided along church/ sect lines but followed a continuum from the traditional to modern. In contrast to Weber's theory of continuity, Troeltsch's thesis derived partly from the assumption of a sharp, economically and socially based distinction between church and sect. The sect type represents an expression of the lower classes to economic motivation. A. T. Boison, following Troeltsch's original suggestion that the sects tended to work from below while churches worked from above, tried to show that there is a direct correlation between the economic conditions and the number of sects that emerged.[25]

This idea has recently been elaborated in the common man orientation that obtained during the Reformation, especially in connection with the Peasant Revolt in Germany.[26] The common man motif is a development that, like Kautsky's Marxism, takes social and economic considerations into account. It is important that this aspect of Mennonite history receive fair attention in the face of the historical revisionism that some are proposing under the label of evangelical Anabaptism, which emphasizes the other-worldly doctrine it shares with the rest of Christendom, including verbal conformity to highly ritualized expressions of personal belief in the received dogmas, but all too often without any deeper understanding of the ethos of brotherhood essential to Anabaptism. This is a problem (as we have seen from Marianne Weber's estimation of Max Weber's thinking) that is endemic to modern Christianity. Exponents of the other present strident social revolutionary action as the defining Anabaptist theme. As Packull said, "Early Anabaptism sponsored by Hut, it may be argued, fed on resentment against the rich and powerful. Initially, the hope remained alive for a reformation of society that would benefit the broad mass of ordinary people."[27]

Both antinomies contain vital elements of truth. Mennonite religious ideology—especially the aspect of an adult confession of faith to attain full membership in the community—is the basic reason Weber considered it a contributor to modern individualism. And modern, as opposed to Greek, individualism means the liberation of bodies for the labor market. On the other hand, before dismissing the Marxist consideration of social and economic conditions we must remind ourselves that the society of medieval Europe was one church family, uniting all classes of society by a communion, as Weber pointed out. Religious revolt, no matter how pure the rhetoric, became *de facto* social and economic revolt. Church, state, and family subsequently became separated in part as a result of the Protestant Reformation. Thus, religious affiliation or preference does not affect family relations or employment opportunities the way it did for the first Anabaptists who rejected the state communion, whether Catholic, Lutheran, or Calvinistic.

H. Richard Niebuhr presented the first non-Marxist analysis of the social deprivation thesis when he proposed that "sects emerge as the result of severe economic deprivation and . . . individuals will leave the sect as their economic conditions improve or the sect itself will change as its members acquire more wealth."[28] Niebuhr steered clear of an economic determinism of religion, but he maintained that social and economic forces determine the direction that religion will take.[29] Numerous other scholars have adopted this interpretation, including Elmer T. Clark, A. T. Boison, Thomas Hoult, Milton Yinger, John B. Holt, and Liston Pope.[30] Yinger's *Religion in the Struggle for Power*, a study of a community in the U.S. South, presented an extended argument of this view.

In essence, the social deprivation thesis suggests a frustration-aggression dynamic that sublimates the real object of aggression—namely, the controllers of wealth—at a religious level in which the goal becomes spiritual release and religious salvation. But the real issue is economic advancement and status. As they are gained, the sectarian rejection of the world is forgotten as the members, individually or collectively, achieve economic success and power. Hence "a sect is a place where religious status is substituted for social status."[31]

This thesis does not apply as well to the situation in North America because of the expanse of geographical territory involved. In North America, as Weber pointed out, sectarian religion functioned as the most important stabilizing element of pioneer society, which was otherwise volatile and lawless. In addition, the premise of the thesis is that as the economic conditions of the members of the particular sects improve sufficiently the sect becomes more denominationlike, or the members who become more affluent join other "respectable" (liberal Protestant) churches, forcing the sect to recruit new members from among the poor. However, the demographic reality is that the respectable or mainline churches are becoming less visible on the American scene and, as Wade Clark Roof and William McKinney demonstrated, are in decline.[32] Meanwhile, Mennonites and other sectarians are flocking to various Pentecostal churches, which have become very "middle class" in terms of social status.

The social deprivation theory has two dimensions, focusing on the collective sect group and *inheritance*, and the individual member and economic *disinheritance*. Let us consider these two dimensions in greater detail.

The Economic Disinheritance Theory and Old Colony Mennonites

Testing the theory on Mennonites proved to be a difficult task. This is readily understandable, given the tremendous complexity and variety of the group. However, several studies of Mennonite subgroups have emerged. The first was undertaken by Calvin Redekop on the Old Colony Mennonites, who live in Canada, Mexico, Paraguay, and Bolivia. Because it is a very small conservative group, the Old Colony Mennonites provide a manageable case study. Redekop concluded that "the Old Colony has in many ways retained the simple life. Individual farms are not much larger than they were when the Old Colony settled in Canada or in Mexico."[33]

Redekop noted further that there is economic striving and achievement among Old Colony members, but this means "specifically conforming to the norms of the Old Colony and its worldview."[34] There are some differences in economic achievement, but they do not affect the social or religious status in the settlement. There are, however, differences between geographical settlements, and these indicate that changes in economic activity or belief affect each other. Hence the Manitoba Old Colony group, which did not migrate to escape the world, became more affluent and in the process also became more liberal and worldly. But whether affluence created worldliness or worldliness allowed the influx of wealth is not clear. Redekop concluded that the economic disinheritance thesis must be rejected for the Old Colony taken as a whole, since the South American Old Colony settlements seem "to be working against economic mobility." [35]

Economic Disinheritance Theory and the General Conference Mennonites

Leland Harder's study of the General Conference Mennonites also included several chapters on the social disinheritance thesis. Using occupational statistics, Harder concluded that the General Conference Mennonites on the whole "have attained the rank of middle class." [36] Harder maintained that since the greatest majority of the Mennonites in the conference are "birth-right" members, there has been no influx of more wealthy converts, so the rise in the status of the group is a collective process.

The difficulty with Harder's premise is that he did not use a time-longitudinal study, so there is no indication of a change in the status of the sect over time, which is at the heart of the thesis. In other words, compared with earlier decades or periods, has the group in fact moved upwardly? In a subsequent study comparing General Conference Mennonites in 1960 and 1970, Harder identified a considerable increase in the percentage of professional and technical but a very small increase in the proprietor and manager categories over the ten-year period. Harder concluded that "we note a significant increase in the proportion of white collar workers and a corresponding decline in the proportion of blue collar workers in the General Conference. Obviously, a new day in the composition of membership in this Conference has arrived, having far-reaching implications for the total program of local congregations and the larger conferences." [37]

Harder's conclusions may be more consistent with the disinheritance theory than he thought. First, his claim that the General Conference of Mennonites has become middle class is exaggerated and is an expression of the American myth that "we are all middle class." Second, the rise in affluence which he documented could be explained by the normal upward mobility of the second generation of Mennonite immigrants. And, finally, although there can be no doubt that the Mennonite society has risen on the socioeconomic scale in the last decades, it is very difficult to separate this from the general rise in economic well-being in North America. Since the U.S. census does not provide information on income identified with religious or ethnic affiliation, it is impossible to establish any definitive baselines. [38]

The Disinheritance of Individual Membership

Even though Mennonite groups may not have collectively moved up the socioeconomic ladder, the basic theory also proposes that it is possible for individual members to enhance their status economically and thereby move up through the sect and into the more respectable denominations, illustrated by Assembly of God members transferring, for example, to the Presbyterian Church.

Does empirical evidence support this notion? In the Old Colony study, Redekop found practically no documentation of upward mobility on the part of individuals since there was no proselytizing and practically no defection, due to the strong community cohesion and discipline. He concluded that individual members rarely leave, and it is the well-to-do who stay, rather than the poor. Typically, a person leaves "because he can no longer subscribe to the way of life of the Old Colony."[39] Whether they are motivated by a desire for economic wealth or more religious freedom is not stated, nor is it very easily demonstrated. In any case, membership additions and losses are so minimal that the circulation of members into and out of the Old Colony society is practically nonexistent.

The Harder study came to very similar conclusions. Harder deduced that General Conference Mennonites have had very little defection and equally few converts and thus little transfer of membership into or out of the society. Since only 2.5 percent of the membership is of non-Mennonite stock, Harder believed that individuals did not move through the General Conference Church as a means of upward socioeconomic mobility.[40]

In a significant study focusing on Mennonite evangelization, John A. Hostetler reported on the education, occupation, and income of converts to the (Old) Mennonite Church as well as the defectors.[41] In all three categories, the converts ranked lower than the members who left. Like Harder's research, Hostetler's study was limited by the lack of longitudinal data.[42] However, in comparing the income of those who joined and those who left, the proportion of higher income members leaving is significantly higher than that of those joining.[43] This indicates that the Mennonite Church is more effective at reaching lower income groups. But because individual careers were not identified, the study did not prove that as the low-income members become more affluent, they abandon the Mennonite Church for a more prestigious or acceptable denomination.

Calvin Redekop's community study of Mountain Lake, Minnesota, did provide some longitudinal data. Redekop's research, which focused on the Mennonites, compared the values and practices in 1900 with those in 1950. In the socioeconomic realms, Redekop found that there was a substantial turning away from the cooperative associations that were operating in the 1920s, although the Mennonite occupations remained closely tied to agriculture. The financial habits changed, including more credit buying and less dependence on mutual aid.[44] Once more, however, there was little empirical evidence indicating how the socioeconomic changes affected defection from the Mennonite Church.

The Applicability of the Social Deprivation and Disinheritance Theories

We must leave the disinheritance thesis with the observation that, just as the Protestant ethic thesis accounted for some general features of the Mennonite landscape but did not address Mennonite reality's central features, the church/sect dichotomy only covered a smattering of Mennonite reality. Its greatest problem is its ahistorical orientation. Because it reflects what appeared reasonable to the liberal theologian and social thinker rather than historical reality, the dynamic of so-called sect type churches evolving into denominations failed to materialize. This was the case for the Mennonites, and it is probably true for the larger North American context as well. This ahistorical dogma is popular because it baptizes individualism and capitalism into the Mennonite communion under the label of evangelical (i.e., individualistic and capitalistic) Anabaptism.

ANABAPTISM–MENNONITISM AS A PRESOCIALIST REVOLUTION

Superficially, the thought and theories of Karl Marx would seem to have little, if any, connection with Mennonites. It is easy to see why one might take this view given that Mennonites historically have been an agrarian movement with no political or economic program. However, historical materialists have carefully analyzed the early Anabaptist movement and scrutinized some of its socioeconomic practices to reveal significant contributions from the Marxist orientation to the understanding of Mennonite economic life. Norman Cohn's *Pursuit of the Millennium*, for example, traced both Anabaptism and socialism back to Joachim of Fiore and the apocalyptic sects within Catholicism before the Reformation.[45] The historical basis for connecting Mennonites and socialist movements (a connection still resisted by Mennonites anxious to purge their heritage from anything remotely resembling socialism) lies in events surrounding the Muenster Rebellion and the Peasant Revolt—events that were intimately related to the essential Anabaptist movement.[46] In *Das Deutsche Bauernkrieg* (translated as *The German Peasant War*), published in 1950, Friedrich Engels first proposed that the Anabaptists were presocialist. He assumed that the Anabaptists were closely involved in the Peasant Revolt and proposed that these revolts were one expression of a change in the structure of economic production in Germany and that the feudal system was breaking down and with it the nobility's control of economic production.[47]

Karl Kautsky made a more careful analysis of the connections among the Peasant Revolt, Anabaptism, and the Muenster Rebellion.[48] He distinguished several strands of Anabaptism and showed the Anabaptists to be motivated as much by religious factors as economic, although he did not deny the material dynamics of their origins. The Anabaptists were not clear on the social and economic bases of their own movements, since the intellectual aspects of the revolution were just being formulated. Thus they were premature in their demands and objectives.[49]

Recent research indicates that Engels and Kautsky were probably more correct than previously thought.[50] That there was a connection between the religious dimension of the Reformation—especially its radical wing—and the socioeconomic forces of the times cannot be denied. The exact nature of the connection is more difficult to establish.[51]

Gerhard Zschaebitz suggested that the defeat of the Peasant Revolt caused the vanquished to turn inward and become "the quiet in the land."[52] "Early Anabaptism became the collective reservoir of the manifold oppositional, radical, and revolutionary responses to the revolution that failed. . . . Thus Anabaptism produced an ideology of the poor, in which the traditions of the Peasants' War had a clear aftereffect and which contained latent within it the potential for another uprising."[53]

The debate continues, and at present it appears that there is more scholarly acceptance of the social and economic revolutionary nature of Anabaptism. Some Mennonite historians and theologians have resisted the introduction of these forces into the discussion. However, non-Mennonite scholars point increasingly to a pluralistic origin of the movement, with much more concern about the common man and the lower classes and the economic oppression of the poor.[54]

Is the presocialist revolutionary model of Mennonite history applicable to contemporary Anabaptist-Mennonite groups? Whether Mennonites were, in fact, socialistic revolutionaries is today more open to analysis; but the empirical work to determine whether the model has any contemporary application remains to be done. When this work is undertaken, the substantial background material on the Marxist-Mennonite debate, flourishing for a number of decades, will prove helpful.[55]

AGRICULTURAL FOLK SOCIETY AND ANABAPTIST ECONOMICS

In the last fifty years, an emerging theme holds (oftentimes more implicitly than explicitly) that Anabaptist-Mennonite society, however radical it may have been in its earlier phases, gradually relinquished its original impetus and became a traditional agrarian folk society, content with self-sufficiency and preservation of its life.[56] This folk understanding of Anabaptist-Mennonite life has been applied to a number of traditional Mennonite groups. For example, John Hostetler described the Amish as follows:

The Folk model lends itself well to understanding the tradition-directed character of Amish Society. The heavy weight of tradition can scarcely be explained in any other way. The Amish, for example, have retained many of the customs and small-scale technologies that were common in rural society in the nineteenth century. Through a process of syncretism, Amish religious values have been fused with an earlier period of simple country living when everyone farmed with horses and on a scale where the family members could work together. The Amish exist as a folk or "little" community in a rural subculture within the modern state.[57]

In describing the Amish societal structure, Hostetler went on to say that the parameters were distinctiveness, smallness of scale, homogeneous culture patterns, and the strain toward self-sufficiency.

Ernst Correll probably came closest to stating the folk approach to understanding Mennonite life. He observed,

A realistic appraisal of Mennonite traditions of faith and practice must take into account the fact that they grew and bore fruit mainly in an environment of rural life and town handicraft economy. Only certain portions of the Dutch Doopsgezinde groups and of the north German movement were more closely and more generally tied to a relatively advanced merchant civilization. Historically, an agricultural occupation predominated; and among genuine Mennonite groups, it still does.[58]

Correll claimed that "through these vanguard achievements [the agricultural communities] shines the voluntary principle of the 'beloved community' by which Mennonite personalities and sociological techniques helped to overcome hazards of pressures of an intenser market economy."[59] Further, he argued that "as a cultural group in history, the economic significance of the Mennonites is a distinct by-product of their religiosociological existence."[60]

Subsequently, scholars have taken up the theme, assuming that the rural community was both the result of the peculiarly Mennonite faith system and the cause of it and that the true ethos could only be maintained in the agricultural setting—hence the studies and writings of scholars such as Correll, A. E. Morgan, Walter Kollmorgen, Charles P. Loomis, and Allen I. Beegle. Mennonite scholars such as Guy F. Hershberger, Winfield Fretz, and Melvin Gingerich reflected this rural community orientation and promoted the Mennonite Community movement, which was to preserve the authentic Mennonite system in the face of the secularization of the modernizing world.

Interestingly enough, this Mennonite orientation was related to a larger rural life movement that reached its apex in the 1940s. Among the Free Churches, it was expressed in the Rural Life Association, headquartered at Quaker Hill in Richmond, Indiana, and long directed by Stanley Hamilton. This organization staged conferences and produced publications promoting and lauding the virtues of agricultural and rural life. The Mennonite Central Committee published the comprehensive *Mennonite Community Sourcebook* in the late 1940s, including many sources on agricultural and community building. It would be interesting to compare the Mennonite interest in its folk consciousness with the larger society's interest in such matters—the back-to-the-land movement of the 1960s and the ecological movement of the 1980s, both of which are resonant with the traditional Mennonite ethos.

Support for the agricultural folk society interpretation of the Mennonite society derives from the historical reality that the Mennonites quickly became rural after their initial burst of radical creativity. Even though the Anabaptist movement was largely urban, it soon became almost totally agricultural in Switzerland, southern Germany, Alsace, Bohemia, western and eastern Prussia, Russia, and North and South America. Scholars holding the folk understanding of Mennonite life have been fascinated with and meticulously detailed the development of Mennonite farming settlements; their landholding characteristics; their crop and livestock techniques and development; their innovations in organic, chemical, and mechanical practices and techniques; their spatial arrangements; and their social structures.

Harold Bender examined the reasons for the development of a folk society:

The widespread settlement of Mennonites on such estates often widely scattered from one another, on the one hand lifted them above the village peasant class and aided in their cultural and religious isolation from the surrounding world, while on the other hand making an organized active congregational life very difficult and throwing much weight on family religion.[61]

Extensive case analyses of these isolated Mennonite congregation-family settlements are just beginning to emerge. Horst Penner's study of the Prussian Mennonites is one example.[62] The most comprehensive study so far which provides information to support the folk agrarian perspective is Jean Seguy's study of the Alsatian Mennonites. He said,

From the beginning of their settlement in France in the second half of the seventeenth century until 1850 or even beyond, the Anabaptists lived within the context of a culture of their own, in a subsociety that was originally [uniquely?] structured. In the span of time mentioned, an "Anabaptist nation" was in existence . . . which was as much an ethnic group as it was a church. It proves that the Anabaptists' social and vocational life was in constant symbiosis with their Anabaptism.[63]

Although the term *folk society* is not used, the description of the social life being formed by a traditional faith, centered in the family and congregation, and supported in a rural agricultural setting isolated from other social groupings is the classic source of the emergence of the folk society.

In analyzing the Mennonites of Prussia and Russia, geographer Harry Leonard Sawatzky arrived at the same conclusion. After describing the history of the Mennonite migrations, rural settlements, isolation from other groups, and the protection of their religious scruples by princes and kings, he concluded, "It was under these conditions, over a period of [two hundred] years and more, that the Mennonites established the cultural solidarity and folk identity (*Gemeinschaftssinn*) which have marked their group coherence ever since."[64]

Kollmorgen concluded his intensive analysis of the Old Order Amish community of Lancaster County, Pennsylvania, with this observation:

Continued stability in the Old Order Amish community bespeaks at least a reasonable degree of continued success in farming and resolving all crucial problems, including economic problems within the primary group. The very nature of some of the deep-seated convictions of these people seems to make this success imperative. Partly because of their outstanding success in farming in the past the Amish and the Mennonites feel that their way of life is the correct one. The difficulty is that economic problems, including those of agriculture, are increasingly complex and less easy to cope with locally.[65]

The folk society perspective clearly assumes the existence of an organic and functional connection among the rural agricultural economic, family, and religious aspects of life—a situation in which an isolated and relatively protected political system, often based on special privileges provided by the government of the host society, exists.

This type of society, considered in isolation (the most serious flaw of this theory as it is expressed to date), is assumed to exist as a simple and harmonic interdependence among a community of families cohering around a religious history and an agrarian economic system, which is oriented to subsistence and self-sufficiency. The norms governing productive distribution and consumption activities are oriented inwardly, with no conscious production of a surplus for an expanding commercial structure. "Farming was not practiced to make money, but money was made to support the farm."[66]

The ideal type of this society has only existed in prehistory and in the mythology of human nature which is part of our intellectual tradition. History begins with the city, and a universal peasant culture such as the agrarian folk model is found today only in the archaeological evidence and scholarly hypotheses regarding the meaning of this evidence. The dynamics of this universal peasant culture evolved into the city-state civilizations of the ancient Near East. The city-states, the centers of the surplus production which made their development possible, acquired political dominance over the originally independent and autonomous peasant villages. This, according to the theory, is the beginning of class society. The challenge facing the folk society approach is to explain how a European Neolithic peasant culture could survive in the context of Wallerstein's long sixteenth century, which, according to the canons of both liberalism and socialism, began the decimation of such peasant societies.

The other problem with the present formulation of this theory is that in it the Mennonite folk society is dependent on the host society for basic technical and economic materials and institutions, exploiting them for its own inner life without contributing back to the host society. There is little question that the Mennonites have been very concerned that the external world not make inroads on its life. As Kollmorgen stated, "They feel their way of life is the correct one." But this view does not take adequate note of the considerable economic and cultural advance and development that has taken place in Prussia, Russia, and North America in the last several centuries.[67] The parasitical relationship that is seemingly implied by the host society/folk society relationship perpetuates a view of Mennonite subjective biases which is, in fact, hostile to the values of the group.

TOWARD A NEW ECONOMIC SOCIOLOGY OF MENNONITE ENTREPRENEURS

In this chapter we have surveyed some of the major theories by which scholars of various traditions have tried to explain Mennonite faith and economic practice. Several observations or conclusions can be drawn from this review. Most obvious is the fact that the Mennonite community has become so varied that generalization is difficult, although not impossible. The basic character or theological presuppositions of all of the groups are very similar. It is not so much in doctrine that Mennonites differ, it is in practice. As Harry Loewen stated, "The comparatively common, consistent theological center [i.e., ideologically literal biblicism] contributes to a truly integrative pluralism in the Mennonite family of faith. Pluralism is rich when there is a firm center."[68] So the differentiation of cultural forms does not pose an insurmountable barrier to social analysis.

Second, our review demonstrates that analyses using Weberian, disinheritance, Marxist, and folk society propositions have not accounted satisfactorily for Mennonite economic ethic and practice. It is impossible to understand or interpret the Mennonites without considering their ideological and belief systems.[69] The greatest weakness with most studies of Mennonite society from an anthropological/sociological perspective is their neglect of the symbolic system that informs Mennonite society in a most intimate way.

That is not to say that the theories reviewed here have not made valuable contributions to our understanding of Mennonite economic life and its context. Rather, our point is that each has a limited application. In fact, the promise lies with our belief that the theories we have discussed can be synthesized into a coherent understanding of the Mennonite psyche, its social and historical context, and the economic system within which it has to function and maintain its identity. Beginning with Max Weber's recognition that the Anabaptists–Mennonites hold the key to the iron cage of the future, we need to work toward a synthesis of these theoretical models which will enable us to unlock the door.

CHAPTER TEN

The Cultural Contradictions of Mennonite Life and Utopian Economics

THE CONTRADICTIONS OF MENNONITE ENTREPRENEURIAL LIFE

In our discussion of the Mennonite entrepreneur and economic ethos, we have confronted a series of conundrums or antinomies. Contemporary North American Mennonites (all immigrant cultures in North America, for that matter) find themselves pulled in different directions. They are drawn to ghetto traditionalism, where patterns from another place and time are held in place through forced authority. At the same time, they want to assimilate into the mainstream of the perceived host society.

To use the language of Daniel Bell, contemporary Mennonites are pulled in different directions by "cultural contradictions."[1] Bell's concern, of course, was with North American society more generally—a society that experiences disjunctions among axial principles governing the economy (ruled by efficiency), the polity (ruled by equality), and the culture (ruled by self-gratification). To the extent that Mennonites are part of North American society, they share something of these same cultural contradictions. However, Mennonites also face cultural contradictions peculiar to them which create their own disjunctions.

Mennonite entrepreneurs are faced with loyalty demanded by the economic system in which they participate. They are also faced with the fact that the Anabaptist-Mennonite economic ethic is diametrically opposed to the values of the British liberal free market system. This contradiction is animated further by the diminishing rural occupational base of the Mennonites, and, correspondingly, it has become increasing difficult for them to maintain an agrarian community.

The traditional Mennonite economic ethos had a pronounced communal emphasis, and the congregation provided a basis of economic activity. This ethos has stood in sharp contrast to its Anglo-American counterpart in which the individual is the basis of all economic activity. In addition, in North America communal sharing is no longer needed to ensure survival, as was the case in the impoverished and persecuted Mennonite society of Europe. Thus, the Mennonite community has lost some of its traditional nurturing function as well as some of its authority/power over the lives of individual members. The modern individualistic market economy has made the discipline of excommunication, or any religious discipline for that matter, ineffective. When the community can no longer function as a nurturing mother, as Durkheim put it, the visage of the disciplining father loses its authority as well.

For a time, the Mennonite communal ethic was retained by strict normative control or by the threat (and follow-through) of ostracism and exclusion from the group. And, for a time, Mennonites were able to maintain what Nietzsche described as "prehistorical" morality (i.e., morality based on a religious-ethnic group's self-consciousness) rather than on modern, rational individualism. The community's total claim on the individual's loyalty demanded by Anabaptist ideology has been undermined, however, in the North American context to the extent that Mennonite communities can no longer meet the material needs of their members, who are consequently forced to participate in the larger market economy. North American Anabaptist-Mennonites—except those who live in enclaves: Hutterites, Old Order Mennonites, Amish—have been forced by history to abandon their communal ethic. The decline of the communal ethic or impulse has created confusion and, in some instances, substantial conflict within the community. It has divided congregations and resulted in a legacy of mutual recrimination.

In recent years, the Mennonite community has worked to resolve this problem through compromise where it is no longer materially capable of enforcing its demands in their strictest form. The command to refrain from participating in the secular economy has been modified to the demand for a contribution toward the welfare of the community from those entrepreneurs who claim to adhere to it. The cosmopolitan entrepreneur who chooses to remain a Mennonite is forced to synthesize, to balance loyalty to community with or against the opportunities and demands of the marketplace—opportunities and demands that become more and more available. The Mennonite community is compelled to expand its concept of acceptable occupations and come to grips with the increasing capacity of its members to generate wealth.

The cultural contradictions of Mennonite life are not beyond synthesis. Mennonite society can adapt to the entrepreneurial world with its cultural identity intact. As our quantitative and qualitative data show, individual Mennonites have done so to survive in the market economy and remain members of Mennonite congregations. The question is: how do we arrive at a synthesis at the theoretical (sociological and theological) level? In this final chapter, we intend to work toward this theoretical synthesis, explaining how Mennonite entrepreneurs can participate in the secular world economy without compromising their Mennonite economic ethos, without relinquishing their Mennonite culture, and without leaving Mennonite society.

ANABAPTISM AS A UTOPIAN MOVEMENT

Scholarly work on the Anabaptists—especially by people outside the Anabaptist tradition—has increasingly portrayed them as followers of religious utopianism. This idea has long been resisted by Anabaptist-Mennonites themselves, who feel that this understanding minimized the religious concerns of the movement's founding figures. The advantage of the utopian designation is that it places the action of early Anabaptists into the larger frame of human goals and strivings based on the historical and social conditions in which the movement emerged. It further helps the scholar elucidate how the chiliastic and millennial roots of European peasant discontent fed ideas into the social reform movement.[2]

Subjectively understood, utopianism is captured in the translation of *Utopos* as *non-place*.[3] The spiritual Israel with which the Mennonites identify themselves is such a non-place. This is why Mennonites are at home—as the history of their wanderings discloses—everywhere in the world. By the same token, Mennonites are condemned to search perpetually for a homeland since—unlike the Jews who have identified a historical homeland—the one for which Mennonites search, which will ultimately realize the kingdom of God, does not exist.

Ernst Troeltsch first proposed that the Anabaptists had utopian motivations because they attempted to set up a holy community in the face of the massive resistance of institutionalized power and tradition—hence its apocalyptic eschatological millenarian nature in many places. "The Anabaptists deliberately opposed the results of this [i.e., that of the state church] compromise, and in so doing they also opposed the whole idea of the church, and of an ecclesiastical civilization."[4] It remained for Ferdinand Seibt to develop the utopian case for the Anabaptists more fully and systematically.[5] Ernst Bloch also supported this position by maintaining the importance of religiously motivated utopian goals and the stress on concrete versus theoretical utopias, the Anabaptists being an example of the former.[6] Karl Mannheim proposed that it was the sixteenth-century Anabaptist movement, through its insistence on individual freedom and congregational autonomy, which introduced political pluralism and finally allowed the utopian ideal (religious and social) to be attempted in real life.[7]

Anabaptist-Mennonites must be understood in the context of sixteenth-century European Christianity, which included a strong strand of utopian, or millennial, ideals and practices.[8] This millennialism is endemic to the dialectical structure of biblical religion, which has broken the cyclical character of natural religion to launch on a linear path to a culmination of history in a future, rather than a past Golden Age.[9] A review of the literature on the concrete nature of utopias, especially the religious utopias, reveals that they had four major dimensions or objectives: (1) communism of production and consumption; (2) personal and social equality (brotherhood); (3) peace and harmony in all human relations; and (4) the meaning and allocation of work subordinated to the benefit and purpose of the collective.[10] Again, most utopian literature and experiments have centered on these four elements as crucially significant. A classic analysis of utopian communities by Charles Nordhoff consistently focused on these four issues as the heart of utopianism.[11] In fact, the names of some of the societies Nordhoff described—the Perfectionists, the Harmony Society, the Inspirationists, and the Bethel Commune—themselves indicate the goals and purposes of the groups. All four of these dimensions or objectives informed Anabaptist-Mennonitism as well.

Naturally, there are economic and social consequences of the utopian community so understood. Most important—and most threatening for individualistic forms of capitalism—is the emphasis a utopian community places on the relationships between human beings rather than the relationship between human beings and things. In the words of a first-generation Anabaptist:

True, devout Christians hold all physical possessions in common, and no one among them should wish to be sole lord of his goods; rather, when a poor brother or sister is in want, his need should be supplied by those who hold more possessions, according to their ability. Where this does not obtain among the brethren and Christians, there is as yet no true Christianity, as John and James say. From this it follows that since members of the Christian congregation share all possessions with the poor, holding them in common because of a deep love and free, good will, how then can they go to law and quarrel with each other because of temporal goods?[12]

Ernst Troeltsch proposed that the sect groups, which included the Anabaptist-Mennonite movement, promoted a "strict radicalism of the ethic of the Gospel, which wholly directed towards self-conquest and brotherly love." He contended that this found expression in social activity "which left no room for secular political and economic inequalities and cruelty."[13]

Living the Utopian Vision: An Imperfect Fit

Of course, no Anabaptist-Mennonite group has ever fully realized the utopian vision. If we consider the commitment to radical egalitarianism or universal equality, we see that it has often been derailed by the tendency to form two classes within utopian religious groups: the ministers or religious leaders, and the rest of the membership. This, as Weber observed, is a problem endemic to all charismatic groups: the routinization, institutionalization, and bureaucratization of the originally personal charisma on which new social groups are usually founded.[14]

There is another step that Weber did not discuss. Once the charisma is thoroughly routinized so that the congregation assumes the necessity of the office, the bearer of the office acquires the personal credit for the charisma: the privilege and status that go with it but without effecting the changes that a charismatic leader must make to substantiate the charismatic status. Thus, as was inevitable, universal equality quickly became more of an abstract ideal than actual practice as the various branches grew and became established. In comparison with the larger society, however, many utopian groups have been able to maintain a relatively high degree of equality. The Hutterites, for example, worked toward an egalitarian society, although notable inequality does exist (e.g., women do not have equal status with men in matters of colony administration and authority).

Among other Mennonite groups in general, women have generally been subordinated to men, although in a way less demeaning than has prevailed in society generally. In congregational life, all baptized members have always enjoyed equal spiritual status, but women only recently received full voting rights in church matters and now can serve in preaching and other roles. Differences in wealth and prestige exist and have been influential in congregational politics and life, but there have been constant attempts to reassert the equality of brothers and sisters in Christ in a standardized lifestyle. The more conservative Mennonite groups have been slower to give women equal status in ecclesiastical matters but have been more insistent and successful in maintaining social equality and economic sharing and mutuality for many generations.

Thus, the fit between the ideals of equality and the realities of utopian life has often been less than perfect. Often, universal equality has truly meant common deprivation. Everyone is equal not because of a universal common-mindedness, but because nobody has anything.

Likewise, the fit between the ideal and reality of communalism has been imperfect, especially with regard to private property. Only the Hutterites have consistently adhered to a total communism of property and make it the basic test of loyalty and membership to this very day. Among Mennonites, the commitment to communalism has varied considerably, and it is an area that has been studied very little. Urban Mennonites of Amsterdam and Rotterdam, for example, as well as those in other places and times, such as colonial America, produced very wealthy families early on. Russian Mennonites achieved a form of semicommunalism in which the church held property titles and controlled the economic activities of the colonies. However, because of the population growth and scarcity of land, a landless class emerged alongside other families who were able to develop huge estates, especially on the margins of the colonies.[15] The conformity to communalism in property slowly eroded in those Swiss, Dutch, and southern German Anabaptist groups that migrated to cities in Europe, Prussia, Russia, and North America and emerged as a uniquely capitalist society (following England, to which, for still unexplained reasons, no Mennonites immigrated). But most groups settled in rural areas in which individualistic ownership of the land soon contributed to differences in economic standing.[16] Even though Mennonite beliefs stressed communal economic practices, in reality the temptation to abuse the opportunities of private property and individual acquisition could not be resisted fully.

In the Mennonite groups that have been less communal in economic dimensions, but no less utopian in other aspects, the evidence points to a strong emphasis on promoting the welfare of the collective membership over the good of the individual. They achieved conformity to this goal by strong norms of mutual assistance and care and by stressing the simple life, free of materialistic accumulation.[17]

Describing Mennonites of all stripes as possessing a degree of communalism is probably an oversimplified way of addressing the problem. Yet it is clear that per capita, Hutterites own less than their Gentile neighbors, and modern Mennonite communal groups probably fall into the same category. The middle semicommunal groups that include the Old Order undoubtedly own less capital than their Gentile neighbors. It is only the more conventional community Mennonites who possibly have material holdings comparing favorably with the larger social community, although hard evidence for this assertion is not directly available.[18]

Of the four dimensions of utopianism among Mennonites, the fit between the ideals of peace and harmony and the lived experience of its members is probably the best. Most Mennonite groups have been committed to the achievement of peace and harmony, both in terms of relations between members and between the Mennonite community and the outside world. Formally, Mennonites consider a commitment to peace testimony and nonresistance to be part of their basic identity. Some groups have lapsed considerably in practice, but all groups adhere to this in theory at least.[19] Holding to the position has been a requirement for membership, and only those groups who are seriously questioning their Mennonite identity are relinquishing their stand on nonresistance. The opening of progressive Mennonite conferences and congregations to nonethnic Mennonites has been one factor that has led to this questioning of identity and the erosion of the peace stance.

Of course, Mennonite congregations and conferences have been plagued by internal friction and dissension too. The early part of the twentieth century saw pronounced conflict between so-called modernists and fundamentalists, and various Mennonite groups became locked in battle with one another.[20] Many schisms resulted in the loss of membership, and the period was marked by both personal and congregational tragedy. Until recently, the conflict within the Mennonite community was downplayed. Stephen Ainlay criticized traditional accounts of Mennonite life for being overly consensual—that is, they ignored the profound conflict between subgroups that compete with one another for cultural hegemony.[21]

The ideal of subordinating individual initiative to the purposes and benefit of the community was self-evident throughout most of Mennonite history and obtains today in most branches. The Hutterite society, which most clearly expresses the ideal, places work totally at the benefit of the community. All existing work positions, roles, and statuses are determined by the will (as expressed through its leaders) of the community. Even personal hobbies generally produce artifacts for the benefit of Hutterite society.

This idea of subordinating personal to group interest is not peculiar to utopian societies. All traditional societies socialize their individual members into unquestioning submission to the common good. Modern, rationally capitalistic society (so Weber's argument goes) has undone this commitment in that the individual has been made into the basis of society, and the individual's psychology is the basis of our scientific ideology of society.[22] Utopianism rooted in biblical ideology, however, articulates a communalism that is based neither on the natural religion of traditional society nor on the individualism of Greek heroic religion or modern bourgeois self-interest as the highest common good (utilitarianism), but on an imitation of Christ's sacrificial life and death. Thus, the ideological origins of Anabaptist-Mennonite subordination are somewhat different from those of other traditional societies.

With the routinization of the charisma, however, the tendency is for the expression of submission, or imitation, to take externally defined forms and meanings. Thus, in the Old Order, or semicommunal groups, the land was owned collectively, and the work was directed individually but controlled very closely by the church.[23] Occupations were approved by the community, and the consequences of work were monitored carefully. For example, someone becoming especially adept at a hobby or work activity and taking great interest in it would be disciplined for having too much pride in what was being done. Hence artistic work was strongly discouraged as well.

Among the more progressive, conventional economic model Mennonites, work has more often been controlled by informal and subtle community norms. Occupations that contradicted the Mennonite standards for nonconformity, such as bartending or manufacturing arms (as somewhat extreme examples), were generally grounds for excommunication. Other occupations that posed too many temptations or demanded questionable conduct—such as law and politics, real estate brokerage, or banking—were discouraged until very recently. Within the last generation, however, the internal discipline of the liberal groups has broken down to become individualistic and accepting of the dominant cultural religious ideology. The work norms of the members of these congregations have come to conform more to prevailing standards, and the congregations have imposed no standards for judging the function and consequences of work for the Christian faith. The individualistic Mennonite communities have no recourse to communal sanctions, so there is no longer effective social control.[24]

The Anabaptist Balance of Private and Corporate Impulses

Early Anabaptists produced little discussion or theological literature concerning economic issues.[25] Nevertheless, such issues concerned them. Their commitment to ethical living (*Nachfolge*) had economic implications expressed through beliefs and practices with concrete consequences. Peter Klassen concluded,

For the Anabaptists, economics formed an integral part of the Christian's life of discipleship. Nothing is so strikingly basic to their attitudes toward economic factors as the firm conviction that all facets of life constituted an indivisible unity that must be permeated by the spirit of Christ. There could be no compartmentalization of the faithful disciple—his whole being as well as his possessions, must be willingly placed at God's disposal.[26]

It is this total unity that helps us understand the Anabaptist ambivalence toward private property and the emphasis on mutual assistance and sharing.

One early Anabaptist stated, "True, devout Christians hold all physical possessions in common, and no one among them should wish to be sole lord of his goods; rather, when a poor brother or sister is in want, his need should be supplied by those who hold more possessions, according to their ability."[27] Peter Reidemann, one of the foremost interpreters of the Hutterite wing of Anabaptism, said, "Thus all those who have fellowship likewise have nothing for themselves, but have all things with their Master and with all those who have fellowship with them, that they might be one in the Son as the Son is in the Father.[28] Menno Simons observed that "we are prepared before God and man with all our hearts to share our possessions, gold, and all that we have, however little it may be: and to sweat and labor to meet the need of the poor, as the Spirit and the Word of the Lord, and true brotherly love imply."[29] Simons' position was that although private property was not forbidden to Christians, it was certainly to be accessible and available for all members of the community.

This emphasis is not merely the continuation of a charity based on carrying individualism to its logical conclusion, but rather is the application of an entirely different, indeed revolutionary, principle regarding the relationship between the community and economic life. As we noted earlier in this chapter, Anabaptist communalism derived from the primacy of the relationship of person to person rather than the relationship of person to thing. Liberal capitalism—ruled by the invisible hand of the relations of production—is, of course, based on the primacy of the relationship of the person to the thing (expressed in the sanctity of private property). And any social system based on the relationship between persons and things would be, by necessity, self-destructive from the Anabaptist point of view.

The Anabaptists consistently believed, whether on traditional or revolutionary grounds, that the institution of private property intentionally put personal desires before those of the community. This sentiment was expressed through the idea that worldly economic action was not Christlike and was actually contrary to the law of love. As Bernard Rothmann stated,

For not only have we put all our belongings in a common pool under the care of the deacons, and live from it according to our needs, we praise God through Christ with one heart and mind and are eager to help one another with every kind of service. And accordingly, everything which has served the purposes of self-seeking and private property, such as buying and selling, working for money, taking interest and practicing usury—even at the expense of unbelievers—or eating and drinking the sweat of the poor, that is, making one's own people and fellow-creatures work so that one can grow fat, and indeed everything which offends against love—all such things are abolished among us by the power of love and community.[30]

The idea that economic profit and advantage came at the expense of the neighbor appears to have a central assumption: that I can only gain in a transaction at the expense of the other. This assumption has been articulated by Polka as *the law of the excluded middle* according to which I need to enslave the other in order to be free; that is, I need to make him into a thing before I can relate to him (i.e., manipulate him for my self-interest). The Roman word for slave—*speaking tool*—expresses this assumption and its form of social life perfectly. For Weber, Israel was the exception; it was the only community of free human beings. Pilgrim Marpeck, another early Anabaptist leader, depicted the modern world system based on post-Christian liberal capitalism:

Would to God, for their sake, that it were not true that today there are worse and even more evil merchants than the Jewish Pharisees, who bought the Lord from Judas because of envy and hate. [But today], whole lands, armies, peoples are betrayed, sold, and bought by their loans, finance and usury. It is done out of avarice, envy and hate, an attempt to preserve their earthly pride and vain honor. Moreover, all the actions . . . are done in the semblance of Christ and his Gospel.[31]

The protest against private property, although central, was not the only economic concern of the Anabaptists. Their protest against the charging of high interest, known as usury, is well documented in their writings.[32] There is no explicit rejection of material life, of work and reward for labor, and for enjoyment of natural desires and appetites, only a very strong resistance to economic actions that in any sense undermined the concern for neighbor.

Menno Simons expressed this concern in the strongest terms:

The wicked merchants and retailers (I say the wicked, for I do not mean those who are righteous and pious), together with all those who are out to make money and to make their living that way, are so bent on accursed profit that they exclude God wholly from their hearts. . . . They lie and swear; they use many vain words, falsify their wares to cheat the people and strip them of possessions, they sell, lend, and secure the needy at large profit and usury, never seriously reflecting or taking to heart what is written. Let no man go beyond and defraud his brother in any matter. I Thess. 4:6.[33]

The overriding objective of the Anabaptist movement was to create a pure church, whose members would be concerned about each other's spiritual and social welfare. Of high priority was the spreading of the gospel of liberation to those who were imprisoned in the Roman Catholic, and Reformed, and Lutheran ecclesiastical hegemony. Included were freedom from priestcraft, from the oppression of the tithe and the accompanying support of the church hierarchy, from exploitation by the princes and lord, and the freedom to structure one's life as commanded in the New Testament. The Anabaptists originally intended to implement this program throughout the whole society. They accepted as an economic principle that the poor anywhere had a right to be helped by the rich. In Troeltsch's view, the Anabaptists shared "an extremely high, almost Utopian ethical ideal."[34] He maintained that the Anabaptists' great desire was "to penetrate the whole mass of the population equally with the miracle of the strict Christian ethic of love" and to include "the most far-reaching mutual material help, and the equality of all church members." The universalism of this conviction raised the significance of mission and helps clarify why there was so little discussion and treatment of the issues of economic activities.

In the end, Troeltsch thought that the essence of Anabaptism was to be found in the following core principles:

1. Formation of the church was to include only truly converted believers.[35]

2. Membership in the church should be voluntary and symbolized by baptism.[36]

3. Church discipline would be necessary for all who had committed themselves voluntarily to join the fellowship.[37]

4. The efficacy of the sacraments was rejected; hence the Lord's Supper became a "festival of Christian fellowship."[38]

5. The emphasis was on a holy life that expressed itself in detachment from the state, including service to it, refusal to swear oaths, refusal to engage in violence of any sort, including capital punishment, but taking up the cross instead and suffering injustice as the Christian disciples' share of the suffering of Christ.[39]

6. Church members were to be considered equal.[40] This expressed itself in absolute equality of male and female, as well as in election of leaders. Equality expressed itself in mutuality, in which there was a common sharing of abundance and assisting each other in need.

7. By following the precepts of the Sermon on the Mount and accepting the life and teachings of Jesus as the norm and model for the Christian life, especially in the denial of selfish desires such as materialistic lifestyles and self-interest, "They practice renunciation as a means of charity, as the basis of a thoroughgoing communism of love . . . a union in love which is not affected by the social inequalities and struggles of the world."[41]

This description—by an outsider to the Mennonite tradition—rings true to the self-understanding of many Mennonites. In fact, the comparison of this list with that penned by Donovan Smucker, a Mennonite theologian-ethicist, is striking:

1. The primacy of biblical authority interpreted Christologically.

2. The nature of Jesus Christ as divine Lord and Savior, revealing both grace and pattern for living.

3. The nature of man as fallen sinner desperately needing salvation in Christ, making possible the Christian life.

4. The church as a gathered, responsible, disciplined, converted, suffering, mutually aiding, apostolic, missionary brotherhood.

5. A conception of Christianity as discipleship.

6. The conception of Christian ethics as the all-embracing application of love and nonresistance.

7. The primacy of the local congregation yet with authority delegated to the elders; the validity of the ordinances as symbols yet without any meaning apart from faith and obedience.

8. The presupposition of religious liberty and toleration for interchurch relationships; but with separation as pertaining to church and state relations.

9. A theology that is biblical, covenantal, confessional, and unspeculative.[42]

We are left with such lists to find the core of Anabaptist-Mennonite belief since Mennonites themselves have never developed a formal creed. Although it is generally assumed that they have accepted all of the classical Christian creeds and doctrines concerning the nature and action of God, His creation, and the purpose of humanity, Mennonites have focused even more on what they believe to be Christ's teachings and life.

SUBSEQUENT MENNONITE ECONOMIC UNDERSTANDING

The economic understandings of the early Anabaptist movement carried over to varying degrees in the different Anabaptist-Mennonite groups. Of these groups, the Hutterite model is probably best known as retaining the utopian and communal elements. It was and is a society living in total community, with the religious, social, political, and economic activities all integrated into a unified whole, achieved so totally that the early period has been termed *the golden years*.[43] After some breakdown, the group settled into an institutionalized routine that has remained practically unchanged to the present, even though technical and structural changes have been introduced.[44]

For the less communal branches of the movement, economic life became quickly domesticated, rural, and agricultural, except in the Netherlands. The Alsatian Anabaptists developed a family and congregational community, the economic base of which was working the land for a prince or lord and gaining protection and a niche on the basis of innovative labor and service.[45] Because of the lack of toleration, there were no entrepreneurial thrusts until the migration to America.[46]

The situation in the Netherlands was drastically different. Soon after the emergence of toleration, the Dutch Mennonites embarked upon a commercialization and industrialization that propelled them rapidly into the forefront of Dutch financial and commercial activities. But the Dutch religious discipline was operative in the early rapid commercialization of Mennonites. For several decades—until materialism began to win out— church discipline and excommunication were the reward for undue or crass pursuit of greed and profit.[47] The Mennonites who fled the Nether- lands for Prussia and then Russia generally conformed to the modest agricultural model of the Alsatian, Swiss, south German, and Mora- vian Anabaptists, although considerable movement into cottage industry, commerce, and business emerged, especially in Russia.[48]

A characterization of the emerging Mennonite economic ideology or charter in the postclassic period would thus include the following points. The Anabaptist economic practice derived from a dualistic world- view that emphasized separation from secular values and practices and the creation of a community of love and service in which mutual love and assistance were motivated by following Christ. To live in the kingdom of God (*Gelassenheit*), the ongoing central goals were to maintain the bonds of love and mutual service and to exclude those pagans outside the "per- fection of Christ." In this vein, Burkholder stated that "Christians must separate themselves from the evil of culture."[49] Troeltsch characterized this ethic as an "intimate social relationship" in which there is "care for the poor and provision of relief funds, so that within these groups no one was allowed to beg or starve."[50] Economic activity that went beyond this man- date was worldly and even satanic. Therefore, the Protestant work ethic did not characterize the Anabaptist-Mennonite tradition, for it rejected the presuppositions of upper-class social dominance.[51] Weber and other social theorists did not look carefully enough at the beliefs and origins of Anabaptism, which were an expression of a revolt against Protestantism and Catholicism alike. Hence, any convergence of Anabaptist-Mennonite membership with the evolving capitalist economies was a deviation from the basic direction of true Anabaptism.[52]

The Anabaptist-Mennonites followed three economic paths: the community of goods model, exemplified by the Hutterites; the radical confrontational model, illustrated by the Amish and Old Colony Men- nonites; and the conventional economics model, which most closely ap- proximates the Weberian model. All three models are presently alive and well and represent Mennonite community attempts to be faithful to the classical vision. The community of goods model still operates among the Hutterites. The radical confrontational model thrives even beyond the cultural borders of Old Order groups, and elements of it exist among many college-educated Mennonites who believe that Christians cannot conform to the existing cultural milieu, especially in its economic aspects, without forsaking or at least seriously compromising their Christian commitment.[53] Most Mennonites adhere to the conventional economic model, in which liberal capitalism is interpreted as God's will expressed in the natural order, including the economic order (i.e., the necessity of land, labor, capital, and entrepreneurship), required for human survival.

Describing the Mennonite religious and symbolic system is difficult because of its relative informality and the lack of any centralized authoritative pronouncements or creeds and because the base of all authority rested in the congregation. Hence each congregation historically defined its own creed. Mennonite society *is* a community of faith, in which the process of social and religious interaction forms the foundation for beliefs and ethics. This is not to deny the great variation in economic practice among congregations and among individuals within congregations.

Again, because of the severe religious, political, and economic suppression, the Anabaptists had neither the time nor the freedom to deal with economics in an objective and orderly fashion. Instead, economic ideology became implicit in subsequent Mennonite history and expansion within the context of harassment and expulsions. The Mennonites of France, south and north Germany, Moravia, and the Netherlands developed an extensive economic base and subculture, resulting almost entirely from the dictates of survival and material sustenance. Contrast this with the long traditions of the Roman Catholics, Lutherans, and Calvinists in which an implicitly or explicitly articulated dialectic between teachings on economics and its application in mundane life arose.[54]

Therefore, it is probably correct to say that the Mennonite movement developed an economic *practice* that expressed a system of norms, even though this was never systematically set forth in any extensive way, as evidenced even by the early and contemporary confessions of faith which are silent on economic matters. Thus, the paucity of economic doctrine is a significant phenomenon. Equally strange is the failure of Mennonite economists to focus on Mennonite economics. As Mennonite economist Roy Vogt said, "There is no question that in the past few decades Mennonites have entered the mainstream of economic life. . . . Mennonite people have responded in very diverse ways to the new opportunities opened up to them."[55] In the face of such diversity, Vogt concluded that no coherent interpretation of economic life has emerged.

Although he is correct in this assessment, it is possible to summarize what latter-day Anabaptist-Mennonites have said about economic activities:

1. Communal property, or modifications thereof in a variety of ways, are to be basically for the benefit of all, especially the needy.

2. An ethic of love and sharing for the members of the *Gemeinde* must abide, in which the welfare of each is the highest good.

3. Ostentation and worldly self-adulation or self-indulgence in material things are to be avoided.

4. Worldly occupations and professions that deflect from the commitment to the community's life and witness beyond the community of the elect are to be avoided.

5. The profit motive and acquisition in all economic transactions and activities are to be downgraded and controlled.

6. There is to be no unequal yoking with unbelievers in business and commerce or in marriage and other relationships.

7. Motives and actions will be submitted to the discernment of the religious community (*Gelassenheit*).[56]

The application and expression of Mennonite economic ethics following the classical period have, of course, varied from locality to locality and from time to time. Here again, Vogt was correct. The continuing evolution of the Mennonite communities from south Switzerland to the northernmost regions of the Netherlands, Prussia, Russia, and North and South America ensured an increasing diversification of economic practice, which became strongly institutionalized. Yet none has ever become self-consciously incorporated into the theological and/or ethical statements of the Mennonite community.[57] Mennonites have therefore often been reduced to the argument, "That's the way it's been done." As Burkholder pointed out, "The Mennonite community has been guided to a considerable extent by traditional attitudes and practices, often in the absence of a reasoned and articulate ethic. Ethical decisions have been made by Mennonites largely from the standpoint of what the church has approved in the past."[58]

The lack of a systematic Mennonite theology and ethics created a void. As a result, the task of filling it was left to Mennonite practice that *reflexively* contributed—especially in the area of economics—to Mennonite doctrine. We are reminded here of the anthropological axiom that religion is often the explanation or rationalization of unconscious or ritual behavior.[59] In the economic sphere, this means that "the economic underpinnings enjoined *limits* on [but did not determine] the kind of [legal, political, and social] superstructure that might be compatible with them."[60] Burkholder maintained that "Mennonites have addressed themselves to world problems only as they have become immediate problems."[61] The Mennonite economic ethic was the result of a system of praxis—a systematic integration of experience and faith in the absence of any coherent a priori or independent rational system from which it could derive. The ultimate source of authority for the Anabaptist-Mennonite society derived from the overarching "biblical command and direct obedience [that] take place within the church, the Body of Christ, under the direction of the Holy Spirit" but has lacked specific application for economic activity.[62]

MAINTAINING A UTOPIAN / COMMUNAL VISION IN THE CULTURE OF NARCISSISM

Numerous cultural critics have fretted about the consequences of a society in which commitment to the common good has waned and the quest for individual self-fulfillment has triumphed. Recently, Robert Bellah and his coauthors of the bestseller *Habits of the Heart* seemed to hit a nerve when they suggested that both the biblical and civic traditions within North American culture had declined and that success for most people today is measured less by the common good than material gain (utilitarian individualism) and self-gratification (expressive individualism). This has led some, like Christopher Lasch, to label North American society a "culture of narcissism."[63]

In such a setting, it is hard to imagine utopian or communal visions surviving, other than as small enclaves of what Peter Berger once called "cognitive minorities" (i.e., small isolated collections of people who are at odds with the prevailing cultural ideology).[64] James Halteman addressed this point in *Market Capitalism and Christianity*. Halteman noted that "given the present state of many churches and the prevailing view that one's financial business is a private affair, some may find it hard to imagine how mutual accountability in finances can become part of the Christian agenda."[65]

Is a synthesis of the utopian/communal and the lived socioeconomic reality of modern America impossible? Many would argue that it is. Consider Carl Kreider's treatment of Mennonite economics in *The Christian Entrepreneur*. Kreider interpreted the traditional Mennonite economic ethos as comprising four aspects of economic activity—land, labor, capital, and entrepreneurship—all necessary and normal. However, he intended his book to show that "the biblical discussion of economic issues is filled with warnings against the spiritual dangers which stem from private ownership. One of the purposes of this book is to examine these warnings as they apply to our current practices [i.e., the milieu in which Mennonites operate today]."[66]

The problem with Kreider's conception of the Mennonite economic ethos is that it was premised on a confusion between religious and economic categories. Land, labor, capital, and entrepreneurship are economic but not religious or moral categories. No *ethos* can be premised on *economic* categories without essentially losing its ethical nature. This is a problem endemic to North American scholarship. Many writers have lost sight of the traditional influence of religious beliefs on economic behavior, which Weber highlighted. The important influence of religious beliefs on economic behavior was in curbing acquisitiveness and in channeling it into community interests rather than private consumption. When a religious ideology is utilized to rationalize acquisitiveness, it is no longer a religious ethos in Max Weber's understanding of the term.

That Kreider has not forsaken his ethos but merely confused his categories becomes clear in his discussion of the "just weight" in business dealings, paying workers just wages, problems of litigation, and business ethics in general. He concluded, "I do not reject the profit system. Instead I believe that [problematic] features of capitalism must be brought under the judgment of Christ so that they serve Christ's purposes in promoting his Kingdom in the world."[67]

Kreider's problem is that he addressed his economic concerns in theological rather than sociological categories. From the point of view of effecting practical action in the world, such a formulation leaves interpretation entirely up to the individual's subjective inclination. What specific economic action would be consistent with the judgment of Christ is a sociological as well as a theological question. The theological answer is the ultimate ground for the sociological solution that will emerge; but the former is certainly not a substitution for the latter.

Bearing these shortcomings in mind, let us consider another emergent attempt at synthesis which urges a return to a position closer to that taken in classical Mennonite experience. This alternative view was best expressed by Halteman in *Market Capitalism and Christianity*. In this book he presented his disinclination to accept the prevailing understanding of economic action as part of a natural order to which individuals must adapt and into which they must inject their Christian/Mennonite ethics. Instead, he proposed an Anabaptist position on economic behavior which includes the conviction that the congregation has a definitive role to play in helping its members decide what they can and should do in the economic sphere. Although the economic sphere expressed in the free market exchange system has much to commend it, Halteman concluded that some activity in the economic arena cannot be guided, determined, and mandated by economic laws but rather must be shaped by Christian ethics that are hammered out on the battle line by individuals as they are nurtured, supported, and even disciplined by the congregation. Thus, Halteman recognized the sociological role of the church in shaping its members' economic ethos.[68]

Mennonite businesspeople themselves have recognized the need for the community to provide advice, education, and moral guidance as more and more people follow the entrepreneurial path. We have seen this in the qualitative data in earlier chapters and also in the various musings of members of the Mennonite Economic Development Associates (MEDA). Articles in their periodical, *The Marketplace*, and speeches delivered to their membership attest that the question for Mennonites is no longer whether Mennonites should be in business but rather what the responsibility of Mennonites in and to the business world should be.[69]

The lead article in the first issue of *The Marketplace* was entitled "Business and Christianity: Is There Hope?" written by Rudolph Dyck, a Winnipeg businessman. After citing the great gap between the "people of thought and the people of affairs," Dyck proposed that this gap would be closed if we realized that all of us "must be economists [business-people] to some degree. Those who think they can escape it are merely placing the burden of their existence onto others." He proposed that "we need to develop an economic theology at our colleges and throughout our community for this very reason. Central to it should be the view that Christians in business fulfill a worthy calling to the extent to which they seek out a need in society that can be legitimately satisfied."[70]

The lead article in the next issue of *The Marketplace* was entitled "Business and Following Jesus?"[71] The author noted, "I like business. I even like making money. What's so unchristian about that? Some say a Christian, a true follower of Jesus, shouldn't be in business. Nonsense. To say a Christian shouldn't be in business is like saying a Christian shouldn't be in teaching or farming or medicine or truck driving." The author, a businessperson and ordained minister, continued by listing ten rules or guidelines that should help to allay the suspicions regarding business activity:

1. Remain ill-at-ease with the system.
2. Confess that Jesus is Lord of all.
3. Conduct business in harmony with beliefs.
4. Provide worthwhile goods and services.
5. Acknowledge the importance of reasonable profits.
6. Seek counsel from the Christian community.
7. Find ways to update biblical nonconformity.
8. Be modest about financial success.
9. Be generous in giving of yourself and money.
10. Adopt a new style of frugality.

Roy Vogt delivered the keynote address, "The Costs and Benefits of Being an Entrepreneur: A Christian Perspective," to the annual MEDA convention in 1980. In it Vogt defined the entrepreneur as being daring, individualistic, decisive, and success oriented. After a thoughtful discussion of how these four characteristics fit into the Anabaptist mode, Vogt concluded,

I have tried to express a simple conviction in these remarks and that is that Christian entrepreneurs, like other Christians, have been given a narrow road to walk in this life. The proper image may be even narrower—that of a tight-rope walker. Our particular characteristics may cause us to tilt a bit, but a move too far to one side may result in disaster. May God grant to you, our entrepreneurs, the moral and spiritual agility that such tight-rope walking requires.[72]

Mennonite businesspeople have accepted the legitimacy of the classical liberal economic system while trying to overlay it with a Christian perspective/commitment. They have not, by and large, seriously questioned the ideological and structural foundations of modern rational capitalism. Rather than integrating faith and business, they have opted for a compartmentalization of life to maintain ideological purity while engaging in economic practices that sometimes seem at odds with the Anabaptist-Mennonite ethos. This compartmentalization, it must be remembered, is not the fault of Mennonite entrepreneurs but is ultimately a collective response of any religious minority group if it is going to exist in the context of the modern, or any, world system.

In fact, entrepreneurs have looked for help from Mennonite intellectuals and complained that those serving the Mennonite institutions (e.g., seminaries, Bible colleges and schools, and churches) have been more concerned with the orthodox aspects of Mennonite life than with the concrete reality of Mennonite practice and the Mennonite context today. This failure of Mennonite intellectuals to take seriously the lived experience of the entrepreneur has contributed to the growing discontent Mennonite businesspeople feel with their scapegoat status.

MENNONITE REALITY, SELF-CONSCIOUSNESS, AND THE FUTURE

It is our contention that the fragmentation of the Mennonite economic ethos as represented by the three models as well as the discrepancies in the ideologically tinged accounts of Mennonite origins attest to the need for synthesis and, indeed, reconciliation. A coherent understanding of the Mennonite past would be most helpful, and a clear vision of the Mennonite future in North America could prove even more important.

Had the Anabaptist-Mennonite religiocultural revolution been allowed to develop according to its inner dynamic rather than being diverted by secular and religious persecutors as it was, it likely would never have become rustic, celebrating cultural isolation and agricultural pursuits. Correspondingly, its economic expressions would have undoubtedly followed different paths or even a single path. Whether that path would most closely resemble the socioeconomic system of the Hutterites is not certain, but we believe it would have been a system premised on an open community from which an ever expanding system of mutual sharing, assistance, and discernment would have emerged.[73] Walter Klaassen argued that the radical implications of the Anabaptist movement were, in fact, derailed. He noted that the Anabaptists' "new attitude to property," although they did not advocate extending it to the whole of society—as this would have required force, precisely what the Anabaptists were opposing—"certainly [would] have had major economic repercussions" had the movement not been thwarted by the established secular and ecclesiastical authorities.[74]

The irony of the routinization of the Anabaptist charisma (taking the form of rustication, rather than bureaucratization, as in the classical Weberian paradigm) is that the Mennonites unintentionally came to defend the traditional, compulsory, economic ethos of the European Neolithic peasant tradition which was part of their cultural baggage on the individualistic, voluntary, grounds of New Testament teaching.[75] This irony is further exacerbated by modern defenders (i.e., those attempting to maintain the traditional agrarian ethos in the modern context) idealizing the historical vicissitudes of this movement to defend the externals (the agrarian way of life) without having arrived at the awareness that this is an essential regression from the biblical point of view to that characterized by what Ruth Benedict called *cultural neurosis*.[76]

Of the three major economic paths that Anabaptist-Mennonites have taken, only the radical confrontational model maintains any dialectical elasticity in relation to the classical paradigm. The community of goods model has lost this quality in its appropriation of the rural way of life as essential. The conventional economics model has likewise lost this quality, having implicitly abandoned the communal ethos that liberal capitalism corrodes like an acid whatever it touches.

The greatest value of the radical confrontation model is that it provides the material basis for synthesizing the classical expression of the Anabaptist ethos with modern life—a synthesis that is often overlooked because classical Anabaptist concerns are more often seen as antithetical to modern living. Furthermore, this value is often missed since the radical confrontational model is most often associated with groups that are in transition from the strict community of goods to Weberian economic individualism, or with individuals who seem to adhere to it by default, being alienated from both the community of goods model (finding it oppressive) and the acceptance of conventional economics, which they consider an abandonment of Mennonite practice. Can the community of goods model be expressed consistently without being tied to an agrarian environment? Can the radically confrontational way of life sustain a culture without becoming defensive and oppressive? For its potential to be fully realized, the radical confrontation model needs to be reformulated on a historical-cultural basis so that it does not merely exist *contra* dominant culture.

The Schleitheim Confession and a number of other major statements of the Anabaptist position talk about separation from the world, meaning separation from the evil practices and institutions, not from the world of culture and society itself.[77] Anabaptists never formally stated that human institutions were evil, only that certain practices within them were inconsistent with the faith. It remained for subsequent generations of Anabaptist-Mennonites to introduce other understandings. Deprived of clear teaching to the contrary, they confused aspects of culture and society with their abuses.[78] Furthermore, the rejection of the Mennonites by the larger society caused them to express their economic ideas within their own communities which in time became unique, quaint (almost incestuous in cultural terms), and ultimately irrelevant for meeting the needs of today's society at large.

The essential Anabaptist-Mennonite economic ethos is the result of a profound dialectic between the norms and beliefs of the utopian reformation and the socioeconomic context of the emerging world system beside which it stood in tension. Anabaptism was committed to becoming a world and societal movement, but only on its terms: a world and society based on equality, communalism, peace, and mutual assistance. Since these goals were unachievable without political violence, they were forsaken as goals for the larger world and became goals for the inner life of the society, which attempted to pursue its goals with as little disruption from the larger society as possible. Modernity, with its individualistic and nationalistic organization of social life, has made the traditional Mennonite community somewhat of an anachronism.[79]

The boldest and most visible challenge to this anachronistic expression of the Anabaptist economic ethos has taken the form of the Mennonite entrepreneur, who attempts to practice a traditional ethos in contexts that demand a radical or even revolutionary response. In a way, Mennonite entrepreneurs embody the tension of the dialectic that must exist between an ethos rooted in a utopian religious system and existence in the secular economic world order. This is not to say that entrepreneurs always see themselves and their lives in this manner. They are not self-conscious of living out this dialectic or of their prototypical quality. In fact, the utopian ideal has often become badly blurred as a generation of successful Mennonites adjusts to life in a capitalistic society. Amazingly, however, it keeps emerging in their lived experience. Entrepreneurs continue to forsake their heady trajectories and turn to communal tasks and volunteer service. Young people continue to dedicate themselves to lives of service within church institutions, including voluntary service. There is little question that the dialectic is being played out in Mennonite experience. The question is whether Mennonite institutions and intellectuals are up to the task of both articulating this dialectic and guiding the members they serve toward some sense of synthesis.

The odds of developing a distinctive and coherent Anabaptist-Mennonite ethos depends, in large part, on how the community comes to terms with the emergence of the entrepreneurial role within its ranks.

If those responsible for official ideology isolate and alienate the entrepreneur—as they often have seemed bent on doing—their instructive function as point guards will be lost. On the other hand, if the entrepreneurial role is recognized as paradigmatic for the challenges faced by all members of the congregation, a Mennonite understanding of and coherent position toward the postmodern new world order will be far more likely.

MENNONITE ENTREPRENEURS AND A CHALLENGE FOR OUR TIMES

The Mennonite utopian social experiment and its accommodation with the modern world should be of special interest to other religious-ethnic groups in North America which are facing destruction because the traditional communal ethos of their homeland cannot stand against society's mass media, mass education, and mass production of consumer goods. But the attempt to reach some sort of synthesis between an adherence to traditional beliefs and a commitment to community and the demands of the modern economic system is instructive to us all. To be sure, society at large has reasons to pay attention to the Mennonite synthesis. Again, many cultural critics have called our attention to the dilemmas posed by a culture bent on individualism, self-realization, self-fulfillment, self-promotion, and self-aggrandizement. As the authors of *Habits of the Heart* instructed us, the problem is not so much with individualism per se.[80] The problem is that the individualistic impulse is no longer balanced against community commitments (civic or biblical). Bellah and his co-workers told us that we cannot simply go back (nor would most of us want to) to a time when community membership was held in place through oppressive demands for conformity. "We face a profound impasse. Modern individualism seems to be producing a way of life that is neither individually nor socially viable, yet a return to traditional forms would be to return to intolerable discrimination and oppression. The question, then, is whether the older civic and biblical traditions have the capacity to reformulate themselves while simultaneously remaining faithful to their own deepest insights."[81] Is it possible, however, for the people, who are themselves products of modern individualistic/materialistic culture, to recognize the advantage of a society organized according to principles of biblical communalism?

We should add here that we would stop short of saying that the crisis of North American individualism has caused a complete breakdown of moral discourse. As Jeffrey Stout argued in *Ethics After Babel*, moral diversity is not the same as the lack of morals or moral discourse. Nevertheless, as the sales of *Habits of the Heart* attest, there is a substantial audience that feels ambivalent, skeptical, and, at times even forlorn. Thus, although writers such as Bellah or Alasdair MacIntyre may overstate the case, they do speak to tension in American life.[82]

It is difficult for the non-Mennonite, non-Anabaptist to imagine the Mennonite experience, let alone learn from the lessons of that experience. To do either it first becomes necessary to rethink the biases concerning folk societies. Sociological analysis, in particular, too often treats religious and folk societies, ethnic cultures, and traditional morality with condescension or even overt hostility. Instead we must somehow see our common struggle. As Bellah and his coauthors advised, we do not need to return to traditional societies, but we certainly need to be "open to learning from the wisdom of [them]."[83] To use Chomsky's terminology, we must look for a "deep" commonality rather than being misled by "surface" diversity.[84]

According to the foreword to *The Cultural Contradictions of Capitalism*, "We stand . . . with a clearing ahead of us. The exhaustion of Modernism, the aridity of Communist life, the tedium of the unrestrained self, and the meaninglessness of the monolithic political chants, all indicate that a long era is coming to a slow close. The impulse of Modernism was to leap beyond: beyond nature, beyond culture, beyond tragedy—to explore the apeiron, the boundless, driven by the self-infinitizing spirit of the radical self."[85] Bell went on to note that the new era is more characterized by the recognition of a need for limits: "limits to growth, a limit to the spoliation of the environment, a limit to arms, a limit to the tampering with biological nature." Mennonite entrepreneurs afford us all a model in this regard. The critical aspect of the Mennonite synthesis is its tempering of the pursuit of private interests, if not private gratification, on which free market economy capitalism rests, by consciously rationalizing entrepreneurial commitment to collective interests, common goals, and common needs. Although we may not all be able to embrace the Anabaptist vision, we *must* all find our own synthesis of personal and collective interests. Such is the challenge of our times.

Appendix
Methodological Notes

For this project we used three different sources of previously unpublished data. Each of these sources provided somewhat different information regarding the experience, attitudes, and values of Mennonite entrepreneurs.

REDEKOP ENTREPRENEURIAL RESEARCH (RER)

The entrepreneurial research conducted by Calvin Redekop, identified in the text as Redekop Entrepreneurial Research (RER), began in 1984 with a proposal presented to a number of scholars for critique. A research proposal was constructed and subsequently funded by the Social Sciences and Humanities Research Council of Ottawa, Canada (1985–86, grant 410-84-1217). The project, "Entrepreneurialism and the Sectarian Ethos," also received support from the Office of Research, University of Waterloo, Ontario, Canada.

An in-depth interview, including a number of objective and subjective questions, was administered to one hundred Mennonite entrepreneurs. Interviews lasted two hours on average. Entrepreneurs were intentionally and carefully selected to represent the major geographical areas of Mennonite concentrations in Canada and the United States. They resided in Alberta, British Columbia, Manitoba, Ontario, and Saskatchewan provinces and in the states of Arizona, California, Florida, Indiana, Kansas, Ohio, Oregon, Pennsylvania, and Virginia. The respondents were also selected to represent the various Mennonite groups and business and industry categories proportionately. Both men and women were interviewed.

The questions were constructed with an eye toward isolating the significant aspects of economic behavior and its influences on religious life, especially the sectarian dimensions. The interview schedule was based on one that was used in a study by Evelyn Kallen and Merrijoy Kelner (1983). Questions were added to the Kallen/Kelner instrument to identify unique Mennonite factors and to provide data that could be compared with the Church Member Profile studies of J. Howard Kauffman, Leland Harder, and Leo Driedger (Kauffman and Harder 1975; Kauffman and Driedger 1991). The qualitative interview materials were transcribed fully for analysis.

KAUFFMAN/REDEKOP STUDY

This research was part of a larger research project conducted by Calvin Redekop during the 1970s while he was on the faculty at Goshen College. The project was entitled "Business-Labor Problems in Christian Perspective." Dan Kauffman, a student in Redekop's sociology of religion course, originally designed a research instrument in 1969 which was sent to thirty randomly selected entrepreneurs. The questionnaire was later (1975) adapted and administered in several Mennonite communities to small groups of entrepreneurs in California, Kansas, Manitoba, Ohio, and Ontario. The instrument used close-ended responses, and questions covered a range of topics. Seventy people completed the questionnaire. Their responses comprise the data presented in this book. The research was sponsored by the Mennonite Economic Development Associates.

CHURCH MEMBER PROFILE
STUDIES I AND II

This examination of Mennonite entrepreneurs used data from the Church Member Profile studies. Study I was a survey of five Mennonite and Brethren in Christ denominations (the Mennonite Church, the General Conference Mennonite Church, the Mennonite Brethren Church, the Brethren in Christ Church, and the Evangelical Mennonite Church). The study was designed and conducted by sociologists J. Howard Kauffman and Leland Harder. Data collection, involving the use of a lengthy questionnaire, was carried out between March and June 1972. Questions pertaining to personal religiosity, church involvement, views on theological and social issues, social concerns, moral attitudes and behavior, and background information were included. Responses from 3,591 people were analyzed. Kauffman and Harder reported their findings in their book *Anabaptism Four Centuries Later*. In it they detailed the methods utilized in their study and sample characteristics in an appendix.

Seventeen years later, in 1989, Church Member Profile II was conducted by J. Howard Kauffman, Leland Harder, and Leo Driedger. Once again, these sociologists surveyed the same five Mennonite and Brethren in Christ denominations, asking many of the same questions that were asked in 1972 and adding others. Study II provided comparative data that are all too rare in sociology and the sociology of religion in particular. 3,083 respondents participated in the second study. Results were reported in Kauffman and Driedger's book, *The Mennonite Mosaic*. Kauffman and Driedger also detailed the survey methods and sample selection procedures in an appendix.

Entrepreneurial Subset of Church Member Profile Studies

Kauffman, one of the architects of the two Church Member Profile studies, provided previously unpublished data comparing Mennonite entrepreneurs (defined as those in the proprietor and manager occupational category) with the Mennonite population as a whole.

Notes

Chapter One: Historical and Theological Perspectives

1. See Calvin Redekop's discussion of the conceptual difficulties involved in the term *Mennonite* in his book *Mennonite Society* (1989: 3).

2. Bender (1957a: 586–87).

3. See Simons (1956).

4. Bender (1957a: 587).

5. Bellah et al. (1985: 41–44). Bellah and his coauthors discussed four representative characters: the independent citizen, entrepreneur, manager, and therapist.

6. With the exception of the Hutterites, who are often viewed as aberrant.

7. Anthony Giddens made this contention the centerpiece of his review of the works of Marx, Weber, and Durkheim. See Giddens (1971).

8. Again, there is some conceptual confusion in this regard. The movement is referred to alternatively as the Swiss Brethren, Anabaptist, and Mennonitism. For more elaborate introductions to the origins of the Mennonites, see Clasen (1972); Dyck (1981); Smith (1981); and Durnbaugh (1985).

9. Clasen (1972).

10. Goertz (1993: 75–89).

11. Littell (1952). The young radicals repudiated the name, insisting that it was not re-baptism because infant baptism did not constitute true baptism.

12. Simons (1956: 300).

13. Friedmann (1957: 785).

14. Matthys was attempting to bring about the prophecies of Hoffman, who had originally specified that Strasbourg, not Muenster, would be the site of the New Jerusalem. Dyck (1981: 99ff.). See also van der Zijpp (1957a: 777–83).

15. Zablocki (1980).

16. Hege and Bender (1957: 529–31). There is some debate over the exact nature

of the synod, with some arguing that it was actually a series of separate meetings. A number of key leaders were also absent from this meeting.

17. Dyck (1981: 67).

18. Dyck reported that some claim that Hut accidentally lit the fire in an attempt to summon his guards to his cell as part of a planned escape. His son suggested the fire was lit by guards.

19. Redekop (1989: 10).   20. Braght (1951).

21. See Dyck (1981: 50ff.).   22. Redekop (1989: 15).

23. See Clasen (1972); Packull (1986); and Stayer (1991).

24. In more indirect ways in the Ephrata communistic movement in Pennsylvania as well as the Plockhoy experiment in New York.

25. Bender (1957b: 686).

26. For an extensive treatment of Mennonite migration to America, see MacMaster (1985).

27. MacMaster (1985: 34).

28. Bender (1957b: 686).

29. For a discussion of the Amish-Mennonite split, see Nolt (1992). The Charming Nancy brought the first major Amish group to America in 1737 after an eighty-three–day voyage.

30. MacMaster (1985: 111).

31. For a discussion of Mennonite migratory patterns and motivations during the nineteenth century, see Schlabach (1988).

32. The differences among five major subgroups have been well documented in two surveys of North American Mennonites: Kauffman and Harder (1975); Kauffman and Driedger (1991).

33. Hostetler (1980); Redekop (1969).

34. Klassen (1964: 129).

35. Hege (1955: 405).

36. Krahn (1968: 236).

37. Cited in Kauffman and Driedger (1991: 29).

38. Peachey (1954); Geiser (1956: 310–11); Kauffman and Driedger (1991) made quite a bit of these occupational differences, arguing that they contribute to persisting differences among Mennonite groups in North America today.

39. Hostetler (1974); Friedmann (1956b: 149–50); Gross (1980).

40. Braun (1956: 153–57); Harder (1949); Regher (1988).

41. Krahn (1956: 293–95); Kauffman (1957: 295–99); Redekop (1989).

42. Bender (1956: 303–6); Correll (1925); Hostetler (1974); Seguy (1977).

43. Bender (1956: 305); see also Correll (1925); Seguy (1984).

44. Bender (1956: 305).

45. Penner (1978); van der Zijpp (1955: 483).

46. Bender (1955b: 482).

47. van der Zijpp (1955: 483).

48. Redekop (1973).

49. Rempel (1933). For a recent survey and analysis of Russian commonwealth history and life, see also Urry (1989).

50. Krahn (1959a: 388–89).

51. Braun (1956: 153–57). The agricultural school was sponsored by the Agricultural Association. Outstanding leaders in this development of education included Johann Cornies, Philipp Wiebe, Andreas Voth, Johann Klatt, and Heinrich Unruh, among many others.

52. Krahn (1959b: 939).   53. Krahn (1957: 33).
54. Ibid.: 33–34.   55. Quiring (1955: 717).
56. Krahn (1957: 33).   57. MacMaster (1985: 39).
58. Bender (1955c: 483).   59. Ibid.
60. Klassen (1964: 30).

61. For diverse approaches see: Clasen (1972); Engels (1967); Kautsky (1966); Goertz (1984); Stayer (1991).

62. Bender (1955a: 113–14); Friedmann (1955: 658–62); Klassen (1964). The renaissance of interest in Anabaptist-Mennonite origins stemmed in part from a speech, "The Anabaptist Vision," delivered by Mennonite historian Harold Bender as his presidential address to the American Society of Church History in 1943. For a discussion of its impact, see Hershberger (1957). Some even refer to the Anabaptist Vision School, an allusion to those who accepted Bender's version of early Anabaptism and developed its implications for contemporary Mennonite life.

63. Hershberger (1958: 286).
64. Ibid.: 284–85.

65. Tawney (1920, 1954); Nelson (1969); Heilbroner (1976). For a recent review of the literature, see Tiemstra (1993: 227–47).

66. Hershberger (1958: 292).   67. Redekop and Steiner (1988: 5).
68. Ibid.: 10–11.   69. Hershberger (1958: 226).
70. Ibid.: 192–200.
71. Cronk (1981: 5–44); Friedmann (1956a: 448–49).
72. Franck (1981: 196–97).   73. Friedmann (1956a: 448–49).
74. Maker (1987).   75. Van Leeuwen (1964).
76. Eby (1986: 12).   77. *CIBA Newsletter*, February 1975.
78. Ibid., May 1975.

Chapter Two: Religion and Entrepreneurial Activity: Congruous, Contradictory, or Paradoxical?

1. Marshall Sahlins may be correct in his assertion that hunters and gatherers were relatively free and affluent, meaning that they worked at these things far less than modern humans do. Sahlins thereby challenged social scientists to rethink their notions of progress. See Sahlins (1972).

2. Firth (1956: 41).   3. Ibid.: 50.
4. Ibid.: 74.   5. Goode (1951: 87).
6. Firth (1956: 74).
7. Weber (1947, 1958); Heichelheim (1965); Polanyi (1944).
8. Sorokin (1928: 514).   9. Ibid.: 514–99.
10. Heichelheim (1965).   11. McLuhan (1965).

12. Gamwell (1986: 52). Anthropologist Levi-Strauss listed the exchange of goods, the exchange of women, and the exchange of messages as the three most important transactions.

13. See Marx and Engels (1967).

14. Weber (1947: 158). This concept of economic activity can only make sense in a culture in which the necessities of everyday life are made into commodities.

15. Berger and Luckmann (1966: 48).

16. Ibid.: 51.

17. Davis (1948: 451). Sociologists have, of course, debated the causal relationship between ideas and economy.

18. Sorokin (1928: 369).

19. Heilbroner (1961: 6).

20. Ibid.: 8.

21. This ideology emerged with the Protestant Reformation, the discovery of the New World, the discovery of the heliocentric universe, and, as Marx argued, as the superstructure was erected on the economic base which all these developments brought in their wake. Thomas Hobbes and Adam Smith essentially laid the foundation for modern individualism, with Locke, Bentham, Spencer, and Sumner, to mention only a few, building on it.

22. Sexuality is another important area of life which religion seeks to regulate, a point that was made by J. W. Mohr in a personal letter to Robert Siemens in 1990. Both economics and sexuality embody the contradiction of being vital to the survival of the species and, at the same time, vitally disrupting as they make the individual conscious of "its" alienation from the whole. We want to consider economic life and the encapsulation of this contradiction between individual rights and the common good, which Western reflection on economic reality truly is.

23. Berger (1967).

24. Ibid.: 65ff. Berger described the Hindu religious system as being at the rational end of the rational-irrational continuum of theodicies.

25. Annemarie de Waal Malefijt provided anthropological illustrations of these three aspects of economic life and the manner in which religion has regulated them. See de Waal Malefijt (1968: 312ff.).

26. Berger, Berger, and Kellner (1973).

27. Bellah et al. (1985: 44).

28. Weber spoke of this disenchantment, and Peter Berger developed the implications of it for the breakdown of people's sacred canopy. See Berger (1967).

29. Giddens (1971: 221).

30. White (1979: 97ff.). Berger (1967: 138ff.) described this as a market situation fostered in part by the increasing pluralization of religious beliefs in society.

31. Berger (1967: 145). Swedish filmmaker Ingmar Bergman carried this preoccupation with personal subjectivity to its logical conclusion in "The Silence," which addressed human despair in the face of the absence of God, and in "Through a Glass Darkly," in which God reveals himself as a spider to a schizophrenic woman.

32. Writing on this point is extensive both in literature and in social analysis.

Marquand's (1949) *Point of No Return* and Fitzgerald's (1925) *The Great Gatsby* are two examples in literature.

33. See Margaret Poloma's (1989: 216ff.) sympathetic analysis of the problems posed by the scandals in televangelism.

34. Ironically, the savings and loan scandal disclosed that the capitalist sector of society was fleecing the public on an even greater scale!

35. Weber (1958) made this observation at the conclusion of *The Protestant Ethic and the Spirit of Capitalism.*

36. Siemens (1989).

37. Whether capitalism caused this view or whether the two were simply elective affinities as Weber maintained is the stuff of classic debates in sociology.

38. Weber (1958). For the most recent analysis of Anabaptist-Mennonite economics, see Redekop, Krahn, and Steiner (1994).

39. Halteman (1988).

40. These have become greatly exaggerated in their collective consciousness as the legacy of the severest persecution. This is expressed, for example, in an abhorrence of communism by the North American emigrés from postrevolutionary Russia. The film "When They Shall Ask" (David Dueck Productions, Winnipeg) makes a feeble attempt to come to terms with this collective paranoia.

41. Casson (1982: 1). An entirely satisfactory definition of entrepreneurship may not be possible at this time, partly because of the novelty of the theoretical analysis of the field. A perusal of the field produces the conclusion that the definition depends upon the objective of the inquirer. The concept can be made too broad, so that everybody can be so defined; on the other hand it can be defined so narrowly as to result in a specific theory or hypothesis on the nature of the entrepreneurship. See Kent, Sexton, and Vesper (1982).

42. This definition is taken from the *American Heritage Dictionary* (1983), but other dictionaries provide similar definitions. The word *entrepreneur* comes from the Old French *entreprendre*, which means *to undertake.*

43. Heichelheim (1965).

44. Hugh (1963: 5).

45. Shapiro and Sokol (1982: 75–77).

46. Drucker (1985: 27–29).

47. Hornaday (1982: 25).

48. Barth (1963: 6).

49. Another, less restricted definition of such individuals is denoted by Weber's concept of charismatic authority in which the inner resources of an individual empower him or her to gain a following—sometimes even against the "hero's" will! In modern society, our charismatic heroes—athletes, movie actors, scientists, politicians—are motivated entrepreneurially in both senses of the term. In the classical sense, they attempt to amass enough capital during their brief professional careers to launch a business; and in the neoclassical or anthropological sense, they are gifted in that they possess talents, qualities, and abilities for which their fellows are willing to reward them, whether with respect, obedience, gifts, or whatever. The modern market economy has rationalized this psychological quirk

of human nature into the commodities of capitalistically organized entertainment, religion, sports, and politics.

50. Shapiro and Sokol (1982: 75–77).

51. Stayer (1991: 123–28).

52. Hostetler (1974); Stayer (1991).

53. Zablocki (1980). We are fully cognizant of the fact that this creates some theological problems. For example, Christ's apostles became businessmen (except for Paul, who was too astute a Pharisee to blunder into such a trap). We never solve the problem of the difference between an apostle and a genius (Kierkegaard), our only guiding clue being that we can recognize a genius by his genius at making money. Furthermore, we obscure the difference between a martyr for the truth (the extreme type of charismatic leader according to Zablocki) and an ecclesiastical cannibal (Kierkegaard). The latter capitalizes on the witness of the former.

54. See Hunter (1982).

55. For a discussion of cultural bargaining and the Amish, see Kraybill (1989).

56. Kraybill (1989: 25ff); Redekop (1989: 53).

57. Merton (1957: 233).   58. Kallen and Kelner (1983: 12).

59. Hostetler (1980: 142).   60. Kraybill (1989: 91).

61. Interview by Calvin Redekop, Redekop Entrepreneurial Research (RER), conducted between 1984 and 1989.

62. RER.

63. Franck (1981: 201).

64. Epp (1977: 35).

65. See Joseph Beiler, *Old Order Shop and Service Directory of the Old Order Society in the United States and Canada*, for a comprehensive discussion of entrepreneurship among the Old Order Amish.

66. Communication with Donald Kraybill, June 28, 1993. AMISH research project.

67. Fretz (1989).   68. Ibid.: 204.

69. Epp-Tiessen (1982).   70. Ibid.: 55–67; 126–35.

71. RER.

72. Berger (1963: 52–53). Berger, of course, spoke of this cosmopolitan motif as an important way of *being* a sociologist. Although his intent in introducing the phrase was different from our own, it still provides the flavor of what it means to be cosmopolitan.

73. Ward and Jenkins (1984).   74. Hostetler and Huntington (1967).

75. Kraybill (1989: 11).   76. Redekop (1969).

77. Kauffman and Harder (1975: 21).

78. Kauffman and Driedger (1991: 36).

79. Kauffman and Harder (1975: 329).

80. Kauffman and Driedger (1991: 238) concluded that residence is a weak but still differentiating factor. Even when educational level was controlled, residence continued to have some effect.

81. Kauffman and Harder (1975: 293).

82. Kauffman and Driedger (1991: 236).

83. Kauffman and Harder (1975: 292).

84. Kauffman and Driedger (1991: 236).

85. Ibid.: 133.

86. Donald Kraybill noted the positive effect of Mennonite education. See Kraybill (1978). Kauffman and Driedger (1991: 134–35) reported that those who were educated in Mennonite schools showed stronger adherence to Anabaptism and pacifism as well as higher Bible knowledge, support of church colleges, and church participation.

87. See the work of Karl Mannheim and Kurt Wolff.

Chapter Three: The Ethos of the North American Mennonite Enterprise

1. Yoder (1990: 778).

2. Bender (1956: 304).

3. One such example is Russian Mennonite poet Fritz Senn's "Hinterm Pflug/ Stimungen" ("Behind the Plow/Songs and Poems") epic of nine hundred lines. The literature on this romantic epoch and the resultant self-analysis are only now emerging. See Loewen and Reimer (1985: 149).

4. Clasen (1972); Peachey (1954); Stayer (1991).

5. Correll (1942). See also Yoder (1990: 779); Redekop (1993b: 4); Seguy (1973: 179–224); Penner (1978).

6. Redekop (1985, 1993b). Redekop's work supplemented earlier work by Paul Peachey, who pictured the first-generation Anabaptists as relatively urban. See Peachey's doctoral dissertation, "Die Soziale Herkunft der Schweizer Tauefer in der Reformationszeit," published in 1954.

7. Yoder (1990: 778).

8. Epp-Tiessen (1982); Urry (1989); Enns (1984); Penner (1978); Rempel (1933).

9. Gingerich (1942). 10. Juhnke (1989: 306).

11. Loewen (1946: 38–40). 12. Gingerich (1963: 12).

13. Harder (1971: 45). 14. Raid (1964: 186–87).

15. Of course, the more conservative Old Orders and the Hutterites are still predominantly agricultural, although the Hutterite farms can also be characterized as highly modernized agribusinesses. The Hutterites embody the paradox that, having become rather urbane and sophisticated in their utilization of the modern technical and material culture available in the area of agriculture, they have also retained all of the necessary mechanical, technical, and social organizational procedures they need to retain their communal economy and its supporting ideology. See Bennett (1967); Bender (1956: 303–6); Hershberger (1940: 214–23); Gingerich (1942: 167–73); Correll (1942: 161–66); Hostetler (1974); Landis (1945: 254–72).

16. Harder (1970).

17. Kauffman and Harder (1975: 60). Unfortunately, no census statistics are available for an earlier period of all five groups.

18. Kauffman and Driedger (1991: 38).

19. The rapid industrialization of these Mennonites in Canada remains practically undocumented.

20. The best general picture of the extent to which Mennonites became in-

volved first in farm-related business and later in nonagricultural enterprises can be gained from the studies that have been conducted in Mennonite communities. The studies of Altona, Manitoba, Canada by Esther Epp-Tiessen, of Waterloo County Mennonites by J. Winfield Fretz, and of Harvey County, Kansas by J. Lloyd Spaulding are probably some of the most significant done to date. They include substantial sections on Mennonite business and entrepreneurial efforts, although there are no statistical tables that would have allowed for comparisons. These studies show the significant degree to which entrepreneurship has increased over the last half-century or so. See Epp-Tiessen (1982); Fretz (1989); Spaulding (1953; 1957: 87–98).

21. Practically no research on this subject has been done. In a study of two very representative Mennonite communities (Hillsboro, Kansas, and Mountain Lake, Minnesota) conducted by the senior author in 1993, auto dealerships and oil/service stations were the two highest nonagricultural occupations engaged in by Mennonites. See Redekop (1993a).

22. As elsewhere, the name is fictitious, but the case is real.

23. See Stein (1964: 199–226).

24. Goulden (1976).

25. One reason is that they required the leisure that devotion to churchwork demands. The other is that agricultural labor, because it required attention on the Sabbath, was ritually defiling. See Weber (1952).

26. Buhr (forthcoming).

27. A discussion of the research methods is included in the Appendix. The reputational method of identifying entrepreneurs involved questioning a number of community leaders classified as entrepreneurs by using such indicators as: risk taking, innovation, business success, or undertaking a considerable action. This procedure appeared to create no difficulty for any of the informants.

28. Featherman (1971: 207–22).

29. Warner (1963); Kahl (1957); Curtis and Scott (1973).

30. Kahl (1957: 236; see especially Chapter 8); Dillard (1966).

31. Ward and Jenkins (1984).

32. See, for example, Andrew Greeley's discussion of the various models in *American Catholic* (1977). It might be argued that the larger or host society—whether we conceive of it as melting pot or multicultural mosaic—is largely a mythic creation. The national state—a bureaucracy dependent on direct and indirect taxation to sustain it—and the cultural form of life required to maintain it are, for the purposes of our consideration, one religious-ethnic group among others, albeit occupying a special place in the world system, from the perspective of the ethnic minority group member.

33. Ward and Jenkins (1984: 205).

34. Ibid. Ward and Jenkins spoke of the receiving society.

35. For example, Mennonite Educational Institute—a small Mennonite high school in southern Manitoba—boasts three computer laboratories.

36. Fretz (1955: 481). The emergence of entrepreneurship in the Netherlands, northern Germany, and Russia has been alluded to and needs to be kept in mind as a strong countermovement.

37. Bender (1957c: 895–97).

38. Poettcker and Regehr (1972: 157–58).

39. Vogt (1972: 160). The latter is also exemplified by the writings of Burkholder and Friesen.

40. Burkholder (1989); Friesen (1986).

41. Carl Kreider (1980: 12).

42. Interview, April 1986.

43. Redekop (1989).

44. Fretz (1979).

45. Hostetler (1974).

46. Redekop (1969); Vogt (1983: 64–78).

47. Krahn (1988).

48. Hostetler (1980); Redekop (1969).

Chapter Four: *The Entrepreneur and Work: Community or Self-Advancement?*

1. Pfeiffer (1979: 2).

2. Giddens (1973: 593).

3. And, more specifically, a masculine curse. *Women's work*, in the traditional biblical understanding, was essentially the bearing of children.

4. For a review and analysis of Christian attitudes toward work, see Redekop and Bender (1988).

5. Weber (1958: 108).

6. The sudden flowering of capitalism in northwestern Europe was not only the result of an understanding of work as an end in itself on the part of the Protestant bourgeoisie, but a global event precipitated by the discovery of the New World. This discovery gradually shifted the center of gravity of world trade and commerce from the Italian Mediterranean to the Atlantic of the Netherlands and England.

7. "Values are modes of organizing conduct—meaningful, effectively invested pattern principles that guide human action. . . . Values concern the goals or ends of action and are, as well, components in the selection of adequate means" (Williams (1955: 375–76). *Instrumental work* refers to work that would be a means for the achieving of an ultimate value, whereas *terminal work* would be seen as achieving values present in the work activity itself. See Rokeach (1973).

8. Ironically Mennonite entrepreneurs were among the most significant contributors to these projects, as for example in the Russian Commonwealth.

9. Weber (1958: 104).

10. Klassen (1964).

11. We acknowledge that our description here is at odds with some traditional approaches to the Anabaptist-Mennonite attitude toward work as it relates to salvation which have assumed that Anabaptist-Mennonites simply reflected the Lutheran position.

12. Oyer (1991: 256–86).

13. Ibid.: 267.

14. Cronk (1981: 9).

15. Ibid.: 5–44.

16. Klaassen (1981: 235). See also Redekop, Krahn, and Steiner (1994).

17. Cronk (1988: 21).

18. Ibid.: 1.

19. Fretz (1989: 124).

20. Fretz (1979: 116).

21. Featherman (1971: 207–22); McClelland (1961).

22. Smucker (1986: 285).   23. Ibid.: 274.
24. Ibid.: 274.   25. Weaver (1994: 233).
26. Kauffman and Harder (1975); Kauffman and Driedger (1991).
27. Braudel (1980).
28. The names of entrepreneurs discussed here are fictitious.
29. Weber (1946: 357).   30. Ibid.: 356.
31. Ibid.: 355–57.   32. Ibid.: 357.
33. Cronk (1981: 8).

Chapter Five: Entrepreneurial Upward Mobility and the Dilemmas of Success

1. For a critical review of some of the issues, debate, and furor generated by the Bishops' Letter, see the June 1988 issue of the *Journal of Business Ethics*.
2. Mullin (1983: 82–85).   3. Ibid.: 9.
4. Hershberger (1958: 287).   5. Drucker (1985: 27–28).
6. We recognize that some might argue that the crass goals of power and status would never be stated overtly by Mennonites but would rather be expressed more subtly in actual behavior.
7. Williams (1955: 388–438).
8. Ainlay (1990: 135–53).
9. The names given to these entrepreneurs are fictitious.
10. Lasch (1987).   11. Campbell (1993).
12. Urry (1989: 138–52).   13. Redekop (1993b).
14. Ibid.
15. Hiebert (1973); Juhnke (1989); Schlabach (1988); Steiner (1988).

Chapter Six: Heroic Conformity and Community Alienation

1. Penner (1978); Redekop (1993b); Sprunger (1994).
2. Groenveld, Jacobszoon, and Verhew (1980); Dyck (1981: 100ff.); Penner (1978); Sprunger (1994); van der Zijpp (1957b: 824–44).
3. Penner (1978: 177).   4. Hershberger (1958: 284–85).
5. Horsch (1950: 255).   6. Penner (1959: 923).
7. Hostetler (1980: 106).   8. Redekop (1969: 127ff.).
9. Harder (1970: 28).   10. Ibid.: 95.
11. Kauffman and Harder (1975); Kauffman and Driedger (1991).
12. The responses of the subsample of entrepreneurs from the CMP2 study are previously unpublished. Kauffman separated out the entrepreneurs, defined here as all those falling into the proprietors and managers category.
13. Klassen (1964: 70).
14. Jeschke (1990: 239–40).
15. The response of the congregation and religious community to the entrepreneur's lifestyle would be an excellent source of information on how the con-

gregation felt about them and would indicate the role the congregation played in the alienation process; however, this information was not available.

16. Again, we would note that the occupational homogeneity of Mennonites, especially in the early years of the movement, has been exaggerated.

17. See Juhnke (1989: 108–23). See also the "Bible Conferences" and "Revivals" entries in *The Mennonite Encyclopedia*.

18. For a full discussion of religious accommodation and its consequences, see Hunter (1982). For a discussion of accommodation within the Anabaptist context, see Kraybill (1982).

19. Smucker (1986: 284).　　　　20. Berger (1967).

21. Hamm (1987: 215–18).　　　　22. Wallace (1966: 105–7).

Chapter Seven: Rationalizing Faith and Business

1. Revelation 18: 11–19.

2. Rauschenbusch (1919: 156).

3. Friedman (1962); Hayek (1944); Smith (1937); Spencer (1877); Sumner (1927); and Ward (1963).

4. Hayek (1944: 204).

5. Rasmussen (1965: 3).

6. Goertz (1988b); Redekop (1984: 87–103).

7. Hunter (1991).　　　　8. Hershberger (1955: 650–51).

9. Klassen (1964: 123).　　　　10. Hegel (1961); Maker (1987).

11. Driedger (1982: 234–35).　　　　12. Ibid.: 235.

13. Ibid.: 236.　　　　14. Hiebert (1973: 477).

15. Appavoo (1978: 310–11).　　　　16. Appavoo (1985: 67–93).

17. See the Appendix for a discussion of the Kauffman/Redekop study.

18. The research instrument of Kauffman and Redekop was used in several community settings. We are proceeding inductively in our interpretation of the data. We are moving from the most specific, or purest form of material culture—money—which is wealth that merely exists on paper, and by convention, drawing more general conclusions about Mennonite attitudes toward material culture and the extent to which their attitudes express a *Gelassenheit* ethos (i.e., we are attempting to determine whether Mennonite entrepreneurs value their possessions for their personal or communal value).

19. These findings are from CMP1. CMP2 did not include the question.

20. CMP2 printouts.

21. Callian (1975); Cochran (1967); Cochran and Miller (1961); Grelle and Krueger (1986); Polanyi (1944).

22. Hayek (1944: 92).

23. Ibid.: 93. This modern, liberal individualistic conception of the problem dates from C. Wright Mills' lamentation of the breakdown of both socialism and liberalism as viable options. See Mills (1959).

24. Anthony (1977).

25. As a result there have emerged liberal and humanitarian organizations such as the Employee Stock Ownership Association (ESOP), which attempted to humanize the more blatantly mercenary objectives of corporations.

26. Anthony (1977: 218).   27. Ibid.: 219.

28. Polanyi (1944).   29. Kallen and Kelner (1983: 50–54).

30. RER.   31. Mannheim (1936: 56).

32. Kreider (1980: 32).

33. Anthony (1977; see especially Chapter 4 for a classic statement of this sociological principle).

34. Simons (1956: 349–50).

35. The recent emergence of the Mennonite Economic Development Associates, a merger of three separate spontaneous movements of recent years, is one example of a lay response to the alienation between faith and economic action which unconscious compartmentalization has brought about.

Chapter Eight: Mennonite Faith and Economic Ideologies

1. Burkholder (1959: 1079).

2. Ibid.

3. Ibid.

4. Reimer (1988). See also Weaver (1988).

5. Johnson (1967: 76).

6. Geertz (1964) quoted in Johnson (1967: 76).

7. Johnson (1967: 76).   8. Ibid.

9. Ibid.: 77.   10. Schwartz (1970: 1).

11. Ibid.: 4.   12. Ibid.: 5.

13. Kautsky (1966: 19–20).   14. Ibid.

15. Burkholder (1989: 214).   16. RER.

17. The Amish are somewhat famous for their attitudes toward technology. Don Kraybill (1989) said that outsiders have often misconstrued their approach, suggesting that they make more accommodations than most imagine. For the most recent information on Amish entrepreneurship, see Kraybill and Nolt (1995).

18. Bender (1956: 303–6); Fretz (1957a: 307–9); Redekop (1985).

19. Bender (1956: 303–6). A Mennonite theology of creation/environment is slowly emerging. The Mennonite role in the production, distribution, and consumption of material phenomena is undeveloped, and the implications for Mennonite exploitation of the environment are still not being recognized. See Redekop (1986: 387–403); Redekop (1993b).

20. This is not the place to argue the relative importance of financial wealth in the building of the kingdom of God; however, in the context of the Mennonite community, the role of economic and financial power in religious life has been seriously challenged by the more liberally educated members. But it is very well known that as the Mennonite religious society is becoming increasingly complex and organized, institutionalized financial resources are playing an increasing

role and hence enhancing the status of those members who have the ability to contribute. See Smucker (1976).

21. An analysis of the actual connection between entrepreneurial actions and the purpose and goal of history, as seen by Christianity in general and Mennonites in particular, is still left open. One of the first attempts to focus on business and mission took place at the annual MEDA convention in 1987. For a review of the various positions, see Kroeker (1988: 4–8).

22. Theron Schlabach (1988: 88–105) reported that the effect of pietism on Mennonites has been so strong that many things associated with Mennonites are, in fact, due to pietism's humility theology.

23. A theology of work is also relatively undeveloped in the Mennonite context. Cronk and Kraybill produced analyses of how the Amish understand work as part of their ideology. For a Mennonite interpretation, see Redekop and Bender (1988); Burkholder (1989); Redekop (1994).

24. Burkholder (1989: 214).

25. Ibid.: 133. The *de facto* entrance of Mennonites into commerce and industry is clearly creating a need to articulate and interpret the positions of those who oppose such activity and those who support it. A few entrepreneurial types are beginning to articulate positive orientation, such as Block, DeFehr, Dyck, High, and Strite et al., who have been featured in *The Marketplace*. These are persons who have taken degrees, including MBAs, and feel at home in more academic discussions. Many others have strong feelings but do not articulate them because of their sense of inadequacy in expressing themselves.

26. Business entrepreneurs are by no means the only or central contingent of members who are acculturating. The professions and the successful in other sectors of the Mennonite community are tasting power and influence. Burkholder (1989); Kraybill and Pellman (1982); Loewen (1988).

27. Schwartz (1970: 211).

28. Ibid.: 213–16.

29. Bienvenue and Goldstein (1985: 263); Durkheim (1951); Simmel (1955); Coser (1957).

30. Enloe (1973: 266).   31. Litt (1970: 120ff).

32. Heichelheim (1965).   33. Pollins (1984).

34. Ibid.: 84.   35. Ibid.: 87.

36. Neusner (1987: 332).

37. Burkholder (1989: 133). There is one major exception to this generalization, namely the Russian Mennonite commonwealth, approximately 1800 to 1920, during which the population and resource base were so substantial as to develop into a society resembling the Jewish shtetl in some respects. This society possessed a religious and secular synthesis that resulted in a diversified society, which, although based on agriculture, was fast becoming commercial and industrial. By 1860 "the industrial age complete with steam-powered engines and accompanied by the noise and pollution of the factory system, had invaded the quiet tranquillity of rural Khortitsa"; see Urry (1989: 235). See also Burkholder (1989); Epp (1981: 289–371); Kreider (1951); Rempel (1974: 5–54); Redekop (1989); Toews (1981: 298–

371). The Mennonite commonwealth idea spread in mitigated form to Canada, Mexico, and Paraguay as well.

Chapter Nine: Sociological Paradigms and Mennonite Economic Sociology

1. Wallerstein (1979). 2. Weber (1958: 24–26).
3. Ibid.: 64ff. 4. Ibid.: 109ff.
5. Ibid.: 26ff. This psychology (and we must not forget Weber's debt to Nietzsche and Freud) must be complemented by consideration of the fact that the discovery of the New World as well as of the heliocentric universe in the preceding centuries necessitated a new economic and ideological order as well. Protestantism provided the new ideology and capitalism the new economy. Some have said that Weber was writing *contra* Marx, who had argued that Protestant theology provided a superstructural ideology to rationalize relations of production in which an ascending bourgeois class exploited a pauperized peasantry in a systematic and legal manner. See Polanyi (1944).
6. Weber (1958: 144ff.). 7. Ibid.: 108.
8. Krahn (1968: 211–13). 9. Gerth and Mills (1946: 321–22).
10. Weber (1958: 160). 11. Ibid.: 44.
12. Ibid.: 147.
13. Before we proceed, however, the qualification should be made that the Mennonites specifically are only mentioned very briefly in the context of Weber's entire output. Paradoxically, the allusions are strategic and indicate an interest in and familiarity with the Anabaptists which a simple counting operation fails to disclose.
14. Nafziger (1965: 195–98). 15. Weber (1964).
16. Weber (1975: 323). 17. Appling (1975: 244–47).
18. Stephen Ainlay (1993a) questioned the purpose and usefulness of heritage hunting among Anabaptists. He argued that the tradition has been so dynamic that there is no single heritage waiting to be discovered. Rather, the essence of Anabaptism reflected the priorities of the searcher.
19. Bennett (1967: 159–60).
20. Ibid.
21. Ibid.: 251. As any anthropologist could tell us, this conquest of individualism is an important feature of life in face-to-face societies as well. Thus, in *Totem and Taboo* Freud made most ingenious use of this fact to bolster his theory of the sexuality of the human unconscious. Primitive mythology is preoccupied with the stresses individualism imposes on the social fabric. Freud (Eurocentric, patriarchal) substituted the sexual impulse for this individualism because the culture to which he was selling his psychology was becoming individualistic, secularized, and capitalistic. See Levine (1985). A large part of spiritual work, in the modern church as in the primitive society, is that of integrating the individual's energy (libidinal) into corporate concerns (the cathedrals of the European Middle Ages, the pyramids of ancient Egypt, the factories and freeways of modern America are all monuments to the conquest of individualism—with the most spectacular of

all culminating in individualism's self-conquest). Freud completed the revaluation (poisoning) of all morality by substituting sexuality for acquisitiveness as the basis of our cultural malaise. The difference is that acquisitiveness can be eliminated from culture if we are willing to pay the cost; sexuality cannot.

22. Kauffman and Harder (1975).   23. Harder (1962: 246).

24. Redekop (1989).   25. Redekop (1959: 19).

26. Packull (1986); Stayer (1991).   27. Packull (1986: 60).

28. Redekop (1959: 16).   29. Niebuhr (1957: 22ff.).

30. Redekop (1959: 19ff.).   31. Ibid.: 191.

32. For a recent treatment of the decline of the respectable or mainline Protestant churches, see Roof and McKinney (1987).

33. Redekop (1959: 26–27).   34. Ibid.: 28.

35. Ibid.: 31ff.   36. Harder (1962: 260).

37. Harder (1970: 37–39).

38. These statistics (from Kauffman and Harder, 1975), which we discussed earlier in the book, are the closest we can come to an accurate portrayal. Recall that there are only slight variations and differences from the general population.

39. Redekop (1959: 29).

40. Harder (1970: 260).

41. Hostetler (1954).

42. Adequate proof for the individual disinheritance thesis would require a longitudinal study of congregations and their membership status or a community study of Mennonite congregations in which the individual and/or congregational socioeconomic status could be compared over a sufficient time span. Interestingly, no study of the social mobility among Mennonites has been undertaken, nor has a thorough study of a Mennonite community for this purpose been attempted (Driedger and Redekop, 1983). The community study of Waterloo County, Ontario, Canada, conducted by Fretz (1989) contains considerable description of Mennonite economic life, but there are no indications of how the Mennonite community has changed in its socioeconomic stratification over time. Needless to say, a great deal more hard data are needed before a definitive conclusion to the congregational or individual mobility thesis can be made. Studies are available which show the relative standing of the major religious communions, but none includes the Mennonites because of their insignificant size. As indicated earlier, studies of individual mobility are very sparse indeed, but what there is tends to be negative so it is logical to suggest that Mennonite members have not left the church as they enhanced their socioeconomic situation.

43. This difference is significant at the 0.01 level. See Hostetler (1954: 188).

44. Redekop (1953: 71ff.).

45. Cohn (1970).

46. Mannheim (1936: 211ff.); Niebuhr (1957); Stayer (1991).

47. Friesen (1974).   48. Kautsky (1966).

49. Mannheim (1936: 201ff.).   50. Goertz (1988a).

51. Friesen (1986: 233ff.); Stayer (1991).

52. Zschaebitz (1980).

53. Ibid.: 32.

54. Packull (1986: 51–57).

55. For the latter, representative books include Hillerbrand (1988); Goertz (1984).

56. Kollmorgen (1942: 46).   57. Hostetler (1980: 8ff.).

58. Correll (1942: 164).   59. Ibid.: 165.

60. Ibid.: 162.   61. Bender (1956: 304).

62. Penner (1978).   63. Seguy (1973: 218–19).

64. Sawatsky (1971: 3).   65. Kollmorgen (1942: 104).

66. Ibid.: 46.

67. Rempel (1933); Seguy (1977); Urry (1989); Penner (1978); Loewen and Reimer (1985).

68. Loewen and Reimer (1985: 48).

69. Redekop (1989).

Chapter Ten: The Cultural Contradictions of Mennonite Life and Utopian Economics

1. Bell (1976).

2. Cohn (1970); Mannheim (1936: 211ff.); Ruether (1970); Stayer (1991); Seibt (1972).

3. Mohr, personal letter to Robert Siemens (1990).

4. Troeltsch (1960: 698).   5. Seibt (1972: 166ff.).

6. Bloch (1964, 1980).   7. Mannheim (1936: 251).

8. Cohn (1970); Seibt (1972).   9. Frye (1983).

10. Bloch (1964); Redekop and Koop (1991).

11. Nordhoff (1875).

12. Klassen (1964: 123).

13. Troeltsch (1960: 330). In this context, see Gingerich (1985), which discusses the Reformed and Anabaptist-Hutterite views of property.

14. Weber (1946).

15. Urry (1989).

16. MacMaster (1985); Urry (1989).

17. Klassen, Friesen, Fretz, Goertz, Stayer, and Packull among others have stressed this theme.

18. Kauffman and Harder (1975); Kauffman and Driedger (1991).

19. Ibid. (1991).   20. See Juhnke (1989).

21. Ainlay (1993b).   22. Seeley, Sim, and Loosley (1956).

23. See Chapter Four in this book, in which this theme is explored. See also Cronk (1981); Kraybill (1989); Redekop (1988); Penner (1978); Peters (1990); and Seguy (1973) whose works focus on the role of work in Mennonite community life.

24. Empirical proof for this development is provided by Kauffman and Driedger who observe that "over one-half (55 percent) of the respondents agreed that faith is a private matter." Kauffman and Driedger (1991: 97).

25. Fretz (1957b: 195).

26. Klassen (1964: 114).

27. Ibid.: 123.
28. Sommer (1954: 205–23); Rideman (1956: 43).
29. Simons (1956: 200). 30. Klaassen (1981: 234).
31. Ibid.: 240. 32. Klaassen (1971: 303).
33. Klaassen (1981: 242). 34. Troeltsch (1960: 697).
35. Ibid.: 695. 36. Ibid.
37. Ibid. 38. Ibid.
39. Ibid.: 696. 40. Ibid.: 705.
41. Ibid.: 333–34. 42. Smucker (1945: 5–26).
43. Gross (1980). 44. Hostetler (1974).
45. Seguy (1977). 46. Redekop (1989).
47. Groenveld, Jacobszoon, and Verhew (1980).
48. Urry (1989). 49. Burkholder (1989: 31).
50. Troeltsch (1960: 696). 51. Ibid.: 331.
52. Cronk (1981: 5–44); See also Klassen (1964); Kraybill (1989); Nafziger (1986); Redekop and Koop (1991).
53. Fretz (1979); Kauffman and Driedger (1991).
54. Oyer (1991: 256–86); Schowalter (1957: 521–25).
55. Vogt (1972: 157–60).
56. Halteman's (1988) *Market Capitalism and Christianity* comes very close to providing such an ethos, for although it was written for a general Christian audience, his analysis took a decidedly Anabaptist-Mennonite perspective.
57. Redekop (1989); Vogt (1972). 58. Burkholder (1959: 1082).
59. Wach (1944). 60. Heilbroner (1976: 152–53).
61. Burkholder (1989: 213). 62. Burkholder (1959: 1080).
63. Lasch (1987). 64. Berger (1967).
65. Halteman (1988: 75). 66. Kreider (1980: 41).
67. Ibid.: 170. 68. Halteman (1988).
69. A thoughtful analysis of Durkheim's conception of the Christian Church as the first secular moral community (*Moral Education*)—a community based on personal responsibility—would go far to help bridge the gap between the economic and theological paradigms.
70. Dyck (1975).
71. Rudy (1975: 1–3).
72. Vogt (1980: 1–4).
73. Redekop (1989). Examples of this tendency include the cooperative movement that has taken form in many Mennonite communities and the credit union idea that is rapidly gaining ground in some.
74. Klaassen (1971: 303).
75. Heichelheim (1965); Braudel (1980).
76. Benedict (1946). 77. Redekop (1989).
78. Wenger (1957). 79. Kraybill (1975).
80. Bellah et al. (1985). The thesis of the book is that the biblical and republican forms of individualism advocated by America's so-called founding fathers which modulated the negative effects of pure self-interest have been replaced by utilitarian individualism (the drive for material success) and expressive individualism (the drive for self-actualization). This change in North American life was by no

means a cultural coincidence. With an increasing commitment to egalitarianism, a growing belief that people should rely on their own judgment rather than on a received authority, the emergence of the therapeutic ethos as the dominant ideology, the rise of huge bureaucratic structures, and the handing over of decision making to bureaucratic experts in more and more areas of social life, people's attachments to greater social wholes, such as ethical communities and republics, has declined. Bellah and his co-workers seem to believe that North American society as a whole is at a critical juncture. Americans have not yet fully yielded to modern individualism, and yet most no longer have the mechanism for fulfilling their desire to belong to a community, leaving many Americans with a deep sense of ambivalence.

81. Bellah et al. (1985: 144).

82. MacIntyre (1984).

83. Bellah et al. (1985: 296).

84. This is a malaise of modern (Anglo-American) sociology per se. It does not seem able develop the concepts intellectually, nor are its practitioners experienced existentially, to enable it to perceive a society that is informed by a symbolic world (mythology), having reduced everything to the physical matter that empirical scientists study and capitalists make into commodities. North American sociology has by and large reduced society to a "heap of individuals," out of which no society in any real sense can be generated. Allan Bloom (1987: 113) used the metaphors of the *herd* and the *hive* to characterize the differences between these conceptions of society. A herd animal, to press the metaphor, cannot understand the hive mentality.

85. Bell (1976: xxix).

Bibliography

Ainlay, Stephen C. 1990. Communal Commitment and Individualism. In *Anabaptist-Mennonite Identities in Ferment*, edited by Leo Driedger and Leland Harder. Elkhart, Ind.: Institute of Mennonite Studies.

———. 1993a. Ministry in the Anabaptist Tradition: Theological, Historical, and Sociological Perspectives. Paper presented at the Bridgewater Conference on Anabaptism: A Heritage and Its Twenty-first-century Prospects, Autumn, at Bridgewater College, Bridgewater, Va.

———. 1993b. Mennonite Culture Wars: Power, Knowledge, and Cultural Elites. Paper presented at the Conference on Power: Its Use and Misuse in Anabaptist, Mennonite, and Brethren Communities, July, at Elizabethtown College, Elizabethtown, Pa.

Anthony, P. D. 1977. *The Ideology of Work*. London: Tavistock.

Appavoo, David. 1978. Religion and Family among the Markham Mennonites. Ph.D. diss., York University, Toronto.

———. 1985. Ideology, Family, and Group Identity in a Mennonite Community in Southern Ontario. *Mennonite Quarterly Review* 59: 67–93.

Appling, Gregory B. 1975. Amish Protestantism and the Spirit of Capitalism. *Cornell Journal of Social Relations* 10: 239–50.

Barth, Fredrik, ed. 1963. *The Role of the Entrepreneur in Social Change in Northern Norway*. Bergen, Norway: Scandinavian Books.

Beiler, Joseph. 1977. *Old Order Shop and Service Directory of the Old Order Society in the United States and Canada*. Gordonville, Pa.: Privately published.

Bell, Daniel. 1976. *The Cultural Contradictions of Capitalism*. New York: Basic Books.

Bellah, Robert, Richard Madsen, William Sullivan, Ann Swidler, and Steven Tipton. 1985. *Habits of the Heart: Individualism and Commitment in American Life*. New York: Harper and Row.

Bender, Harold S. 1955a. Anabaptism. *Mennonite Encyclopedia*, vol. 1, 113–14. Scottdale, Pa.: Mennonite Publishing House.

————. 1955b. Business among the Mennonites of Germany. *Mennonite Encyclopedia*, vol. 1, 482–83.

————. 1955c. Business among the Mennonites of North America. *Mennonite Encyclopedia*, vol. 1, 483–84.

————. 1956. Farming and Settlement. *Mennonite Encyclopedia*, vol. 2, 303–6.

————. 1957a. Mennonite. *Mennonite Encyclopedia*, vol. 3, 586–87.

————. 1957b. Migrations of Mennonites. *Mennonite Encyclopedia*, vol. 3, 686.

————. 1957c. Nonconformity. *Mennonite Encyclopedia*, vol. 3, 895–97.

Benedict, Ruth. 1946. *Patterns of Culture*. New York: Pelican Books.

Bennett, John. 1967. *Hutterian Brethren: The Agricultural Economy and Social Organization of a Communal People*. Stanford: Stanford University Press.

Berger, Peter. 1963. *Invitation to Sociology*. Garden City, N.Y.: Doubleday.

————. 1967. *The Sacred Canopy*. Garden City, N.Y.: Doubleday.

Berger, Peter, Brigette Berger, and Hansfried Kellner. 1973. *The Homeless Mind*. New York: Random House.

Berger, Peter, and Thomas J. Luckmann. 1966. *The Social Construction of Reality*. Garden City, N.Y.: Doubleday.

Bienvenue, Rita, and Jay E. Goldstein. 1985. *Ethnicity and Ethnic Relations*, 2nd ed. Toronto: Butterworths.

Bloch, Ernst. 1964. *Geist der Utopie*. Frankfurt: Suhrkamp.

————. 1980. *Das Prinzip der Hoffnung*. Frankfurt: Suhrkamp.

Bloom, Allan. 1987. *The Closing of the American Mind*. New York: Simon and Schuster.

Braght, Thieleman J. van. 1951. *The Bloody Theatre or Martyrs' Mirror*. Scottdale, Pa.: Mennonite Publishing House.

Braudel, Ferdinand. 1980. *On History*. London: Weidenfeld and Nicolson.

Braun, Peter. 1956. Education among the Russian Mennonites. *Mennonite Encyclopedia*, vol. 2, 153–57.

Buhr, Joanna. Forthcoming. Kurt Janz: The Challenges of Success and Failure. In *Mennonite Entrepreneurial Profiles*, edited by Calvin Redekop and Ben Redekop.

Burkholder, J. Lawrence. 1959. Ethics. *Mennonite Encyclopedia*, vol. 4, 1079–83.

————. 1989. *The Problem of Social Responsibility from the Perspective of the Mennonite Church*. Elkhart, Ind.: Institute of Mennonite Studies.

Burkholder, John Richard, and Calvin Redekop. 1976. *Kingdom, Cross and Community*. Scottdale, Pa.: Herald Press.

Callian, Carnegie Samuel. 1975. *The Gospel According to Wall Street*. Nashville: John Knox Press.

Campbell, Joseph. 1993. *Myths to Live By*. New York: Viking Penguin.

Casson, Mark. 1982. *The Entrepreneur: An Economic Theory*. Totowa, N.J.: Barnes and Noble.

Clasen, Claus-Peter. 1972. *Anabaptism: A Social History*. Ithaca: Cornell University Press.

Cochran, Thomas C. 1967. Entrepreneurship. *International Encyclopedia of the Social Sciences*, 87–91. New York: Macmillan.

Cochran, Thomas C., and William Miller. 1961. *The Age of Enterprise*. New York: Harper and Row.

Cohn, Norman. 1970. *The Pursuit of the Millennium*. New York: Oxford University Press.

Correll, Ernst H. 1925. *Das Schweizerische Mennonitentum*. Tübingen, Germany: J. C. B. Mohr.

————. 1942. Sociological and Economic Significance of the Mennonites as a Culture Group in History. *Mennonite Quarterly Review* 16: 161–66.

Coser, Lewis. 1957. *Sociological Theory: A Book of Readings*. New York: Macmillan.

Cronk, Sandra. 1981. Gelassenheit: The Rites of the Redemptive Process in the Old Order Amish and Old Order Mennonite Communities. *Mennonite Quarterly Review* 55: 5–44.

————. 1988. The Meaning of Work in Anabaptist Mennonite Society. Unpublished paper.

Curtis, James E., and William B. Scott. 1973. *Social Stratification in Canada*. Englewood Cliffs, N.J.: Prentice-Hall.

Davis, Kingsley. 1948. *Human Society*. New York: Macmillan.

de Waal Malefijt, Annemarie. 1968. *Religion and Culture*. London: Macmillan.

Dillard, Dudley. 1966. Capitalism. *Encyclopaedia Britannica*, vol. 3, 839–45. Chicago: Encyclopaedia Britannica, Inc.

Driedger, Leo. 1982. Individual Autonomy versus Community Control. *Journal for the Scientific Study of Religion* 21: 226–41.

————. Urbanization of Mennonites in Post-War Canada. *Journal of Mennonite Studies* 6: 70–88.

Driedger, Leo, and Calvin Redekop. 1983. Sociology of Mennonites: State of the Art and Science. *Journal of Mennonite Studies* 1: 33–63.

Drucker, Peter. 1985. *Innovation and Entrepreneurship*. New York: Harper and Row.

Durkheim, Emile. 1951. *The Division of Labor*. Glencoe, Ill.: Free Press.

————. 1961. *Moral Education*. Glencoe, Ill.: Free Press.

Durnbaugh, Donald. 1985. *The Believers' Church*. Scottdale, Pa.: Herald Press.

Dyck, Cornelius. 1981. *An Introduction to Mennonite History*. Scottdale, Pa.: Herald Press.

Dyck, Rudolph W. 1975. Business and Christianity: Is There Hope? *CIBA Newsletter* May: 1–2.

Eby, John. 1986. Must Successful Mennonites Leave the Church? *Festival Quarterly* 13: 11–13.

Engels, Friedrich. 1967. *The German Revolutions: The Peasant War in Germany*. Chicago: University of Chicago Press.

Enloe, Cynthia. 1973. *Ethnic Development and Political Development*. Boston: Little, Brown.

Enns, Gerhard. 1984. *The Rural Municipality of Rhineland*. Altona, Man.: R. M. of Rhineland.

Epp, David H. 1981. The Emergence of German Industry in South Russian Colonies. *Mennonite Quarterly Review* 55: 289–371.

Epp, Frank. 1977. *Mennonite Peoplehood*. Waterloo, Ont.: Conrad Grebel College Press.

Epp-Tiessen, Esther. 1982. *Altona: The Story of a Prairie Town*. Altona, Man.: D. W. Friesen.

Featherman, D. L. 1971. The Socioeconomic Achievement of White Religious-Ethnic Subgroups: Social and Psychological Explanations. *American Sociological Review* 36: 207–22.

Firth, Raymond. 1956. *Human Types*. New York: Barnes and Noble.

Fitzgerald, F. Scott. 1925. *The Great Gatsby*. New York: Scribner.

Franck, Sebastian. 1981. Sebastian Frank on the Anabaptists. In *Sixteenth Century Anabaptism: Defences, Confessions, Refutations*, edited by Walter Klaassen. Waterloo, Ont.: Conrad Grebel College Press.

Fretz, J. Winfield. 1955. Business. *Mennonite Encyclopedia*, vol. 1, 480–81.

———. 1957a. Farming among the Mennonites in North America. *Mennonite Encyclopedia*, vol. 2, 307–9.

———. 1957b. Brotherhood and the Economic Ethic of the Anabaptists. In *Recovery of the Anabaptist Vision*, edited by Guy F. Hershberger. Scottdale, Pa.: Herald Press.

———. 1979. Newly Emerging Communes in Mennonite Communities. In *Communes: Historical and Contemporary*, edited by Ruth Shonle Cavan and Man Singh Das. New Delhi: Vikas Publishing House.

———. 1989. *The Waterloo Mennonites: A Community in Paradox*. Waterloo, Ont.: Wilfrid Laurier University Press.

Freud, Sigmund. 1938. *Totem and Taboo*. New York: A. A. Brill.

Friedman, Milton. 1962. *Capitalism and Freedom*. Chicago: University of Chicago Press.

Friedmann, Robert. 1955. Community of Goods. *Mennonite Encyclopedia*, vol. 1, 658–62.

———. 1956a. Gelassenheit. *Mennonite Encyclopedia*, vol. 2, 448–49.

———. 1956b. Hutterian Brethren. *Mennonite Encyclopedia*, vol. 2, 854–65.

———. 1957. Thomas Muentzer. *Mennonite Encyclopedia*, vol. 3, 785.

Friesen, Abraham. 1974. *Reformation and Utopia: The Marxist Interpretation of the Reformation and Its Antecedents*. Wiesbaden: F. Steiner.

Frye, Northrop. 1983. *The Great Code: The Bible and Literature*. Toronto: Academy Press.

Gamwell, Franklin I. 1986. Freedom and the Economic Order: A Foreword to Religious Evaluation. In *Christianity and Capitalism*, edited by Bruce Grelle and David Krueger. Chicago: Center for the Scientific Study of Religion.

Geertz, Clifford. 1964. Ideology as a Cultural System. In *Ideology and Discontent*, edited by David Apter. Glencoe, Ill.: Free Press.

Geiser, Samuel. 1956. Farming among the Mennonites in Switzerland. *Mennonite Encyclopedia*, vol. 2, 310–11.

Gerth, H. H., and C. Wright Mills. 1946. *From Max Weber: Essays in Social Theory*. New York: Oxford University Press.

Giddens, Anthony. 1973. *Capitalism and Modern Social Theory*. Cambridge, England: Cambridge University Press.

Gingerich, Barbara. 1985. Property and the Gospel: Two Reformation Approaches. *Mennonite Quarterly Review* 59 (July): 246—67.

Gingerich, Melvin. 1942. Rural Life Problems and the Mennonites. *Mennonite Quarterly Review* 16: 167–73.

———. 1963. *The Mennonite Family Census of 1963*. Goshen, Ind.: Mennonite Historical and Research Committee.

Goertz, Hans-Jürgen. 1984. *Alles Gehoert Allen*. Munich: C. H. Beck.

———. 1988a. Das Bild Thomas Muentzer. In *Reformation Europe*, edited by Steven Ozment. St. Louis: Center for Reformation Research.

———. 1988b. The Confessional Heritage in its New Mold: What Is Mennonite Self-Understanding Today? In *Mennonite Identity: Historical and Contemporary Perspectives*, edited by Calvin Redekop and Samuel Steiner. Lanham, Md.: University Press of America.

———. 1993. "Religioaese Bewegnungen in der Fruehen Neuzeit. *Enzyklopaedie Deutscher Geschichte*. Band 20. Munich: Oldenbourg Verlag.

Goode, William. 1951. *Religion among the Primitives*. Glencoe, Ill.: Free Press.

Goulden, Joseph. 1976. *The Best Years, 1945–60*. New York: Atheneum.

Greeley, Andrew. 1977. *American Catholic*. New York: Basic Books.

Grelle, Bruce, and David A. Krueger. 1986. *Christianity and Capitalism*. Chicago: Center for the Scientific Study of Religion.

Groenveld, S., Jacob P. Jacobszoon, and S. L. Verhew. 1980. *Wederdoper, Menisten, Doopsgezinde*. Zutphen: De Walburg Pers.

Gross, Leonard. 1980. *The Golden Years of the Hutterites*. Scottdale, Pa.: Herald Press.

Halteman, James. 1988. *Market Capitalism and Christianity*. Grand Rapids: Baker Book House.

Hamm, Peter G. 1987. *Continuity and Change among Canadian Mennonite Brethren*. Waterloo, Ont.: Wilfrid Laurier University Press.

Harder, Leland. 1962. The Quest for Equilibrium in an Established Sect: A Study of Social Change in the General Conference Church. Ph.D. diss., Northwestern University, Evanston, Ill.

———. 1970. *Steinbach and Its Churches*. Elkhart, Ind.: Mennonite Biblical Seminary.

———. 1971. *Factbook of Congregational Membership*. N. Newton, Kans.: General Conference Mennonite Church.

Harder, M. S. 1949. The Origin, Philosophy, and Development of Education among the Mennonites. Ph.D. diss., University of Southern California, Los Angeles.

Hayek, A. Friedrich. 1944. *The Road to Serfdom*. Chicago: University of Chicago Press.

Hege, Christian. 1955. Wolfgang Brandhuber. *Mennonite Encyclopedia*, vol. 1, 404–5.

Hege, Christian, and Harold S. Bender. 1957. Martyrs' Synod. *Mennonite Encyclopedia*, vol. 3, 529–31.

Hegel, Georg Wilhelm Friedrich. 1961. *Vorlesungen ueber Die Philosophie der Geschichte*. Stuttgart: Philipp Reklam.

Heichelheim, F. 1965. *An Ancient Economic History: From the Paleolithic Age to the Migrations of the German, Slavic, and Arabic Nations*. Leyden: A. W. Systhoff.

Heilbroner, Robert. 1961. *The Worldly Philosophers*. New York: Simon and Schuster.

————. 1976. *American Civilization in Decline*. New York: W. W. Norton.

Hershberger, Guy F. 1940. Maintaining the Mennonite Rural Community. *Mennonite Quarterly Review* 14: 214–23.

————. 1955. Committee on Economic and Social Relations. *Mennonite Encyclopedia*, vol. 1, 650–51.

————. 1957. *The Recovery of the Anabaptist Vision*. Scottdale, Pa.: Herald Press.

————. 1958. *The Way of the Cross in Human Relations*. Scottdale, Pa.: Herald Press.

Hiebert, Clarence. 1973. *The Holdeman People: The Church of God in Christ, Mennonite 1859–1969*. Pasadena, Calif.: William Carey Library.

Hillerbrand, Hans. 1988. *Radical Tendencies in the Reformation*. Kirksville, Mo.: Sixteenth Century Publications.

Hornaday, John A. 1982. Research about Living Entrepreneurs. In *Encyclopedia of Entrepreneurship*, edited by Calvin Kent, Donald Sexton, and Karl Vesper. Englewood Cliffs, N.J.: Prentice Hall.

Horsch, James, ed. 1992. *Mennonite Yearbook*. Scottdale, Pa.: Herald Press.

Horsch, John. 1950. *Mennonites in Europe*. Scottdale, Pa.: Herald Press.

Hostetler, John A. 1954. *The Sociology of Mennonite Evangelism*. Scottdale, Pa.: Herald Press.

————. 1974. *Hutterite Society*. Baltimore: Johns Hopkins University Press.

————. 1980. *Amish Society*. Baltimore: Johns Hopkins University Press.

Hostetler, John A., and Gertrude Huntington. 1967. *The Hutterites in North America*. New York: Holt, Rinehart, and Winston.

Hugh, Gibb J. 1963. "The Future of Entrepreneurial Research." *Explorations in Entrepreneurial Research* 1 (Fall): 3–9.

Hunter, James Davison. 1982. *American Evangelicalism*. New Brunswick, N.J.: Rutgers University Press.

————. 1991. *Culture Wars: The Struggle to Define America*. New York: Basic Books.

Jeschke, Marlin. 1990. Church Discipline. *Mennonite Encyclopedia*, vol. 5, 239–40.

Johnson, Harry M. 1967. Ideology. *International Encyclopedia of the Social Sciences*, vol. 4, 76–85.

Johnston, Jon. 1980. *Will Evangelicalism Survive Its Own Popularity?* Grand Rapids: Zondervan.

Juhnke, James. 1989. *Vision, Doctrine, War*. Scottdale, Pa.: Herald Press.

Kahl, Joseph. 1957. *The American Class Structure*. New York: Rinehart and Company.

Kallen, Evelyn, and Merrijoy Kelner. 1983. *Ethnicity, Opportunity, and Successful Entrepreneurship in Canada*. York, Ont.: York University Press.

Kauffman, J. Howard. 1957. Family in Mennonite History and Life. *The Mennonite Encyclopedia*, vol. 2, 295–99.

Kauffman, J. Howard, and Leland Harder. 1975. *Anabaptism Four Centuries Later*. Scottdale, Pa.: Herald Press.

Kauffman, J. Howard, and Leo Driedger. 1991. *The Mennonite Mosaic*. Scottdale, Pa.: Herald Press.

Kautsky, Karl. 1966. *Communism in Central Europe in the Time of the Reformation*. New York: Augustus Kelly.

Kent, Calvin A., Donald L. Sexton, and Karl Vesper. 1982. *Encyclopedia of Entrepreneurship*. Englewood Cliffs: Prentice-Hall.

Klaassen, Walter. 1971. The Nature of the Anabaptist Protest. *Mennonite Quarterly Review* 45: 291–311.

———. 1981. *Anabaptism in Outline*. Scottdale, Pa.: Herald Press.

Klassen, Peter James. 1964. *The Economics of Anabaptism, 1525–1560*. The Hague: Mouton.

Kollmorgen, Walter. 1942. Culture of a Contemporary Community: The Old Order Amish of Lancaster County, Pennsylvania. *Rural Life Studies No. 4*. Washington, D.C.: U. S. Department of Agriculture.

Krahn, Cornelius. 1956. Family. *Mennonite Encyclopedia*, vol. 2, 293–99.

———. 1957. Industry among Mennonites. *Mennonite Encyclopedia*, vol. 3, 33–34.

———. 1959a. Russia. *Mennonite Encyclopedia*, vol. 4, 381–93.

———. 1959b. Wheat. *Mennonite Encyclopedia*, vol. 4, 939.

———. 1968. *Dutch Anabaptism*. The Hague: Martinus Nijhoff.

Krahn, Victor. 1988. The Effect of Small Businesses upon the Old Order Mennonite Community of Waterloo County. Unpublished paper, Conrad Grebel College, Waterloo, Ont.

Kraybill, Donald. 1975. Ethnic Socialization in a Mennonite High School. Ph.D. diss., Temple University, Philadelphia.

———. 1978. *Mennonite Education: Issues, Facts. and Changes.* Scottdale, Pa.: Herald Press.

———. 1989. *The Riddle of Amish Culture*. Baltimore: Johns Hopkins University Press.

Kraybill, Donald, and Stephen Nolt. 1995. *Amish Enterprise: From Plows to Profits*. Baltimore: Johns Hopkins University Press.

Kraybill, Donald, and Phyllis Pellman. 1982. *The Perils of Professionalism*. Scottdale, Pa.: Herald Press.

Kreider, Carl. 1980. *The Christian Entrepreneur*. Scottdale, Pa.: Herald Press.

Kreider, Robert. 1951. Anabaptist Conception of the Church in the Russian Mennonite Environment. *Mennonite Quarterly Review* 25: 17–33.

Kroeker, Wally. 1988. When Business Becomes Mission. *Marketplace*, January, 4–8.

Kropotkin, Peter. 1955. *Mutual Aid: A Factor of Evolution*. Boston: Extending Horizon Books.

Landis, Ira David. 1945. Mennonite Agriculture in Colonial Lancaster County, Pennsylvania. *Mennonite Quarterly Review* 19: 254–72.

Lasch, Christopher. 1987. *Culture of Narcissism: American Life in an Age of Diminishing Expectations*. New York: W. W. Norton.

Levine, Donald. 1985. *The Flight from Ambiguity*. Chicago: University of Chicago Press.

Lichdi, Dieter Goetz, ed. 1990. *Mennonite World Handbook*. Carol Stream, Ill.: Mennonite World Conference.

Litt, Edgar. 1970. *Ethnic Politics in America*. Glenview, Ill.: Scott Foresman.

Littell, Franklin. 1952. *The Anabaptist View of the Church*. Philadelphia: American Society of Church History.

Loewen, Esko. 1946. *Mennonite Community Sourcebook*. Akron, Pa.: Mennonite Central Committee.

Loewen, Harry. 1988. *Why I Am a Mennonite*. Scottdale, Pa.: Herald Press.

Loewen, Harry, and Al Reimer, eds. 1985. *Visions and Realities*. Winnipeg, Man.: Hyperion Press.

MacIntyre, Alasdair. 1984. *Marxism and Christianity*. Notre Dame, Ind.: University of Notre Dame Press.

MacMaster, Richard. 1985. *Land, Piety, and Peoplehood*. Scottdale, Pa.: Herald Press.

Maker, William, ed. 1987. *Hegel on Economics and Freedom*. Macon, Ga.: Mercer University Press.

Mannheim, Karl. 1936. *Ideology and Utopia*. New York: Harcourt Brace.

Marquand, John. 1949. *Point of No Return*. New York: Little.

Marx, Karl, and Friedrich Engels. 1967. *The Communist Manifesto*. Baltimore: Penguin Books.

McClelland, David. 1961. *The Achieving Society*. Glencoe, Ill.: Free Press.

McLuhan, Marshall. 1965. *Understanding Media: The Extensions of Man*. New York: McGraw-Hill.

Merton, Robert K. 1957. *Social Theory and Social Structure*. Glencoe, Ill.: Free Press.

Mills, C. Wright. 1959. *The Sociological Imagination*. New York: Oxford University Press.

Mullin, Redmond. 1983. *The Wealth of Christians*. Maryknoll, N.Y.: Orbis Books.

Nafziger, Estel Wayne. 1965. The Mennonite Ethic in the Weberian Framework. *Explorations in Entrepreneurial History* 2: 187–204.

———. 1986. *Entrepreneurship, Equity and Economic Development*. Greenwich, Conn.: JAI Press.

Nelson, Benjamin. 1969. *The Idea of Usury*. Chicago: University of Chicago Press.

Neusner, Jacob. 1987. *Death and Birth of Judaism: The Impact of Christianity, Secularism, and the Holocaust on Jewish Faith*. New York: Basic Books.

Niebuhr, H. Richard. 1957. *The Social Sources of Denominationalism*. New York: Living Age Books.

Nietzsche, Friedrich. 1968. *The Anti-Christ*. Middlesex, England: Penguin Books.

Nolt, Steven M. 1992. *A History of the Amish*. Intercourse, Pa.: Good Books.

Nordhoff, Charles. 1875. *The Communistic Societies of the United States*. New York: Harper and Brothers.

Oyer, John. 1991. Michael Schneider, Anabaptist Leader, Hymnist, Recanter. *Mennonite Quarterly Review* 65: 256–86.

Packull, Werner. 1986. In Search of the "Common Man" in Early German Anabaptist Ideology. *Sixteenth-Century Journal* 17: 51–67.

Peachey, Paul. 1954. *Die Soziale Herkunft der Schweizer Taeufer in der Reformationszeit*. Karlsruhe, Germany: Schneider Verlag.

Penner, Horst. 1959. West Prussia. *Mennonite Encyclopedia*, vol. 4, 920–26.

———. 1978. *Die ost- und westpreussischen Mennoniten in ihrem religioesen und sozialen Leben*. Weierhof: Mennonitischer Geschichtsverein.

Peters, John F., ed. 1986. *Work in Canada*. Waterloo, Ont.: Wilfrid Laurier University Press.

———. 1990. Economics of the Canadian Old Order Mennonites. Unpublished.

Pfeiffer, Richard. 1979. *Working for Capitalism*. New York: Columbia University Press.

Poettcker, Henry, and Rudy A. Regehr. 1972. *Call to Faithfulness*. Winnipeg, Man.: Canadian Mennonite Bible College.

Polanyi, Karl. 1944. *The Great Transformation*. Boston: Beacon Press.

Pollins, Harold. 1984. The Development of Jewish Business in the United Kingdom. In *Ethnic Communities in Business*, edited by Robin Ward and Richard Jenkins. Cambridge, England: Cambridge University Press.

Poloma, Margaret. 1989. *Assemblies of God at the Crossroads: Charisma and Institutional Dilemmas*. Knoxville: University of Tennessee Press.

Quiring, Walter. 1955. Johann Cornies. *Mennonite Encyclopedia*, vol. 1, 716–18.

Raid, Howard. 1964. Economic Trends in Mennonite Communities. *Mennonite Life* 19: 186–87.

Rand, Ayn. 1946. *Capitalism: The Unknown Ideal*. New York: New American Library.

Rasmussen, Albert. 1965. *Christian Responsibility in Economic Life*. Philadelphia: Westminster Press.

Rauschenbusch, Walter. 1919. *Christianizing the Social Order*. New York: Macmillan.

Redekop, Calvin. 1953. The Cultural Assimilation of Mennonites of Mountain Lake, Minnesota. M.A. thesis, University of Minnesota, Minneapolis.

——. 1959. The Sectarian Black and White World. Ph.D. diss., University of Chicago.

——. 1969. *The Old Colony Mennonites*. Baltimore: Johns Hopkins Press.

——. 1973. Religion and Society: A State within a Church. *Mennonite Quarterly Review* 47: 339–57.

——. 1984. The Mennonite Identity Crisis. *Journal of Mennonite Studies* 2: 87–103.

——. 1985. The Mennonite Romance with the Land. In *Visions and Reality*, edited by Harry Loewen and Al Reimer. Winnipeg, Man.: Hyperion Press.

——. 1986. Toward a Mennonite Theology and Ethic of Creation. *Mennonite Quarterly Review* 60: 387–403.

——. 1988. The Sociology of Mennonite Identity: A Second Opinion. In *Mennonite Identity: Historical and Contemporary Perspectives*, edited by Calvin Redekop and Samuel Steiner. Lanham, Md.: University Press of America.

——. 1989. *Mennonite Society*. Baltimore: Johns Hopkins University Press.

——. 1993. Mennonites, Creation, and Work. *Christian Scholars Review* 22, no. 4 (June): 348–66.

——. 1996. Jacob A. Shenk: Business Was Servant to the Church. In *Entrepreneurs in the Faith Community: Profiles of Mennonites in Business*, edited by Calvin Redekop and Benjamin Redekop. Scottdale, Pa.: Herald Press.

Redekop, Calvin, and Urie A. Bender. 1988. *Who Am I? What Am I?: Searching for Meaning in Your Work*. Grand Rapids: Zondervan.

Redekop, Calvin, and Al Koop. 1991. The Streams of Anabaptist-Mennonite Utopianism. Unpublished.

Redekop, Calvin, Victor A. Krahn, and Samuel J. Steiner. 1994. *Anabaptist-Mennonite Faith and Economics*. Lanham, Md.: University Press of America.

Redekop, Calvin, and Samuel J. Steiner. 1988. *Mennonite Identity: Historical and Contemporary Perspectives*. Lanham, Md.: University Press of America.

Regher, Ted. 1988. *For Everything a Season*. Winnipeg, Man.: Canadian Mennonite Bible College.

Reimer, James. 1988. Mennonite Theological Self-understanding, The Crisis of Modern Anthropocentricity and the Challenge of the Third Millenium. In

Mennonite Identity: Historical and Contemporary Perspectives, edited by Calvin Redekop and Samuel Steiner. Lanham, Md.: University Press of America.

Rempel, David G. 1933. The Mennonite Colonies in New Russia: A Study of Settlement and Economic Development from 1789 to 1914. Ph.D. diss., Stanford University.

———. 1974. The Mennonite Commonwealth in Russia: A Sketch of Its Founding and Its Endurance, 1879–1919. *Mennonite Quarterly Review* 47: 259–308; 48: 5–54.

Rempel, Elfrieda. 1981. An Examination of Where and How Winnipeg Mennonites Earn Their Living. *Mennonite Mirror* March/April/May, 7–28.

Riedemann, Peter. 1956. *Account of Our Religion, Doctrine, and Faith.* London: Hodder and Stoughton.

Rokeach, Milton. 1973. *The Nature of Human Values.* Glencoe, Ill.: Free Press.

Roof, Wade Clark, and William McKinney. 1987. *American Mainline Religion: Its Changing Shape and Future.* New Brunswick, N.J.: Rutgers University Press.

Roth, Willard, ed. 1994. Mennonite and Brethren in Christ World Directory. *Courier* 9: 15.

Rudy, John. 1975. Business and Following Jesus? *CIBA Newsletter*, May.

Ruether, Rosemary. 1970. *The Radical Kingdom.* New York: Harper Brothers.

Sahlins, Marshall. 1972. *Stone Age Economics.* Chicago: Aldine.

Sartre, Jean Paul. 1991. *Critique of Dialectical Reason.* London: Routledge, Chapman, and Hall.

Sawatsky, Harry Leonard. 1971. *They Sought a Country.* Berkeley: University of California Press.

Schlabach, Theron. 1988. *Peace, Faith, Nation: Mennonites and Amish in Nineteenth-century America.* Scottdale, Pa.: Herald Press.

Schowalter, Paul. 1957. Martyrs. *Mennonite Encyclopedia*, vol. 3, 521–25.

Schwartz, Gary. 1970. *Sect Ideologies and Social Status.* Chicago: University of Chicago Press.

Seeley, John R., R. Alexander Sim, and Elizabeth W. Loosley. 1956. *Crestwood Heights.* Toronto: University of Toronto Press.

Seguy, Jean. 1973. Religion and Agricultural Success. *Mennonite Quarterly Review* 47: 179–224.

———. 1977. *Les Assemblies des Anabaptist-Mennonites de France.* Paris: Mouton.

———. 1984. The French Anabaptists: Four and One-Half Centuries of History. *Mennonite Quarterly Review* 58: 206–17.

Seibt, Ferdinand. 1972. *Utopica.* Düsseldorf: Verlag L. Schwann.

Shapiro, Albert, and Lisa Sokol. 1982. The Social Dimensions of Entrepreneurship. In *Encyclopedia of Entrepreneurship*, edited by Calvin Kent, Donald Sexton, and Karl Vesper. Englewood Cliffs, N.J.: Prentice-Hall.

Siemens, Robert. 1989. Introduction to Paideumatic Sociology. Unpublished manuscript.

Simmel, Georg. 1955. *Conflict and the Web of Group Affiliations.* Glencoe, Ill.: Free Press.

Simons, Menno. 1956. *The Complete Writings of Menno Simons.* Scottdale, Pa.: Herald Press.

Smith, Adam. 1937. *An Inquiry into the Nature and Causes of the Wealth of Nations.* New York: Modern Library.

Smith, C. Henry. 1981. *The Story of the Mennonites*, revised and enlarged by Cornelius Krahn. Newton, Kans.: Faith and Life Press.

Smucker, Donovan. 1945. The Theological Triumph of the Early Anabaptist-Mennonites. *Mennonite Quarterly Review* 19: 5–26.

———. 1976. Gelassenheit, Entrepreneurs, and Remnants: Socioeconomic Models Among the Mennonites. In *Kingdom, Cross and Community*, edited by John Richard Burkholder and Calvin Redekop. Scottdale, Pa.: Herald Press.

Smucker, Joseph. 1986. Religious Community and Individualism: Conceptual Adaptations by One Group of Mennonites. *Journal for the Scientific Study of Religion* 25: 273–91.

Sommer, Don. 1954. Peter Rideman and Menno Simons on Economics. *Mennonite Quarterly Review* 28: 205–23.

Sorokin, Pitirim. 1928. *Contemporary Sociological Theories.* New York: Harper and Brothers.

Spaulding, J. Lloyd. 1953. Profiles of a Mennonite Community: A Survey of Moundridge, Kansas. *Proceedings of the Annual Conference on Mennonite Educational and Cultural Problems* 9: 78–88.

———. 1957. The Changing Economic Base of Mennonite Community with Special Reference to Certain Kansas Communities. *Proceedings of the Annual Conference on Mennonite Educational and Cultural Problems* 11: 87–98.

Spencer, Herbert. 1877. *The Principles of Sociology.* New York: D. Appleton.

Sprunger, Mary. 1994. Dutch Mennonites and the Golden Age Economy: The Problem of Social Disparity in the Church. In *Anabaptist-Mennonite Faith and Economics*, edited by Calvin Redekop, Victor A. Krahn, and Samuel J. Steiner. Lanham, Md.: University Press of America.

Stayer, James. 1972. *Anabaptists and the Sword.* Lawrence, Kans.: Coronado Press.

———. 1991. *The German Peasants' War and Anbaptist Community of Goods.* Montreal, Que.: McGill-Queen's University Press.

Stayer, James M., and Werner Packull. 1980. *The Anabaptists and Thomas Muentzer.* Dubuque, Iowa: Kendall/Hunt Publishing Company.

Stein, Maurice R. 1964. *The Eclipse of Community.* New York: Harper and Row.

Steiner, Samuel. 1988. *Vicarious Pioneer: The Life of Jacob Y. Shantz.* Winnipeg, Man.: Hyperion Press.

Stout, Jeffrey. 1988. *Ethics after Babel.* Boston: Beacon Press.

Sumner, William G., and Albert G. Keller. 1927. *The Science of Society.* New Haven: Yale University Press.

Tawney, Richard Henry. 1920. *The Acquisitive Society.* New York: Harcourt, Brace and World.

———. 1954. *Religion and the Rise of Capitalism.* New York: Mentor Books.

Tiemstra, John P. 1993. Christianity and Economics. *Christian Scholars Review* 22: 227–47.

Toews, John B. 1981. The Emergence of German Industry in the South Russian Colonies. *Mennonite Quarterly Review* 55: 298–371.

Troeltsch, Ernst. 1960. *The Social Teachings of the Christian Churches*. New York: Macmillan.

Urry, James. 1989. *None but Saints*. Winnipeg, Man.: Hyperion Press.

van der Zijpp, N. 1955. Business among the Mennonites of Holland. *Mennonite Encyclopedia*, vol. 1, 483.

———. 1957a. Munster. *Mennonite Encyclopedia*, vol. 3, 777–83.

———. 1957b. Netherlands. *Mennonite Encyclopedia*, vol. 3, 824–44.

Van Leeuwen, A. 1964. *Christianity and World History*. New York: Charles Scribner's Sons.

Vogt, Roy. 1972. Economic Questions and the Mennonite Conscience. In *Call to Faithfulness*, edited by Henry Poettcker and Rudy A. Regehr. Winnipeg, Man.: Canadian Mennonite Bible College.

———. 1980. The Costs and Benefits of Being an Entrepreneur: A Christian Perspective. *The Marketplace* (September): 1–4.

———. 1983. Mennonite Studies in Economics. *Journal of Mennonite Studies* 1: 64–78.

Wach, Joachim. 1944. *Sociology of Religion*. Chicago: University of Chicago Press.

Wallace, Anthony F. C. 1966. *Religion: An Anthropological View*. New York: Random House.

Wallerstein, Immanuel. 1979. *The Capitalist World-Economy*. New York: Cambridge University Press.

Ward, Lester Frank. 1963. *Lester Frank Ward: Selections*. New York: Crowell.

Ward, Robin, and Richard Jenkins. 1984. *Ethnic Communities in Business*. Cambridge, England: Cambridge University Press.

Warner, W. Lloyd. 1963. *Yankee City*. New Haven: Yale University Press.

Weaver, J. Denny. 1988. Mennonite Theological Understanding: A Response to A. James Reimer. In *Mennonite Identity: Historical and Contemporary Perspectives*, edited by Calvin Redekop and Samuel J. Steiner. Lanham, Md.: University Press of America.

Weaver, Laura. 1994. Hard Workers: Mennonite Women in Academic and Other Professional Fields. In *Anabaptist-Mennonite Faith and Economics*, edited by Calvin Redekop, Victor Krahn, and Samuel J. Steiner. Lanham, Md.: University Press of America.

Weber, Marianne. 1975. *Max Weber: A Biography*. New York: John Wiley and Sons.

Weber, Max. 1946. *From Max Weber: Essays in Sociology*. New York: Oxford University Press.

———. 1947. *The Theory of Social and Economic Organization*. Glencoe, Ill.: Free Press.

———. 1952. *Ancient Judaism*. Glencoe, Ill.: Free Press.

———. 1958. *The Protestant Ethic and the Spirit of Capitalism*. New York: Charles Scribner's Sons.

———. 1964. *The Sociology of Religion*. Boston: Beacon Press.

———. 1988. *The Agrarian Sociology of Ancient Civilizations*. New York: Verso.

Wenger, J. C. 1957. Nonconformity. *Mennonite Encyclopedia*, vol. 3, 891–97.

White, John. 1979. *The Golden Cow: Materialism in the Twentieth Century*. Downers Grove, Ill.: Inter-Varsity Press.

Williams, Robin. 1955. *American Society: A Sociological Interpretation*. New York: Knopf.

Yinger, J. Milton. 1947. *Religion in the Struggle for Power*. Durham, N.C.: Duke University Press.

Yoder, Michael. 1985. Findings from the 1982 Mennonite Census. *Mennonite Quarterly Review* 59 (October): 307–49.

———. 1990. Rural Life. *Mennonite Encyclopedia*, vol. 5, 778–80.

Zablocki, Benjamin. 1980. *Alienation and Charisma*. Glencoe, Ill.: Free Press.

Zschaebitz, Gerhard. 1980. The Position of Anabaptism on the Continuum of the Early Bourgeois Revolution in Germany. In *The Anabaptists and Thomas Muentzer*, edited by James M. Stayer and Werner Packull. Dubuque, Iowa: Kendall/Hunt Publishing Company.

Index

SUBJECTS